T0357575

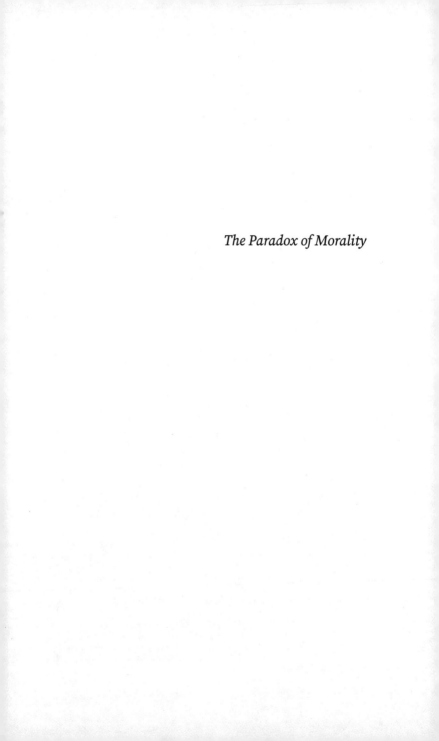

The Paradox of Morality

VLADIMIR JANKÉLÉVITCH

The Paradox
of Morality

Translated from the French by Andrew Kelley

A MARGELLOS
WORLD REPUBLIC OF LETTERS BOOK

Yale UNIVERSITY PRESS | NEW HAVEN & LONDON

The Margellos World Republic of Letters is dedicated to making literary works from around the globe available in English through translation. It brings to the English-speaking world the work of leading poets, novelists, essayists, philosophers, and playwrights from Europe, Latin America, Africa, Asia, and the Middle East to stimulate international discourse and creative exchange.

Yale University Press books may be purchased in quantity for educational, business, or promotional use. For information, please e-mail sales.press@yale.edu (U.S. office) or sales@yaleup.co.uk (U.K. office).

Set in Source Serif type by Motto Publishing Services.
Printed in the United States of America.

Library of Congress Control Number: 2024940520
ISBN 978-0-300-26926-0 (hardcover : alk. paper)

A catalogue record for this book is available from the British Library.
This paper meets the requirements of ANSI/NISO Z39.48-1992 (Permanence of Paper).

10 9 8 7 6 5 4 3 2 1

Contents

Translator's Introduction

The Paradox of Morality (*Le paradoxe de la morale*), which first appeared in 1981, is the last philosophical work that Vladimir Jankélévitch (1903–85) published before his death. Even with a dedicated following of students, an endowed chair at the Sorbonne, and a large number of publications in philosophy as well as on music, Jankélévitch never achieved the celebrity status that many intellectuals with similar pedigrees often have in France. Those who knew him provide glowing accounts of Jankélévitch the professor, the philosopher, and the person. He was unique, and as a result found himself outside the mainstream in postwar French philosophy. However, now, in the early twenty-first century, Jankélévitch's works are beginning to attract more attention in France and the rest of Europe, as well as in other parts of the world—even in Anglophone countries.

There are several reasons why Jankélévitch's thought has received less attention than it deserves. His writings and the influences on them were firmly rooted in the Western philosophical canon, yet Jankélévitch was an independent thinker, and he oftentimes cited authors and works that were not in style at the time. He unabashedly penned studies on Henri Bergson's works at a time when Bergson's status was already waning. After the horrors of World War II, Jankélévitch published an idiosyncratic, 850-page treatise on the virtues (*Traité des vertus*). Moral philosophy, and in particular the supposedly "antiquated" approach known as "virtue ethics," were among the most central elements of Jankélévitch's philosophical corpus. But these were not in fashion in France in that era. Jankélévitch further distanced himself from his contemporaries because he did not take his inspiration from many of the thinkers on whom postwar French intellectual life was focused: Heidegger, Hegel, the Marxists, and others. Ironically, before World War II, Jankélévitch championed certain thinkers from Germany, even though to do so was not popular, given the strained relations between their two countries. He was acquainted with the phenomenological movement, but referred more often to Max Scheler than to Husserl or Heidegger. Jankélévitch even makes explicit mention of Heidegger in 1933 in the first edition of *The Bad Conscience* (*La mauvaise conscience*)—a reference that was removed in later editions—and he includes a critical jab at Heidegger in his 1938 book *L'Alternative*.

In 1940, after being wounded during the German invasion of France, Jankélévitch was denied permission to teach because of his Jewish heritage. He subsequently went into hiding in the southern city of Toulouse, worked with the French Resistance there, and continued to hold clandestine lectures in the back rooms of the city's cafés. After the war and especially on account of the Shoah, Jankélévitch purged all things German from his life. He would never set foot in Germany again, he stopped playing music by German composers, and he deleted references to certain German thinkers from subsequent editions of his books. At the end of his career, he marched with students during the May 1968 protests and appeared on radio and television, but he still remained an outsider within French philosophy.

Jankélévitch's work is difficult to pigeonhole into an easily categorized movement or school of thought. This is partly due to the wide array of authors and books he mentions in his texts, where his references might run the gamut from ancient Greeks to more recent philosophers, theologians, poets, novelists, movies, and pieces of music. Sometimes these are well-known people or texts, but at others they may be obscure writers, composers, or artists. His style, too, is unique. If we listen to recordings of Jankélévitch's lectures, we can hear that his spoken presentations mirror his written words; both are constructed almost as if they were musical compositions: there are crescendos and diminuendos, themes that are repeated, and changes of pace, all of which can build into a high point at the end of a passage or chapter. Style is crucial for Jankélévitch, and his was certainly one of a kind. But for him style was not a matter of some potentially superficial undertaking (as studies of fashion or cultural trends can sometimes be). Instead, for him, the way in which something was said, written, composed, painted, presented—its style—was tied to the content itself. For example, the manner in which two musicians play the same passage of a piece of music can radically alter what is conveyed to the listener. And as we can see in *The Paradox of Morality,* as in almost all Jankélévitch's texts, he does not write in a deductive fashion, in the way that, say, Descartes proceeds in *Meditations on First Philosophy* or how Spinoza composes his *Ethics.* Jankélévitch does not begin with an indisputable truth of fact and then deduce his way to other truths. But this should not be interpreted as a lack of rigor: Jankélévitch is not so much concerned with *telling* us what is the case as if he were an oracle. Rather, just as Kierkegaard does in his texts or Plato in his dialogues, Jankélévitch wants to compel us to think, to see, to feel our way *around* a problem. In his texts, Jankélévitch never provides us with easy answers. Instead, he shows us the complexity of a certain topic and makes us wrestle with it for ourselves.

Given Jankélévitch's affinity for Bergson's writings, it is no stretch to read *The Paradox of Morality* as an elaboration upon key themes that Bergson discusses in 1932 in his last book-length work of philosophy, *The Two Sources of Morality and Religion,* which appeared one year after the publication of Jankélévitch's first book, about Bergson's philosophy. In "Moral Obligation," the opening chapter of *The Two Sources,* Bergson provides his account of how human beings come to be aware of duty. He takes pains to show that our acquaintance with the concept of moral obligation does not arise by means of reason. Instead, our awareness of duty is due to the interaction of two nonrational forces. First is the social pressure that is exerted upon each of us as a member of a contained group or community. This is Bergson's well-known notion of a "closed morality," which he deems "infra-intellectual." As we become members of larger groups, the social pressure of the smaller group is expanded to create greater concentric circles around the original group. However, Bergson emphasizes that there is no "circle" or contained community that gives rise to any type of fellow feeling for all humanity. So for Bergson, a different type of force is required, one that hearkens back to the "morality of the Gospels," and this is an "open morality," which turns the person into a lover of every human. This type of morality is one not of pressure but rather of "aspiration," and it is the morality that is embodied in certain people, so-called saints and heroes. "Open morality" is supra-intellectual, and it involves breaks or ruptures from the social pressures of groups. Love of one's neighbor, according to Bergson, cannot be preached.

Instead, as he goes on to say, "heroism may be the only way to love," and such a heroism "has only to show itself." In the end, for Bergson, we can form a rational conception of duty. But we mistakenly believe that reason lies at the origin of duty, when the origin is actually the byproduct of infra- and supra-intellectual forces.

Jankélévitch knew *The Two Sources* well, having published in 1933 in the prestigious *Revue de métaphysique et de morale* one of the earliest reviews of Bergson's book. The ideas and themes of that article were later incorporated in the 1959 revised edition of Jankélévitch's *Henri Bergson.* Much of Jankélévitch's own moral philosophy and, hence, much of *The Paradox of Morality,* involves a discussion of "open morality," of which love is the source. His manner of addressing love is tied to the fact that love is impossible to pin down by a concrete, rational definition. Love, like time, free will, the absolute, or even forgiveness is, by its very nature for Jankélévitch, a "mystery" or paradox. As opposed to a "secret," which is simply something that is hidden, but which entails the possibility of being uncovered and comprehended at some point in time, a "mystery" is something whose essence or existence necessarily cannot have a rational explanation. As a result, Jankélévitch often employs the negative or apophatic method, saying what something is *not* so as to point us in the direction of being able to glimpse the mystery or paradox. But a rational account of a mystery will always arrive at a dead end, faced with contradictions and inconsistencies.

Jankélévitch attempts to point his readers in the direction of the mysteries that reside at the extremes of our experience and are tied to the very foundations or ground of what he is attempting to discuss. It is therefore fitting that his final philosophical book addresses morality's paradoxes. As is the case with so many of his texts, Jankélévitch provides no introduction to the work; he simply jumps into his analyses forthwith. Beginning with the first chapter, he underscores the omnipresence of morality in all philosophical judgments, comparing it to Descartes's arguments tied to the idea "I think, therefore I am." For Jankélévitch, that is, the act of denying morality itself entails an implicit moral judgment—a value judgment—in the same way that, for Descartes, the act of doubting one's existing or the act of being deceived by some "evil genius" automatically proves that at least one thing exists, namely, the very consciousness that doubts or is deceived. And so for Jankélévitch, even a questioning or a denial of the validity of morality or ethics carries with it an implicit judgment of value. Morality is never absent.

But even given the ubiquity of moral judgments, another paradox arises. If morality could be reduced to rational self-interest, whereby doing what is right for the majority amounts to what is right for ourselves, and vice versa, then it would come down to nothing more than egoism, and all we would need to do, in the end, would be to follow the social pressures of our community (to put it in Bergsonian terms). However, for Jankélévitch the essence of morality is not self-interest but altruism: putting the interests of other people ahead of our own. If morality were no different from self-interest, what would be the point of giving it a different name or pretending it was a different type of activity? Thus, the root of morality for Jankélévitch, if it is to be anything, must be something akin to Bergson's "open morality." In fact, Jankélévitch, following Bergson, acknowledges that we cannot arrive at a concern for all humanity through reason, for if we had a rational "reason" for promoting such a concern, then a rational person would automatically perform the appropriate actions out of self-interest. Therefore, there must be a different "reason," one at which we do not arrive via intellection or deductive proof, for putting the interests of the other person before our own. In the end, this nonrational reason—if it can be called a reason at all—is love. Love defies any rational accounting or deductive proof; love loves because it loves.

According to Jankélévitch, we do not love humans in the abstract. Rather, love for another is aimed at a concrete person, a "Thou" if you will, even if this "Thou" might be a complete stranger. But love is somewhat problematic because, as Jankélévitch points out with yet another contradiction, love can harbor within itself its own negation. In other words, if the lover loves so much that the lover becomes engrossed in the beloved, then the love itself could bring about the end of the one who is loving. To love wholly and without reserve, the lover might need to divest him- or herself entirely of his or her own selfhood. But if this were to happen, there would be no more loving, for the lover would cease to exist. As a result, the lover must always wrestle with a sense of restraint. Does the lover hold back a bit of self in order to be able to continue to love? Or does the love literally vanish in the act of love? Hence, we arrive at the formulation found in the last lines of Chapter 3, in which Jankélévitch mentions that one possible option for avoiding our own permanent demise in loving is to inject "the most love into the least possible being." That is, the lover performs the acrobatic maneuver of loving up to the point of near-nonexistence, while not quite reaching it so as to continue to love.

This aforementioned paradox is related to two more paradoxes. First, the love that we would profess for another cannot be based on any kind of criterion, bias, membership, or *prosopolepsia,* a term from Christian Scriptures to which Jankélévitch often makes reference in the text. In other words, love or duty toward others must be universal and admit of no exceptions; otherwise, it is not universal. But here again, Jankélévitch points to a potential problem: if love and hence duties are incumbent on others, and if I myself am part of this universal moral community, then it would seem that I can demand that rights and obligations *toward myself* be fulfilled by others; if I am a human, like those to whom I owe duties, then can I not demand that others fulfill their duties toward me? The obvious problem is that in making such demands, I can find a reason for no longer performing what love or duty would require of me toward others. That is, if I can make demands of others based on my own rights, then I might use these so-called rights as a way of not performing my duty until those duties are performed for me. This kind of reasoning takes us back to ethics as some type of quid pro quo or a rational egoism, and so we have returned to ethics as simply a form of selfishness, of cost-benefit analysis. So, as Jankélévitch notes, in order to maintain a near universality of moral action I must make an exception to rights owed to me. In such a way, I am no longer able to place my own needs above those of another. To maintain the universality of such an ethics, Jankélévitch claims that my attitude must be: I have all the duties and you have all the rights; duties belong to me and rights belong to you. Taking such a position defies rationality and, thus, the impetus for morality must come from somewhere else.

Ironically, Jankélévitch is not wholly critical of egoism. One of the most germane ideas throughout his writings, one that he claims to have found in Bergson's thought, is that of the paradoxical "organ-obstacle." An organ-obstacle is something that by its very nature serves both to hinder and to give rise to something else. So, for example, air resistance both allows for and hinders the lift of an airplane wing. Likewise, death marks the end of a life. But without the fact of death, then living things cannot be said to be alive; death is both a condition of life and that which destroys it. The same holds for egoism in relation to love, altruism, and duty. Egoism can destroy love and a sense of duty. But if there were no egoism and no tendency for a person to focus solely on his or her own pleasures, there would be no merit in love or duty. Thus, not only must there be egoism for there to be morality, but we may need to be a bit "selfish" in order to be able to give more love or fulfill more duties.

In the present work, like most virtue theorists, Jankélévitch says that a person's actions must reflect the person's character; one's actions must be chosen and undertaken with the "entirety of one's soul," as he so often writes, loosely quoting Plato and also Bergson. But unlike Aristotle, Jankélévitch does not believe that an action performed out of habit or as a reflex is virtuous. When a person does something reflexively or unconsciously, that person is not making the commitment to the action with the entirety of her or his soul. The person must make the choice each and every time with the entirety of who he or she is. Jankélévitch's argument is that we are more than mere rational beings: reason is an important part of who each of us is, but it is not the only part. In turn, whereas Aristotle preaches moderation and a "golden mean," Jankélévitch would see virtues as lying at the extremes. It is not practical wisdom (Aristotle's *phronesis*) that undergirds moral behavior but love. It is love that, in the end, creates values. However, love is neither a Form nor a fixed entity. Love must be made and remade with each instant. In Jankélévitch's conception of morality, there are no easy answers. Moreover, what is important is not what we have done but what we are going to do. And as soon as we have performed an action, then we must act again. If we are basking in the glory of past actions, so to speak, then we are not attending to what needs to be done here and now, but rather are stuck in nostalgia for days gone by. We can never rest on our moral laurels.

A Note on the Translation

Because of Jankélévitch's unique style, my goal in this translation has always been to remain as close to the French text as possible. That style, in both Jankélévitch's writing and his speaking, is so singular that French readers can often identify the author simply from reading a passage in a book or hearing an audio excerpt. "Style" and "appearance" are important tenets of Jankélévitch's writings. For him, style is not a matter of constructing a facade or appearance or keeping up with fashionable trends; in fact, he stood for the opposite. Jankélévitch sees style as the way in which a thing is done or expressed; the "style" he feels can drastically alter the sense of what was written or uttered. Jankélévitch was an accomplished pianist and student of music, and his philosophical works are often constructed along the lines of a musical composition rather than as strict, deductive arguments. There are crescendos and pianissimos, repetitions and alliterations throughout his writing.

Jankélévitch's paragraphs can sometimes span several pages, and his sentences too can be quite long, with the main ideas—often complete sentences—separated by semi-colons or colons. Likewise, he might simply set a word or two or a phrase in place of a sentence. I have intentionally chosen not to alter these aspects of his writing.

I have preserved Jankélévitch's idiosyncratic use of parentheses and quotation marks. Words or phrases that appear in parentheses occur that way in the French text, and the same holds true for words and phrases set off by quotation marks. Words or text in square brackets or set off by single quotation marks represent my own additions or clarifications. Finally, it should be noted that the French word *conscience* can mean both "consciousness" and "conscience" in English. My choice of which to use in the translation depended upon the context. But the multiple meanings of the word must be kept in mind whenever either word appears.

The Paradox of Morality

1

Moral Evidence Is Simultaneously Encompassing and Encompassed

We are assured by all sides that moral philosophy presently occupies a place of honor. A moral philosophy that is honored by public opinion being, a priori, questionable, we must welcome such comforting talk with some suspicion. First one might doubt whether the crusaders of this new crusade really know what they are saying. At the heart of philosophy, already so controversial in itself and so occupied with defining itself and assuring itself of its own existence, moral philosophy appears as the height of ambiguity and of that which is intangible: it is the intangible of intangibles. Moral philosophy is indeed the first problem of philosophy: it would thus seem necessary to clarify its problem and to reflect upon its raison d'être before pleading its case.

1. An Omnipresent and Forestalling Set of Problems.

In fact, it is easier to say what moral philosophy is not and with which substitute products one is tempted to confuse it. It is thus with this "negative" or apophatic philosophy that we ought to begin. Moral philosophy is obviously not the science of mores, if it is true that the science of mores contents itself with describing mores in the indicative mood and as an established fact, and (in principle) without taking sides or formulating preferences or proposing judgments of value: it exposes without proposing, be this only indirectly, clandestinely, and with insinuations; rites, religious traditions, juridical customs, or sociological uses—everything can serve as preparatory documentation in view of moral discourse strictly speaking. But how do we go from the indicative to the normative and, a fortiori, to the imperative? In the immense collection of absurdities of the barbaric or ridiculous prejudices for which history and ethnology roll the picturesque film for us, how do we choose? Faced with this ocean of hypothetical and in the end indifferent possibilities in which all the aberrations of tyranny seem justifiable, will we ever find a single principle of choice? a single reason for acting? And why the one *rather than* the other? one concept *rather than* the other concept? The principle of preferability in its elementary form would be capable of explaining the tropism of action and of magnetizing the will: but it does not find a way to be employed in a world founded on the capriciousness, the arbitrariness, and the isosthenia of motives.

Well, here our embarrassment, at the point of turning into despair in the face of the incoherence of the dictates and the stupidity of prohibitions, allows us to glimpse a light; and the more we grope about, the more the glimpse becomes clearer, in and on account of the ambiguity itself. The moral *set of problems,* with respect to other *problems,* plays the role of an a priori, whether we mean the a priori as *chronological priority* or as *logical presupposition.* In other words, the moral set of problems is simultaneously *forestalling* and *en-*

compassing; spontaneously, it goes ahead of the critical reflection that pretends to contest it, but not the way prejudice
in reality precedes judgment, nor yet under the pretext that
taking a moral stand, in its explicit actions, would go beyond
critical reflection in quickness and agility: paradoxically,
each of these two is quicker than the other! Quicker over
and over again, that is, infinitely . . . On the other hand,—
and this amounts to the same thing—morality is co-essential
with consciousness [*conscience*], consciousness is wholly submerged in morality; it is proven after the fact that the moral
a priori had never disappeared, that it was still there, that it
was always there, apparently asleep but at every moment on
the verge of awakening; morality, speaking the language of
normativity, or even of bias, *forestalls* the critical speculation
that contests it, because it tacitly *preexists* it. And not only
does it shroud it with its diffuse light and, moreover, from
another perspective, and using other metaphors, it impreg-
nates the entirety of the speculative problem; it is the quin-
tessence and the inner core of this problem.

2. Thought Goes Ahead of Moral Evaluation. And Vice Versa!

Thought, according to Descartes, is always there; it too—it
especially—implicitly or explicitly, immanent and continually thinking, even if one does not expressly realize it; but it
discovers itself present in deed to itself in a reflexive return
to itself, owing to an interrogation or on the occasion of a
crisis. Thought thinks axiology, thought thinks judgments of
value, just as it thinks anything: doesn't axiology link to evaluation (*axioun*)[1] a logos, that is, a certain form of rationality?

Doesn't a "judgment of value" evaluate in the form of a judgment? In the ambiguity of "judging," the logical operation and the axiological evaluation influence one another. Without a doubt, the former "logic" is a logic lacking rigor and of poor quality: it is, or so it seems, something partial, approximative, or even a bit degenerate. Nevertheless, it is still reason that determines the speculative status of the evaluation here . . . Let us remember that Spinoza wanted to demonstrate ethics in the manner of geometers!—But the reciprocal is no less true: morality, in turn, which expresses itself concerning the normative mood, and even in the imperative, brings speculative reason in front of its tribunal, as if reason and logic could be answerable to such a jurisdiction, as if they had to justify themselves to it. Better yet: morality wonders about the moral value of science! Isn't this the height of it all? the height of impertinence and derision? Let us still insist: when morality demands explanations from reason, it is not by virtue of an exorbitant or royal privilege that it would arbitrarily arrogate to itself . . . Who knows? It perhaps has the right to do that. Pascal, considering the irrationality of death and the nothingness to which we are destined, wondered whether philosophizing was worth the trouble. Yes, of course, philosophy is worth the trouble, on condition that it not evade the radical problem of its own raison d'être, which is always moral to some degree. The question can rather be posed in this form: Is truth as good as it is true? Because man is a weak and passionate being, there will always be a deontology of truth and a mysterious relation between truth and love. This deontology and this love are not the least unsettling paradox of the moral set of problems. All that is human, sooner or later, in one way or another, in one form or another, thus poses a moral problem.

For morality is relevant everywhere . . . and especially in the affairs that do not concern it; and when it does not have the first word, it will have the last word. Taking a moral position does not tolerate any abstention, any neutrality, at least ultimately and theoretically.

Man is a potentially ethical being who exists *as such,* that is, as a moral being, from time to time, and here and there— distant heres and theres. For intermittences are abnormally frequent here, and the eclipses of conscience inordinately protracted: during these long pauses, the conscience, apparently void of any scruples, seems struck by moral anesthesia and moral adiaphora, that is to say, seems incapable of distinguishing between "good" and "evil." Or, to use the traditional language of moral theology: the *vox conscientiæ* remains silent as long as the absence of conscience [*inconscience*] of the speculative consciousness [*conscience speculative*] lasts. What has become of the voice of conscience, generally so loquacious, according to theologians? It has become mute and aphonic—it is broken, this voice of the conscience; its infallible oracles fall silent. To live from a truly moral and, as a result, *continually* moral existence such as it is—in the sense in which one says: to have a religious life—is perhaps within reach of the ascetics and the saints who are in the good graces of holiness and thanks to supernatural resources, if such a chimera were conceivable . . . Tolstoy aspired to a Christian "life" and despaired about never being able to attain it, or if, for an instant, he attained it, about not being able to hold on to it. What do the austere person and the mystic do between two observances? What are their ulterior motives? As the days pass by, the average man, whom we can call *Homo ethicus,* goes about his business, pursues his simple pleasures, and does not pose any problems for himself; he is not even a "Sunday morning Christian"! The thinking being is a long way away from thinking all the time. Even more so, instinct, in the moral animal, only sleeps with one eye open: the retaliations of naturality, sensuality, and voracity are frequent; no less frequent are the repercussions of self-love; and as concerns the somnolences and the lapses in concentration of the moral conscience, they occupy the major part of our daily life.

3. A "Moral Life." Continuous or Discontinuous? The Inner Core. The Circle of Temporality.

Having said that: the entire question is to know, with regard to the moral being, what meaning it is necessary to give to the qualifying, attributive, or predicate adjective. The moral being, *is* he moral in the ontological sense—moral from head to toe and from one end to the other? Moral at all times and in all the instants of these times? Is he moral even when he eats his soup or when he plays dominos? One can, with Aristotle, believe in the permanence of a manner of being (*hexis*) that would be chronic, as is every manner of being: when this manner of being is moral, it would merit the name of virtue. Wonderful! But virtue is in no way a habit: for as it becomes habitual, the moral manner of being withers and drains itself of any intentionality; it becomes a tic, an automatism, and the drivel of a virtuous parrot. It is thus much worse than the rite [*geste*] of holy water that, at least, is not meant for anyone on earth: it is rather the gesture [*geste*] of the devout person, who, without even looking at the beggar, drops a penny into his bowl. Even more so, cannot one speak of a second nature that would substitute for the first

one, for the natural nature, and that would be the supernatural nature of supermen (or angels!). Aristotle himself
agrees: a moral disposition becomes virtuous only if it exists in action (*energeia*): in other words, it is actualized on the
occasion of an event or a crisis. Such would be the dangers
of war, such would be the exceptional circumstances of life
that reveal the courage of the courageous man; without the
German invasion, without the ordeals of the occupation, of
the deportation, of the humiliation we would perhaps never
have known that some young resister was a hero; no one is
judged to be a hero simply by his good appearance or his
speech (except when the speaking itself indicates the engagement of the entirety of his being): we do not give credit
to a potential hero if he has only ever been but a candidate:
heroism is not written in advance on the face or in the gait
of this laborer, or of this modest functionary, whom we will
have discovered after the fact was capable of the most sublime abnegation in the face of a most implacable enemy.

For it is after the fact and in the future perfect that *heroism,* as with vocation and merit in general, will have been
a "potentiality"; it is retrospectively that it affirms its excru-
ciating, its mysterious obviousness with the supreme sacrifice. When a patriot has been felled by salvo, a voice within
us clamors louder than the assassins' guns: this was a righ-
teous man! Virtue, then, was neither an inert and purely logical potentiality, strongly aroused by some chance accident,
nor an inimitable aptitude, a predestined aptitude inscribed
in advance in one's character: the situation adds something
synthetically, and adds nothing to what we were able to know
about the hero—the two together; it is necessary to say at
the same time that bursts of courage, like surges of sincerity,
need an occasion or a difficulty in order to exist in action, that

is, meritoriously, expensively, dangerously, and yet a manner of being courageous maintains all its sublime obviousness. Virtue remains paradoxically chronic even if it springs up and disappears in the same instant. Let us add: a moral sense is present potentially in all humans even if it seems to be in a state of lethargy in all of them. When one considers less exceptional, less hyperbolic forms of moral life, one never knows if it is necessary to maintain confidence in man or despair about him: one is rather returned back indefinitely from confidence to misanthropy. The surges of the most spontaneous and most sincere *pity* in an apparently insensitive being sometimes reconcile us to what is human in man; one was not expecting such happy surprises; we begin again to believe in the "good foundation" of human nature, or rather we oscillate between two opposite theses about it. And likewise, the permanent possibility of a violent moral insurrection, capable of breaking out at any moment and of crossing the threshold of scandal, attests, although in a way that is always a little ambiguous, to our need for justice; the flame of anger and moral *indignation* was not extinguished, it was only on the back burner. It is here, in the passing outburst of emotion, in the tenderness of pity, and in the heat of anger, that a moral life is suddenly awakened from its apathy. But sometimes this awakening happens without a feverish burst of activity in the chronic passion of *remorse* or *shame*. Remorse is a moral persecution that pursues the guilty person in all places and at every instant, and does not leave him any respite. However much Cain could flee to the end of the world or shut himself away a thousand miles underground, he inexorably remains alone with the haunting memory of his misdeed: moral life, instead of being concentrated in an outburst of anger, in an anger [*colère*] that is wholly ready to fade [*décolorer*], is immobilized in the obsession of remorse. But the burning of remorse is an exceptional torment. More commonly, remorse burns on the back burner and, thus, it is called *bad conscience:* hidden under the ashes of indifference and sordid interests, the infinitesimal glowing coals of the bad conscience are rekindled from time to time: man is then racked with inner reproaches that have not ceased to haunt his nights with insomnia. The bad conscience stands guard: so earlier theology called it *synteresis:* a faithful paragon of virtue, "synteresis" watches over the sacred fire that has become latent and can at any moment reignite the flame. A moral life that would be identified with the bad conscience can be called retrospective or consequent, since it is turned toward the past of the misdeed; and so it is proper to set it in opposition to an *antecedent moral conscience* that would be turned toward the future of problems to be resolved, and notably toward "crises of conscience": the moral problem here is lived not in the stagnation of suffering and the ruminations of anguish by an unhappy conscience, but in hesitation and perplexity by a worried conscience that is not always stationary. The moral conscience and the bad conscience thus form the web of an unreal life: the moral life is like the remorse of an elementary or "primary" life; and it has as its object neither the conservation of the being itself nor pleonexia. As for this orphan dressed in black whose solitude the poet invites us to acknowledge, one will permit us to call it *conscience.* The conscience is a dialogue with an interlocutor, a dialogue in a hushed voice, which in truth is a monologue. And what name should we actually give to this double that keeps me company everywhere, following me or preceding me, and yet leaves me alone with myself? What name should we give to the one who is both myself and another, and who, however, is not the *alter ego,* the Aristotelian *allos autos?* It is always present, everywhere absent, omnipresent, omni-absent. For the me [*moi*] never escapes this tête-à-tête with itself . . . This object-subject that looks at me with its absent look, one can only call it by a name that is simultaneously intimate and impersonal: the "Conscience."[2]

And not only does the a priori of moral evaluation get ahead of and impregnate all the steps of the conscience, it even seems, by the effect of an ironic ruse, that the rejection of every evaluation accentuates the impassioned character of it: as if, in secrecy, axiology had regained powers and acquired a new vitality; suppressed, hunted down, persecuted, it only becomes more fanatical and more intransigent; chase it out the door and it comes back in through the window, or by the chimney, or by the keyhole; or better yet, it never left; it only pretended to do so; it remained sitting tranquilly at our table under the lamp . . . *Dubito ergo cogito.* Thought is affirmed in its presence and its plenitude at the very interior of the doubt that claims to deny it. Doubt sends us immediately and in one fell swoop back to thought, to that thought of which it is the essential function, if it is true that contestation, or rather problematization, is thought itself, thought as it is exercised, thought at it works: this thought that is constitutionally in the action of doubting itself refutes doubt and restores the first truth; before one has had the time to say it or merely become aware of it, doubt has already reconstituted the inexterminable truth of which it was hoping to be rid. The thought that doubt can no longer, at least without contradicting itself on the spot, be doubtful in turn: and so, doubt, by its very definition, saving the thought that is its speculative backbone, involuntarily will have reestablished a first truth; upon this first truth, as is the case with Des-

cartes, all truths will be constructed! Doubt contradicted itself in thinking. But it is perhaps to be feared that thought
contradicts itself in doubting: thought, hardened by the ordeal and having become conscious of itself in this ordeal,
is tempted to refute itself and to repudiate itself, to apply to
itself the supplementary arguments and instruments of a
doctrinal skepticism; man now uses his critical faculties to
doubt even more deeply. But perhaps it was sufficient to distinguish carefully between a vicious circle and a healthy circle. The feverish circle, a diallel or a circular argument, indefinitely sends us from doubt to thought and from thought
to doubt: this circle is a sophism, in other words, a clandestine game with logic, one that plays clever little games with
this logic the way a smuggler does with customs agents. Epimenides' Paradox, condemning the mind to spin around in
a bewitched circle until the end of time, results in a type of
malicious logic, a shameful logic, a black logic. Doesn't such
an accursed circle make us think of the torture of Ixion on
his wheel? If the accursed circle resembles a machination
of the evil genius, the healthy circle would be a type of malicious ruse. It is perhaps this malicious genius who, having
taken refuge in the Cogito, puts up an inscrutable resistance
to the corrupt undertakings of the evil genius. Instead of di-
abolically refuting every truth, including thinking thought
itself, we stick to thought and ceaselessly come back to it;
also, it is the supreme instance of it; everything ends at it,
everything follows from it, everything arises from it; it is the
alpha and the omega, it is the first and the last . . . The negation of the negation is no longer a nihilistic and destructive
dialectic: it is turned toward the positivity of sense, toward
the plenitude of mind, and toward the continual enrich-
ment of thought. Thought is an instance of supremacy, and

we hold fast to this instance . . . We will not let go of it! Indeed, it turns out after the fact that we had never let go of it! . . . Such is benevolent malice, such is the beneficial malice of the healthy circle.

Let us recap the movement of coming-and-going, which is not a mere oscillation in situ but also a deepening. The more I doubt, the more I think: and vice versa, the more I think, the more I doubt; but here, once more, I think by beginning again to doubt, and more and more actively: the circle is closed, is partially opened, and is closed again continually, but each time with a bigger exponent; the auction price does not cease to grow and the bidding to climb; doubt and thought challenge one another over and over, and outdo each other to become stronger . . . But in all cases the fractures will be fused again, the discontinuities will be filled in. Thought will have the last word.

The omnipresence of moral evaluation, despite its pronounced and apparently quite subjective qualitative specificity, or because of its very specificity, is not dissimilar to the omnipresence of the Cogito. The more I deny it, the more passionately it exalts itself. But on the other hand, moral evaluation, like temporality, is a type of category of language; axiology adheres so closely to the logos that we cannot dissociate it from it; before setting our sights on what is impalpable in one's inner core, we first discover it in discourse. It is impossible to characterize time other than with words that are already temporal: a definition, in such matters, inevitably presupposes that which is defined! Isn't time an ultimate, irreducible instance that always refers to itself and that is defined, circularly, by itself? An analysis cannot go beyond. Monsieur Jourdain, in order to define prose, expresses himself in prose and tacitly supposes the problem to be resolved. But begging the question is a fortiori legitimate when the concern is time, since time is an "a priori." It is impossible to speak of time without the discourse itself taking time, without reasoning in time, without using words of time, verbs and adverbs, without a forestalling time furtively having itself gone ahead of our analysis and our reflection. When one defines time as the succession of the anterior and the ulterior, complex and indivisible temporality has already surged back in each of these three concepts and then in each of the infinitesimal instants of the present where philosophers will want to pursue it and catch it. This regress goes ad infinitum . . . We were saying: it is to propositional logic that judgments of value owe their status. It is certainly not a question of uncovering axiology, even in the form of untraceable tracks, even in minuscule homeopathic doses, in a geometrical treatise. And yet, the principle of finality permits Leibniz to speak the language of morality in physics. Incidentally, it is speculative discourse in general that is steeped in normativity, permeated by axiology. When we say axiology, it is not at all a matter of tables, scales, or value judgments inspired by the needs and desires of man. The preference will remain anthropocentric and relative as long as the principle of preferability remains morally undetermined; and the "principle" of what is better, far from being a principle of choice, will never be but an indifferent, physical tropism, that is, a natural attraction, if one does not discover within it a "supernatural" principle, or ideal motivations or rational grounds; certainly the "monad," being (as Leibniz says) a unilateral point of view, prefers this or that, is attracted here or there according to the whims of unequal tensions in the environment in which it evolves and according to the disparity between the attractions that solicit it. But if one speaks this language, then where are the moral activity and the moral autonomy of the will? And what is "better"? Better for whom and for what reason? Better from which point of view? Better for one's health? Or more useful and in conformity with my general interest? Or recommended by the administration? That which is desired, is it desired because it is desirable or as the source of a greater pleasure? Desir*able*, prefer*able* . . . It is quite difficult not to justify the real attraction by a priority of right, by a normative legitimacy that remains implied and that is the consecration of the attraction. But conversely, one can fear that moral evaluation, with its hierarchies, its unevennesses, its comparatives, and its adverbs of manner, is recuperated by logic as formal modality . . . But modality is a form of assertion; and a judgment of value itself is of a wholly different order; and it is not enough to say that this modality, if there are modalities, is not evaluative: it expresses a normative exigency of a subject confronted with certain behaviors, certain words, certain ways of living or feeling—better yet, it is a nascent gesture, the first steps of the rejection or the adoption that is its militant and drastic manner of participating in a fight. But the action itself would not have any ethical meaning if we were not able to give a name to the values that remain implicit in the evaluation and that tacitly justify the axiological normativity of the "possessing value." In any case, this impalpable and invisible responsibility of valorization insinuates itself into words and sometimes even rushes into them; all of our objective rigor does not suffice to hold back such an overflowing. Viewed from above and afar, in other words by approximation, the innumerable nuances of manner are summed up in the dramatic and somewhat Manichaean polarity of benevolence and malevolence; but it is language in general that always reveals to some degree the taking of a stand, an infinitesimal taking of sides, an imperceptible partiality. The indicative, without even slipping into the imperative, indirectly suggests a normative choice, a preference that does not dare speak its name. The judgments of value that are denounced by the scientific mind are re-created ad infinitum.

4. From Negation to Refusal. Refusal of Pleasure, Refusal of the Refusal.

But here is the height of irony: moral exigency is all the more urgent given that one pretends to deal with it more carelessly; the advocacy for the defense was in the indictment itself, and it does not, thus, need supplementary arguments. It is this economy of proofs that is ironic: for the revenge that it has in store for moral exigency was implicated in the questioning itself! Let us here recall that for Descartes, thought nihilized negation practically without moving, without taking a single step outside itself, and, to a certain extent, on the spot. Better still: man sometimes claims to be matter, and nothing but matter, a thinking machine, a desirous gelatin; and the more he persists in this affirmation, armed with the resources of reflection and reasoning, the more he proves the suzerainty of a mind that alone is capable of conferring meaning. For the negation of thought is still thought . . . And how very complex this is! And how much thinking is involved! Negation, states Bergson in *Creative Evolution,* is an affirmation in the second degree (I say: an affirmation with an exponent), an affirmation of an affirmation that remains implied, an affirmation that one utters to the subject of an affirmation that one does not utter. Beyond pure and simple affirmation, which is a tautology, and independent of every series, we distinguish three degrees of negation according to the intensity of the past: 1st: Negation is an indirect, complex, secondary affirmation that is expressed via a detour or in the modesty of an embryonic periphrasis ("snow is not black"); it can be of the same order as understatement; affirmation is made up of two parts, but the second part is all the more dynamic because it remains tacit. Bergson demonstrated it well: this complication of words, which seems superfluous or needlessly aggressive, gives it a pedagogical and sometimes even polemical character: the negative statement, so as to forestall a very unlikely error and defend something clearly obvious that hardly has need of being defended, is raised in advance against the paradox and, in fact, shatters the absurdity. Without a doubt, I had my reasons for expressing myself in such a manner . . . In any case, negativity here implies a protest of common sense which, for this or that reason, judges itself to be threatened by nonsense. 2nd: The negation of the appearance, rejecting the appearance as erroneous, is located on the plane of the paradox: it protests against something falsely obvious, against a specious appearance, against a superficial resemblance that hides a superficial dissemblance. No, appearance is not the truth, appearance is not the being. 3rd: And here we have the negation of the negation. Yes: snow is, indeed, white. The mind returns to the appearance, but in professing an empiricism that is conscious of itself.

Leaving aside the naive adhesion to instinct and naturality that is on the side of ethics, in moral life we find the second and third stages already distinguished: but negation will henceforth be called *refusal*. And why "refusal" rather than "negation"? Because moral life puts into question the tumultuous, emotional, contradictory, biological energies with which the will is grappling in its experience of duty; it is then pleasure that is in play, pleasure, desire, and vital affirmation. Negation, a logical operation, and, as such, notional and Platonic, would not be sufficient for nihilizing these orgiastic forces! To deny is *to say that . . . is . . . not,* and for the rest, to leave it up to a Platonic wish or to an enchantment; but to refuse is *to say no,* with a sharp word; and this word is an act; and this act, independent of all rationality, can be a fit of anger; for the monosyllable "no" is indeed a real act, a deliberate and decisive act in the interior of the action or better yet the *drastic* gesture of someone who, by banging his fist on the table, puts an end to transactions and to prevarications; it is the brutal gesture of pure and simple rejection: this rejection is a nascent aggression. Gathering together the scattered members of negation (*to say that . . . is . . . not*), refusal uses them like a weapon, so as better to strike and to wound. I respond no to that which had the pretension of seducing me, the insolence of tempting me. The assaults are not far away! The no is a type of magic.

1st: The first refusal is situated at the level of supernatural morals, whether they are intellectualistic, ascetic, or rigid. On this matter, Plato's no, in contrast to Aristotle's *yes . . . but,* echoes Kant's unconditional no in contrast to the indulgent optimism of the eighteenth century. The words themselves indicate the entirety of the gulf that remains between the negation (or the simple questioning) of appearance and the categorical refusal of pleasure: skepticism toward appearance readily makes exceptions for nuances, degree, point of view, in a word, for more or less; and on the other hand, it does not necessarily have practical consequences: it is the

earth that turns, and yet men, despite knowing this, continue to act as if it were the sun that rose and set, and they
conform their behavior to this anthropocentric appearance.
In contrast, the repudiation of pleasure responds to the alternative of the all-or-nothing . . . And to intimidate and send
shivers down the spines of those who would be tempted by
the bad solution in spite of everything, theologians invent
the most abominable words; they speak of a concupiscence
of the flesh. Appearance is not truth, even though it can par-
ticipate in it; but pleasure is absolutely not the Good, on no
account, in no degree, in no fashion, even if it so seems . . .
What am I saying? Especially if it so seems! Besides, appearance can be partially false or specious, but strictly speaking
it is neither fallacious nor deceptive; it wishes no evil upon
me; it is, moreover, neither malevolent nor benevolent—it
is what it is, that is all, and in itself rather indifferent; it is
the interpretation of the dazzled or astounded man who at-
tributes intentions to it. On the contrary, the attraction of
pleasure is more than an error: it is a deception. Around
this attraction, a complex of perfidious beauty, intent upon
harming me, has formed; around this complex, a myth of
the seductress has formed. With regard to the seductress, we
feel not defiance [*défiance*] but rather mistrust [*méfiance*]: not
a justified, measured, reasoned defiance toward news that is
open to question or with respect to a doubtful piece of information that it would be necessary to verify and to correct,
to interpret with the help of customary reducing agents—
but rather an infinite and irrepressible mistrust. The highly
suspect object of our mistrust is called ill will.—This is the
first refusal. This first refusal is the beginning in us of the
first complex and of the first ambivalence: the repression
instituted by law transformed naive pleasure into a shame-

ful temptation and voluptuousness without any complexes into a more or less cloudy desire. Temptation is all that remains of pleasure after the censure. The moral man . . . and the tempted one . . . feels aversion toward what is naturally attractive and what he truly wants. This situation of a being who is torn apart, secondarily attracted by reason and held by desire, we say that it is passionate: we call this indecisive situation, in which the movement *toward,* which is the attraction, impedes the movement of avoidance, which is aversion, phobia. Two voices, of which each one is, depending on the case, the regret or the nostalgia of the other, two voices, for which the one is subordinate to the other, are in some way combined in the polyphony of a complex; when it is a question of the first complex, then it is the voice of desire that is, if not the ulterior motive [*arrière-pensée*], then at least the aftertaste [*arrière-gout*], and that is expressed quietly; and it is, consequently, pleasure that is repressed, forbidden, and condemned to an illegal and subterranean existence; desire will have to live according to a regimen of secrecy along with poor, contraband pleasures and imaginary satisfactions. The ambivalence of the first degree, tormented by the internal contradiction that tears it apart, engenders violence of the first degree. This is an induced violence . . . Since the prohibited pleasure is not absolutely exterminated and, besides, is not nihilizable, then exterminating asceticism, which is not content with suffocating it, savages its corpse, hunts down its shadow everywhere, persecutes its very memory, all the way to the memory of this memory. As for pleasure per se, one can deprive oneself of it, erase it, renounce it . . . But as for temptation, which is a mental game with the possibility of, a gentle stroke of, the imaginary, barely a "flirtation," how does one stop oneself from thinking about it? The person who is tempted does not have hold of a will [*volonté*] that is flirtatious with the opposite, subconscious will [*subvolonté*] and that is secretly a velleity or even an absence of will [*nolonté*]; it wages an impossible battle against an intangible, impalpable, imponderable hypocrisy concealed within the deepest depths of itself. It is this infinitesimal hypocrisy that produces our impotence; and it is this impotence that explains the almost desperate passion of asceticism, its holy fury, the infinite torture to which it indefatigably subjects the body. It would resurrect its victim, if it were able, for the mere pleasure of killing him again . . . For there are dead people whom it is necessary that we kill!

2nd: Refusal number two is the refusal of the refusal, that is to say (at least in appearance), the refusal of "idealistic" morality. Before showing how the stand against morality [*l'antimorale*] itself restores the most fanatical of moralities, let us attempt to untangle the dense and complex ulterior motives of the refusal that has an exponent. For the refusal of a refusal encompasses a complex as does the first refusal, but the terms of the ambivalence are now reversed. In reality, with the ambivalence itself varying according to the respective proportions of the two elements that constitute its ambiguity, innumerable transitions fluctuate between the simple complex (the first refusal) and the "complicated complex" (the refusal of the refusal), between the absolute, intransigent, and unconditional No and the nuanced refusal, the herald of a Yes. One glides, almost without perceiving it, from fanatical extremism to a mischievous asceticism that multiplies the allusions in the direction of the sin; but still (or again) in extremist asceticism, the allure is mixed with disgust and comprises with it a type of sacred horror. At one end of the series, asceticism vomits up the cloying lemonade and syrups of pleasure; halfway between this supernaturalism and radical naturalism, it sometimes happens that the conscience smiles timidly on suavities and looks askance at them; in line with the *Philebus* rather than the *Phaedo,* Baltasar Gracián, simultaneously faithful and unfaithful to Plato, agrees to mix pleasure with truth. Complacency toward pleasure is a first step in the direction of hedonism. Converted by the first complex, the ascetic feels an unnatural aversion toward that which is naturally attractive; converted a second time, but by a complication of the complication, the voluptuous person, conversely, recognizes the attraction of what is natural and fails to recognize the supernatural value of the norm. Nevertheless, the second conversion is not a perversion that would be the symmetrical opposite of the first conversion. The two ambivalences both favor the proliferation of paradoxes and the exuberance of monsters, but they are hardly comparable: the first ambivalence was the clandestine duplicity of the ascetic who is tempted by lascivious images—Saint Anthony in the desert! And the second ambivalence is that of the voluptuous person who has moralizing pretensions. In the wake of the virtuous-vicious person and his libertine accomplices, here is the vicious-virtuous person who recruits his accomplices from the camp of puritans. Such are the two generations of monsters, like the double teratology, begat not strictly speaking by the redoubling of refusal but by its division in two [*dédoublement*]: for to renounce [re*nier*] is not at all to deny [*nier*] two times by increasing the negation and by extending it to other objects of the same order that are capable of being denied; it is, on the contrary, to deny the very effects of the act of denying by almost always completely annulling, but sometimes only partially, the nullifying effects of the act; renunciation is not a second negation that would be added arithmetically to the first one, it is a reflexive retreat and one that refutes rearward or backward; in a word, the negation of the negation is not repetition but *reflection*. The negation of the negation, having ended in the emancipation of desire, renders the protests of the body superfluous: passion no longer has need of an outlet; however, the complex that has an exponent is just as orgiastic and passionate as the first complex: but the terms of the contradiction that inhabit it are reversed. Pleasure, reduced to the secrecy of temptation, was the aftertaste [*arrière-goût*] of austere idealism: the ideal, or the law, will be the ulterior motive [*arrière-pensée*] and the innermost intention [*arrière-intention*] of unrestrained voluptuous pleasure . . . —the innermost intention and, who knows, perhaps the remorse; if one dares say it, by way of expressing oneself, that persecuted pleasure is the scruple of the ascetic, then even more is the ridiculed ideal the scruple of the libertine, and this in the proper meaning of the word. Each of the two wills, thus, prolongs in itself the repercussion and the echo of its own ulterior will [*arrière-volonté*]. For conscience has a good memory: converted to asceticism, it has not forgotten the taste of pleasure; reconverted to pleasure, it has retained the lessons of reason. The secret voice that was whispering the persuasive counsels of pleasure into our ear now whispers the reproaches of reason into pleasure's ear. Asceticism thought that it had exterminated pleasure, but pleasure was still breathing; a wisp of life was remaining in it, a sensitivity, a remainder of heat . . . It was only too easy to reanimate it. Now that the orgy of pleasure, like an irresistible tidal wave, has inundated everything, it is the law's turn to protest: but of course, the ideal testifies in a soft voice, and its weak voice barely makes itself heard in the tempest of desires. The negation of the negation does not entirely undo what the first negation had done. Grammar tells us that two negations, the second one annulling the first, are equivalent to an affirmation—an affirmation in two steps. But—which grammar does not tell us—the second negation can quite well leave intact certain positive benefits of the first one and, in this particular case, the ideal for which the denigration of the pleasure will have served as a foil; if the negation with an exponent annuls the first negation and, consequently, restores the pleasure, it neither necessarily nor completely annuls the correlative affirmation that matches it; it can quite well remain something of the ideal . . . unless, of course, this affirmation formally contradicts the sovereignty of the pleasure; outside of this incompatibility, it is not absurd that a residue of normativity, that a type of halo still idealizes the life of instinct. In any case, the negation of the negation, at the end of its circuit, will not have restored "identically" the world of common sense: its world is another world, its pleasure another pleasure, and one which, like the Prodigal Son, takes into account ordeals undergone, bears the stamp of adventures lived, and holds on to the lesson of them.

The unusual presence of duty in full sensual fury as well as, in turn, the unmentionable presence of temptation deeply hidden in moral intimacy generates explosive promiscuities, breathtaking contradictions, and above all scandalous violence. Here the induced violence is a violence of the second degree, an almost exaggerated violence. The sacrilegious person experiences a semblance of respect and even a remnant of gratitude toward these values that it furiously tramples upon, spits out again, and renounces today; and this devotion that does not want to speak its name is seasoned with a vague aftertaste of remorse. The survival of respect complicates still more the second complex by making a better offer on its complexity, by multiplying it, by itself. However, the bizarre nostalgia of a law that is now renounced makes us go from regret to aversion, mockingly sends us back from veneration to hatred. The liberation of instincts is not only a signal of deliverance, it announces an extreme tension. The austere aggressiveness that is directed against the body is no longer but a memory, it now kindles a reverse aggressiveness, a profane and sacrilegious aggressiveness; I continue to have it in for values after their failure, despite their failure, and sometimes because of this failure itself—and that indefatigably; I am angry at myself for my own remorse and for my secret respect; and the more I show respect, the more I am angry at myself. This short-lived weakness stirs up still more the rancor of sacrilege against the long-standing prohibition and against the hypocritical deceptions that robbed us of our simple pleasures for so long. The simple pleasures, having been persecuted for so long, now take their revenge on obligations and deprivations. Thanks to vengeful debaucheries, thanks to provocative orgies, the time of penitence will be quickly forgotten. A cynical provocation echoes the ascetic provocation, the cynical counterviolence that spits on values responds to the ascetic violence that tramples the body and manhandles the body's pleasures; instead, ascetic relentlessness is made of maledictions, of mortifications, and of tortures—cynical relentlessness, rather of blasphemies, sarcasms, and affronts, but acute ambivalence inhabits both of them. In the ambiguous and ambivalent meaning of the word "horror" the lascivious person loathes morality as the ascetic person loathes voluptuous pleasure: exoterically, duty horrifies the lascivious person, but the constraints of duty, esoterically, tempt him; the moral law is for him somewhat untouchable; this horror, a "sacred" horror, a loving horror, is thus most suspicious, just as the phobia is suspicious that distances us from a taboo and an appealing aversion, that is, the irrational outcome of terror and attraction.

5. The Prohibition. Prohibition of the Prohibition.

Sometimes it happens that man, sent from one to the other, and then from the other back to the one, is struck with vertigo and no longer knows the saint to which he should dedicate himself; with this indefinite oscillation between two poles having deprived him of every frame of reference, man is given over, body and soul, to the frantic contradiction, to the orgiastic confusion, to the chaos of the absurdity. It is prohibited to prohibit: it is what the infinite questioning formerly inscribed on the walls in black letters, black like the black flag of anarchy. Just as the negation of a negation merits an affirmation, and the refusal of a refusal merits an approval, so the prohibition of a prohibition is equivalent to an authorization: it is the periphrasis in a modest way of an authorization that does not want to speak its name. If the accent is on the interdicts themselves, lifted one after the other, then the refusal of all prohibitions leads, if worse comes to worst, to universal lawfulness and thus to caprice, to what is arbitrary, and in the end, to quietist indifference; the *rather-than* (*potius quam*) is obsolete; freedom was defined only in relation to certain prohibited things: a prohibited direction, a prohibited crossing, a prohibited entry; what is not expressly prohibited is tacitly permitted; and, in fact, permission, in this regard, has a determinate meaning. Every determination is a negation and implies a limitation that consecrates the advent of the finite to existence. But when everything is licit, there is no longer space except for licentiousness, and the latter is hardly preferable to total paralysis. Everything is permitted, even the contradictions that destroy each other and refute one another. General lawfulness, but also the Bacchanalia that ensues, prevents an order from being formed, even if it be the order of disorder, [or prevents] a reign from being instituted, be it the reign of anarchy. And can one even speak of "institution"? The situation is no less blocked when, instead of achieving, through extrapolation or generalization, universal lawfulness by gradually knocking down all vetoes, one begins with the prohibitive assertion itself: what is prohibited now is not this or that prohibited thing—it is not a question of prohibiting this or that—prohibitions concerning details, the lifting of which would gradually extend our latitude for acting—no! what is, as it were, prohibited to the second power is the fact of the prohibition in general and globally, and this is the very intention of prohibiting. Every velleity to prohibit, even if it is nascent, is a priori suppressed. *It is prohibited to prohibit* is a general assertion, and this assertion with an exponent is not, in turn, subsumed under a new interdiction that would render it discretionary; there would be here an absurd infinite regression, and perhaps a vicious circle similar to the way Epimenides' Paradox makes us turn in circles; *it is prohibited to prohibit* is thus a one-way veto, an irreversible assertion; no veto in the opposite direction is reborn in the wake of this general prohibition of annulling it or devouring it; no regressive prohibition comes to neutralize the prohibition of the prohibition. Even so, when all is said and done, if everything is permitted, then the prohibition of the prohibition as well is permitted; it is not prohibited, but quite the opposite, it is useful, even recommended, to remember that the prohibition is in principle systematically prohibited; this prohibition is affirmed without appeal, but the affirmation of the veto of vetoes itself escapes a veto. This is a necessary exception so that discourse has a sense. If this venting is not granted to us, silence is our only recourse. It is prohibited to prohibit: you cannot prevent me from professing it, from justifying the right to prohibit every prohibition, and in the end, in the name of a dangerously dogmatic philosophy of freedom, from upholding this law and, if need be, from punishing every infraction of the veto of vetoes; it is prohibited to think otherwise, prohibited to obstruct the philosophy of universal lawfulness, to sabotage it through trickery, to limit it hypocritically. This prohibition to prohibit anything is itself formulated in menacing terms; absolute permissiveness, assuring the exercise of all freedoms, without limits or hindrances, is a guarantee, if necessary, of bludgeonings. Freedom is thus imposed in an authoritarian manner, and in a threating language designed to intimidate the undecided. An all-is-permitted freedom and a virtuous terrorism thus come together or, better yet, become one. The prohibition to prohibit, reduced to impotence by its internal contradiction, at least finds its foundation in a libertarian moral philosophy.

Prohibition more or less always harbors a terroristic temptation. Now, the prohibition that is not only the direct prohibition of prohibited things but the prohibition of the very intention of prohibiting, and not only the prohibition of this intention but a radical prohibition of every prohibition,—this prohibition paves the way for the one-upmanship of moralizing fanaticism. However, the restoration of a virtuous terrorism can take place in a much more simplistic and in some way mechanical manner. Since the moral law became, for the sacrilegious person, a sort of forbidden pleasure (for every virtue is impure and every disinterestedness is suspect), it is pleasure that makes the law. There will be a duty of pleasure, and even a religion of pleasure, and even a theology of pleasure! And so the "reversal" of values amounts to a postponement of value, transferred from one extreme to the other. This reversal, although irreversible (for it does not imply an inversion that at the end of the round trip would reestablish the status quo), is rather an interchanging [*interversion*], a simple exchange of roles. To exchange roles is not to transform intrinsically the meaning of values; to switch jailers and prisoners with each other is not to abolish jailers and prisoners or to do away with the very principle that we call today the "prison system." In prison, the veto! In prison, duty and the moral law! Now that the extravagances of pleasure rule over the place, the veto, in turn, has become the martyr! The last will be the first, beginning with the moment the first have passed last . . . But there will still be first ones and last ones. Isn't this revolution, which consists in a change of the jailers, a sinister derision?

Morality is essentially refusal . . . even though every refusal is not necessarily moral! It all depends upon what one refuses . . . In this particular case, morality is the refusal of egoistic pleasure. And consequently, the refusal that refuses morality is quite generally the refusal of the *moral* refusal, the refusal to renounce one's own pleasure, one's own interest, and one's own self-love: in this case, the first refusal (the refusal to refuse) is not deduced from the first one by subtraction—it annuls it, it cancels it in one fell swoop and in one go. Such is the egoist's *No* in its wretched harshness. But sometimes it also happens that this refusal of the refusal is the refusal of a complaisant austerity, the refusal of useless fasting and of suspect penances. It is in these interested privations that Fénelon recognized the symptoms of "spiritual avarice." Anti-morality itself thus becomes a chapter of morality. For morality has such a great assimilative power that it infinitely recuperates all the *antis* that are capable of refuting it. In Pascal's dialectic, everything proves God and turns to his glory, that which is against as much as that which is for, the objections as well as the arguments: and in the same way anti-morality in many cases is an homage that immorality pays to morality.

The genre painters of the seventeenth and eighteenth centuries who describe the "characters" and the social types of their times we call the "French *moralists*"—and not without reason: La Bruyère and Vauvenargues are not disinterested and amused spectators of the human comedy; they are not dilettantes or amateurs in their armchairs contemplating the theater of the world with opera glasses. And Theophrastus, the disciple of Aristotle, whose name they invoke, is not any more so a detached spectator: the gallery of satirical portraits and picturesque little paintings presupposes, for Theophrastus, another gallery of which this one is in some way the opposite or the negative; all the forms of human pettiness, flatterers, sycophants, blackmailers, cowards, hypocrites, and crooks of all types have arranged to meet on the square and at the harbor: but they refer to a type of better man, who in general remains anonymous—for perversion always seems to be varied, strongly affected, and abundant compared with the ideal. To be honest, the "char-

acterology" or better yet the "characterography" of Theophrastus and La Bruyère is discretely normative and has
Manichaeism as a backdrop: it remains understood (quietly
understood) that loyalty is preferable to hypocrisy; the informer and slanderer serve as foils for the true man. According to the Christian moralists of the Classical Age, notably La
Rochefoucauld and Pascal, this model of the true and pure
man is distorted by the consequences of original sin, that is,
by the Fall, but it is easy to find it again under the grimacing guise of hypocrisy and egoism. Saint Francis de Sales lucidly denounces the poison of pious concupiscence among
the collectors of penances who stockpile perfections with an
eye to their salvation. He reproaches these hoarders for their
spiritual avarice! An eminently moral profession of faith is
thus expressed in misanthropy just as much as in philanthropy. Ethological relativism itself, if it excludes all dogmatism, admits of a type of potential system of reference: it untangles, it thwarts the thousand and one tiny maneuvers and
schemes that comprise the strategy of bad faith.—Gracián
himself notices the misery of man when he proposes to the
courtier, as a last resort, a belligerence founded upon dissimulation and the proper use of pretenses. To resign oneself to the least amount of evil is not necessarily immoralism! More, it is a highly moral undertaking to dismantle the
economic mechanisms of deception. Such is Marx's undertaking: the sublime superstructures that camouflage the
sordid or the basely alimentary interests are foiled. What
would Marxism consist of without the entirely moral opposition of justice and injustice and without the concept of an
alienation that is exploitation, that is to say, spoliation, and
which is founded upon the scandal of surplus value? Spoliation would only be, at worst, an ingenious fraud. In order to

have the courage to create a revolution and descend onto the streets, to pass from speculation to the wholly other order of militant action, to cross this vertiginous threshold, a motivating idea is necessary, and this motivating idea can only be born of moral indignation. Without the intentional element of ill will and deception, spoliation reduced to the sole factor of pay would itself be a mere plot, a plot to dismantle, when it is outrageous trickery.

Taking a stand is discreet and at times lacks leniency if not humor for all these moralists, but it was vehement and violent in the doctrinal immoralism of the cynics. For the "moralists," the variety of innumerable perversions suggests indirectly and as if by allusion the outline of an ideal model. With cynicism (here, of course, we are speaking only of the cynical *doctrine*), it is a matter not of an allusive game but of an aggressive contrast. The cynic, in theory, does not play; he is most serious or at least claims to be. The brutal contrast of immoralism and virtues by no means boils down to an antithesis in aesthetic character or to an effect of relief. The morality of anti-morality can here be interpreted in three different ways: (1) An abrupt irony authorizes us to infer tranquilly, automatically, with a cold insolence from a contradictory to its contradictory and from counter-morality to morality; cynical irony invites us, by itself, to take up the opposite of its pretensions; with a direct reading and an immediate adaptation, we decipher virtue in vice and good moral sense in immoral nonsense: in this case, the contradiction is only the extreme and scandalous form of the correlation. With the cynical affronts being a pretense, the translation of this transparent text is done by sight. (2) And here is our second approach: there is nothing to adapt. There is no dialectic. It is actually evil that *is* good (or vice versa) . . . and forever. The reversal, the cynical perversion, in turn, does not call for any interchanging that is capable of putting what is inside out back to being right-side out, of making sense of nonsense, of steering what is counter-sensical back in the direction of good sense. That is the extremism of the cynical challenge. Is the most absurd of cynical absurdities answerable for this "worst-case scenario" whose workings Clément Rosset analyzes in such an original and penetrating manner?[3] Everyone since Plato, and with Plato, repeats it: the Good is by its very definition the supreme desirable; that is an analytical judgment or quite simply a tautology that the principle of identity imposes upon us; and if I say that what is most supremely selectable is called Evil, it amounts to the same thing, which is that I call the Good an evil and, consequently, that Evil is a good. Nothing has thus changed! The one who claims to "will evil" wills evil as a good: that is how Leibniz's optimism expressed itself. In our second approach, the monster that is the willing of evil can thus appear as an effect of rhetoric, and that which is the worst as what is least evil or as a necessary evil. As for the extremism of the absurd, it is above all verbal. A type of "bluff"! The Good is that to which one responds yes; and if one responds no, it is because the so-called Good is a camouflaged evil: paradoxology is free to reverse the two poles, but it merely displaces the polarity, which alone is important: only the signs and the names of the two poles are reversed; paradoxology thinks that it professes nonsense, but this nonsense still has a sense, to which oratorical insolence lends a scandalous face. No one can defy the principle of identity. And likewise, morality gives us the power of refusal and abnegation, but itself is not made for being refused, or sincerely renounced, or a fortiori contradicted. What one rejects is a false, hypocritical, and puritan morality, therefore, a fraud that one prefers over the *other morality* and other "values," those of instinct, of vital fulfillment, and of naturality. Neither fanaticism nor rigorism will be lacking for this morality. (3) Ill will is as evasive and fleeting as the good one, and yet the perverse will exists: it is called malevolence or wickedness; the conscience, a long way from rebounding from the willing of something bad to the willing of something good, will seem split, torn between the two willings: it is inhabited by the nostalgia of abnegation, but it is tempted by egoistic existence; and the more extensive the nostalgia is, the more irresistible the temptation is. And vice versa. And *more and more.* This paradoxical law of *auction,* which rules over all the passionate disorder, alone explains the inexplicable, disproportionate, excessive furor of sacrilege: the moral law is renounced, ridiculed and insulted, trampled, tormented, dragged through the mud, and massacred. The very exaggeration of this refusal and of these invectives is something suspicious and announces its ambivalence: what is "suspect" is indeed a thought that implicates an ulterior motive behind or under the confessed thought, what is suspect is a first intention that hides an ulterior intention. Cynicism opposes the same refusal to morality that morality opposes to immoralism; not that it simply reversed the roles, but did so in order to hurt itself; the sacrilegious person also acutely bears the tension that results from the sacrilegious plot. This complex of torment and diabolical joy is not unrelated to masochism. The cynic, in his own way, feels the anguishes of parricide. Or in circumstances that are less tragic: he makes a scene of morality the way the lover makes a scene of his mistress . . . Nietzsche's mad rage is perhaps a loving rage, a loving of morality. The violent reaction of dismissal toward normative values is not a reverse moral anger or a caricature of moral indignation, it is rather the frenzy of a conscience split in two, crucified, and torn apart by its insoluble contradiction. The more that value is seemingly sacred and revered as such, the more scandalous and trivial are the manifestations of cynical disgust: spitting, vomiting, and rejecting! No gesture is energetic enough to express cynical disgust or the cynical will to expel from our lives, to eliminate from our being in general, the values reputed to be the most holy: moral values are considered as going in a direction that is opposite to life. The cynic makes himself more wicked than he is. In his impotence to stifle completely the irrepressible moral need, or to silence the "voice of conscience," he covers over, with the din of his imprecations and his anathemas, this weak voice that, in an imperceptible whisper, persists in *murmuring again* within us, as if he were exorcizing, or at least defusing, it loudly . . . or at the top of his lungs. It seems that he magically immunizes himself with the same excesses of language and abominable affronts. Blasphemies verify experientially that God does not have self-love, that God is not "susceptible," that God is not irascible, that God would not be able to be challenged or offended, that what is divine is above our ridiculous ways and impotent anthropomorphisms. Cynical discourse is, in spite of itself, indeed a type of alibi; its intemperance is itself revelatory. So there is no reason to attach excessive importance to the rhetoric of curses and swear words. When speaking about Eudoxus of Cnidus,[4] who was both a theorist of doctrinal hedonism and a scholar of quite austere mores, Aristotle expresses himself almost in the same way as Bergson[5] does: do not listen to what they say, look at what they do. Nothing is convincing, or decisive, or revelatory of a sincere intention except the engagement of the actuality of doing something; the only thing that counts is the example that the philosopher provides by his life and in his actions.[6] There is no testimony more authentic and more convincing than that! Indeed, such was, according to the ancients, the case of Antisthenes, a philosopher split in two, a Cynic by doctrine and an ascetic by the example of his life; and such was, without a doubt, the ambiguity of Cynicism in general, an anti-doctrinal doctrine that preferred exercise and suffering to speculation, and that, beyond all political, social, or verbal conformities, dreamed perhaps of an impossible, of an unlivable, purity.

To avoid the perilous temptations of ambivalence, and so morality is not wrong in any way, hedonism usually takes care to recognize in law and de jure the normative value of pleasure; pleasure and instinct are not only rehabilitated, they are directly sacralized; naturality is not simply justified, it is also sanctified; in advance, an injection of value has transfigured, moralized this appealing object that had been an object of aversion. Hedonism thus becomes a type of religion that the person guided by voluptuous pleasure dares celebrate with black masses. "Forbidden kisses, it is God who commands them." Gabriel Fauré set to music these apparently sacrilegious words in his *Shylock*. When Sade himself invokes instinct, he has undoubtedly found the means of sacralizing the sacrilegious, of valorizing anti-value and the naturality of what is against nature, of conferring a monstrous legality upon the nihilism of the absurd. But above all, one can safely confirm that one envisages the cult of sensible pleasure or the provocative immoralism of the Cynics; they are all moralists, and those who are the most are those who seem to be it the least. It is impossible to find a philosophical doctrine that can rigorously maintain the challenge of indifference toward every moral position taken: a difference, be it infinitesimal, between good and evil, an imperceptible partiality, an invisible polarity, even a bias, can always be detected; without the basic principle of nascent preference, without a minimal rather-than, neither choice nor life nor movement would be possible. So absolute immoralism has something corpse-like to it. Simultaneously, leveling off the drastic decisions of the will and the dramatic disparities of emotion, immoralism is addressed not to passionately concerned human beings but to mummies. The moral cardiogram has flatlined, and the burden of emotionality falls to zero. Morality, pilloried and murdered by so-called amoral groups, takes refuge in other ways in the "codes" of these social categories. Street gangs have their "honor," and prostitutes gratuitously observe certain rules of disinterested camaraderie or filial piety. Morality always has the last word: Hunted down, persecuted by immoralism, but never nihilized, it knows all sorts of acts of revenge and of alibis; it regenerates ad infinitum, it is reborn from its ashes, for our protection. For one cannot live without it.

2

The Conspicuousness of Morality Is Simultaneously Equivocal and Univocal

1. The Ambiguity of Maximalism, the Excellence of Intermediarity

Morality is intangible, not only because, in challenging the spatial alternative of inside-of–outside-of, it is simultaneously encompassing and encompassed and because its place would thus not be localizable or assignable, but also because it is simultaneously equivocal and univocal. This second ambiguity, which makes its intrinsic nature evasive, aggravates the effects of the first one. *An Essay of Paradoxical Ethics* is the subtitle that Nikolai Berdyaev gives to his work *The Destiny of Man.*[1] But can one conceive of an ethics that is not paradoxical and whose sole vocation would be to justify the received ideas and the prejudices and the routine of a "doxical" ethics? Now, isn't the paradoxical reversal but a verbal escape clause[?] . . . it responds to the question by the repetition of this question, that is, by the very pronouncement of the mystery it professes. It goes along with the scandal and the challenge. The agonizing alternative, the insoluble alternative, since it cannot be resolved, is settled by a "Gordian" decision. Such is the "madness" of sacrifice. Yet one would be wrong to consider this dilemma as a wholly theoretical situation: it appears when I am not able to save simultaneously my own life and yours, and when a crisis of conscience obligates me, but from a wholly moral obligation, in other words, from a *discretionary obligation,* to sacrifice my own life. Be that as it may, it is not from Platonic transcendence that one should ask for a justification of conformism! Plato's ethics, like Plato's dialectic, follows the upward impetus that carries it into the sublime region where the sunlight of the Good shines. However, if the purpose of the moral man is not to establish himself at the center of the temperate zone that Aristotle calls the golden mean [*juste milieu*], then neither is his purpose to elevate himself to the peak of perfection or to attain the summit of value. First, what about the culmination? Baltasar Gracián speaks of a hero who typifies the height of perfection, who embodies the perfection of perfections; he is the pinnacle of plenitude; with him, all the virtues are at their height; he himself is the paragon of them; he is eminent grandeur and the wonder of wonders; the bouquet of the rarest of flowers, of the most exquisite scents, and of the most splendid colors make his excellence obvious and manifest. When all the elements of wisdom, without excluding a single perfection, as in, for example, the man of virtue or the elderly man at the end of his life, are gathered together in the same crown, the experience of the sage spreads as sage counsels, as reasonable and serene sayings, like a tranquil river; the all-perfect sage at the zenith of his excellence lets flow a torrent of beneficial and soothing words. Such also is Stoic wisdom in which all the virtues are but one and the same virtue.—However, negativity is already implied in this excellence, as the end (*telos*) is already implied in the perfection: completion sometimes says yes, sometimes no, depending upon whether one looks hither or beyond, that is, according to the aspect being considered. Baltasar Gracián, in talking about his hero,[2] more or less defines the seventh "Excellence" in this manner: the hero is first in everything, the first everywhere; he deserves the award for excellence; he is the greatest of all and breaks all records; one is neither able to climb any higher, nor go farther; whether it is an issue of priority or primacy (which is Plotinus's language), or of majesty or "maximality" (which is the language of Nicholas of Cusa), a tacit limitation is dialectically implied in the supremacy of the relative superlative; or, more simply, the relative superlative is the extreme and supreme limit of the comparative. The limit is thus essentially ambiguous: with respect to the magnitudes of what is empirical, it is the apogee, but with respect to the magnitudes of what is meta-empirical, it is what one cannot go beyond or exceed; it is an unexceedable-unsurpassable (*indépassable-insurpassable*) record, but at the same time it alludes to an impossibility. Such is the weakness of its power! There is in the "maximum" of *maximalism,* just as in the "extremes" of *extremism,* a constitutional duplicity that creates all the misery and all the impotence of the purely quantitative increases. The common man easily puts up with a maximum authorized by fate: in advance he is adapted to this very relative superlative!—The relative superlative is the extreme limit of the comparative, but it is of the same order and the same kind as the comparative: it differs from it simply by the more or less of the ordinal, scalar, and continuous series of their magnitudes. Likewise, and using Aristotle's terminology, contraries, far from excluding one another as do contradictories, are the two extreme poles of one median zone; opposite extremes, both are part of the hither.

Whether one considers contraries, the degrees of comparison, or general temporality, all things remain within the limit of intermediarity: being contrary is an extreme difference, an acute difference, but always a simple difference of degree; the other is another myself and always remains, whatever he does, an egomorphic alterity; the empirical superlative is, all in all, an extreme comparative; and the empirical termination is still a part of the continuation and is a link in the sequence of the interval . . . Every perfection—if there is perfection—is fatally inscribed in the register of immanence and median magnitudes. The perfect thing is the accomplished or finished thing in the static sense of the passive past participle. The dogmatic person has arbitrarily decreed that it is advisable to stop right there: *ananke stenai!* The idolatrous man has designated his idol as the *nec plus ultra* of every comparison and of all research; research is thus finished before having begun; and the idolatrous man tells himself while contemplating the idol, Let us not touch anything more; enough already! To the model itself, admired by all, he dares to say, like the photographer during the shoot, Be sure not to move any more, you are perfect. It is quite obvious that a maximum restored to the dimensions of a determinate, ascribable, and universal quantum has no moral significance! What we were seeking is not a closed totality, a totality in action at the end of a totalization: what we are seeking is infinitely evasive. For our target is situated beyond any horizon.

In an anthropocentric optics, the extremes (*ta akra*) belong to the hither, and, reciprocally, the mean can be in its own way a very relative apogee. If the primacy that simplistic extremism has its heart set on is quite often, in fact, a most bourgeois superlative, then mediocrity or the philos-

ophy of "mediumness" complacently takes hold and is pro-
claimed—this mediocrity can in certain cases be a culmination and a type of summit. But while the maximum of
maximalism is apparently perched on the highest rung of
the ladder, the philosophy of the golden mean aims at its
core for the optimum, and the optimism that is the philosophy of this optimum. An average life, blunted and dull in
its routine, thus tapers off into the fine point of the golden
mean [*juste milieu*]. In contrast to the maximum, a quantitative superlative, the optimum, an axiological superlative,
implies quality and value. Isn't the mean [*milieu*] that Aristotle recommends for us a mean that is *just* [*juste*]? Justice,
after all, is a virtue, and at the same time, in some way, ap-
propriateness [*justesse*] is, too; the golden mean (*mesotes*) is,
therefore, normative. With a keen gaze, the mind [*esprit*]
measures, evaluates, and determines the equidistance of the
median point with respect to the two extremes, excess and
deficiency, situated on both sides. Is not this keen gaze, in
search of a univocal determination, the optical form of the
spirit [*esprit*] of finesse? Equidistance, implying the equality
of relations, and the proportion itself are symbols of justice.
Here, however, the ambiguity of the golden mean emerges.
To be sure, Greek moderation is not, as is Pascal's intermedi-
ateness, lost between two infinites, but in contrast harmoniously adapted to its finitude, perfectly well established in its
golden mean, halfway between too much and not enough,
perfectly in equilibrium, or so it seems, and at the apex of its
optimum . . . Perfectly or, rather, tolerably! "Perfectly" and
"moderately" tend to be confused here. The centrist virtue
is in equilibrium, but this equilibrium is unstable; this equilibrium is a good fortune that is continually renewed; this
equilibrium is threatened from two sides, by the two con-

trasting indeterminations of insufficiency and of the excess that overflow onto it. To this double temptation, it opposes a double resistance which is, like the Skeptics' *epoche,* restraint and modesty. What is the worst is the enemy of what is good, which goes without saying, but also of what is the best, because it is paradoxical and because it does not go without saying. All sorts of virtues prosper within this zone of the hither and of intra-worldly immanence: this zone is the zone of commonness or, if one may express oneself so, of average perfections. And first of all, concerning *modesty:* in contrast to extreme humility, to the mendicant humility of the one who, in his infinite abnegation, renounces every part of his own being and is himself annihilated, modesty reserves its modest part. Such is, above all, the relation of *justice* to charity: heartrending charity, absurd charity acknowledges the right of others by unjustly sacrificing its own right; justice is closer to rational truth and even to logic and arithmetic; the just man does not forget himself and legitimately considers himself as one of these others whom he respects. In contrast to an impossible meta-empirical purity, to a limit-purity that would be something like the spiritual form of asepsis, *sincerity* is content with being serious: it does not claim to be literally, chemically pure, not 100 percent sincere, pure from every reticence and from every ulterior motive, but it takes into account as much as possible the circumstances and the totality of psychological data. There are still a multitude of other virtues, of minor perfections in this valley of average existence: the discretion and the restraint that spare us the jealousy of Nemesis, timidity, modesty, in the end; and above all moderation, which is simultaneously average and sovereign—*metron ariston*—says Cleobulus—; for it is the foundation, in Plato, of a science of measure [*métrétique*], and in this sense it is normative; but at the same time, it says how much, up to what point, and to what degree; and this degree is expressed in a determinate or assignable number. Isn't finitude the condition that makes the science of measure possible?

2. To Live for the Other, Whatever This Other May Be. Beyond Every "Quatenus," Every Prosopolepsia.

In the heart of hearts of a moral life, there is a secret contradiction that the same old, same old of daily continuation and intermediarity rarely allows to emerge, but which here and there flares up at the incandescent height of tragic situations. We can formulate this internal and almost always invisible contradiction with a double axiom that is simultaneously an indemonstrable, evident fact and the height of nonsense, which is thus an impossible-necessary: *to live for you, to live for you so as to die of it,* death included. This dilemma of the all-or-nothing, which is the irrational ultimatum par excellence in hyperbolical sacrifice, this dilemma leads, by right or if worse comes to worst, to an exorbitant and absurd demand. A purely gratuitous demand, so it would seem . . . To live for you, to live for you so as to die of it—these two paradoxes together comprise one single imperative: for the offering that one makes to someone when one lives for him, and does so *thoroughly,* without holding back anything for oneself, in sacrificing everything for him, this implies that one tacitly consents to die for that someone, and in his place, if that is the condition of his survival. This simultaneously double and simple imperative does not expect a Platonic response from me, but an act; I am personally concerned, instantly called out by the drastic urgency of a request in which my whole life is immediately and passionately involved.—Let us begin with the phrase to-live-for-you (without dying of it). Even if one leaves out death, even if the paradox is not meta-empirical, this to-live-for-the-other is already paradoxical in itself. The unconditional preferability of the other cannot be rationally justified. The life of the other has an infinite price, *whoever this other is,* independent of the qualities, talents, or competences of this other; I should thus devote myself uniquely to him because he is another; because he is not me. And can I even say, in general, *because?* As we shall see, it is this inexplicable that explains that which is inexplicable about the second paradox, the absurdity of living-so-as-to-die-of-it. Here is, indeed, the height of arbitrariness! The fact of alterity is not even, strictly speaking, the abstract reason that explains love. If the life of my neighbor were eminently precious, there would be no paradox surrounding the unconditional love I give him; if your life were worth more than mine, my devotion would simply render justice to a truth and would not differ in any way from wisely motivated, reasonable observation. But a rational, justifiable, and demonstrable imperative can only be morally conditional: I deliberately love after having weighed the importance, assessed the value, judged the merit of the beloved. It is the logical conclusion of an argument. But where, then, is the miraculous supernaturality, where are the sublimity and the divine madness of the sacrifice? It is necessary, therefore, to say just the opposite: because the imperative of love is radically unmotivated, it is categorical! I love you because it is you . . . which is obviously not "a reason"! Better yet: it is a bad reason! Or more simply: I love without any reason. And better yet, still: I love contrary to all reason! I love because I love . . . There is no because. The because is a pure and simple repetition of the why. In general, one acknowledges the sublimity of a sacrifice by the derisory fact that the beloved does not merit such a love . . . : That is when mercy is the most heartrending. Unless (there is always an *unless*) this preference for a beloved who is unworthy of our love is itself a supreme affectation and a false humility, something like a suspect one-upmanship of asceticism, sometimes even a challenge and a provocation, the desire to break a record—the record of disinterestedness! Even so, Aristotle, who considers the friend as "another myself" and willingly shuts himself away in the xenophobic *clausura* of Hellenocentrism, finds a paradoxically "altruistic" language for friendship: it is necessary to love the other, it is necessary to be just toward the other . . . Altruism preaches the virtue of friendship without specifying either the nationality, the religion, or the race of the friend. The principle of an infinite opening can already be glimpsed. It will appear in full light only with the universalism and "totalitarianism" of Stoic *philantropia*. "Philanthropy" is paradoxological because it is "paradoxical" to love man *in general* and for the sole reason that he is a man. For this reason, according to the concepts of closed morality, is not "a reason." Most often a man loves his neighbor when this neighbor is his coreligionist, his fellow citizen, or his compatriot, or possibly even his "colleague"! Most often a man loves other men on condition that they belong, both they and he, to the same herd; or, again, on condition that they are members of the same clan, the same tribe, or the same caste. The one who loves his neighbor if this neighbor is a parishioner of the same parish does not like men; the one who loves a woman inasmuch as she belongs to the same caste does not know what love is. The philanthropical paradox is of the same order as the cosmopolitan paradox; the two paradoxes are linked to each other in the same paradoxy, and Stoic wisdom professes them both. The cosmopolitan is a citizen of the world. The citizen of one city and not of another city, now that makes sense. But how can one be a citizen of the *universe?* A citizen of the planet, a citizen of the terrestrial globe—which in no way is a *city,* these are ways of talking, and for a Greek ear, these ways of talking sound rather like contradictions or absurdities. One might as well speak of a patriotism of the galaxy! And yet it is this infinite extension, verging on the absurd and the derisory, that measures [*mesure*] the unthinkable excessiveness [*démesure*] of human fraternity.

The prophet Isaiah says that God does not perceive strangers: for there are no strangers. The New Testament will express an analogous idea by using the Greek word: *prosopolepsia;*[3] prosopolepsia is the deceit that consists in making exceptions for a mask (*prosopon*), in taking into consideration facial aspects and the color of one's skin, which is to say the persona. In a word, *prosopon,* a superficial appearance. That which is inessential or accidental, that which is a look or an "adjectival" membership, God does not take these into account: God takes into account only essence, he takes into account only the humanity of the man, without considering the pigmentation of his skin or the shape of his nose. Because he is above all pettiness and all prosopolepsia, God considers substance and not the more or less picturesque or folkloric epithets. The refusal of prosopolepsia reveals, in the Gospel, the fundamental indifference to all social, professional, or ethnic distinctions and, hence, the double maximalism of the charity—extremism, universalism—that is the source of this indifference. But the moral paradox could be formulated just as well in other philosophical languages even if it was not made for them. One can, for example, adopt the language of monadic relativism: to love someone from such and such a point of view, from such and such an angle and in certain respects, and, correlatively, not to love him in other respects, and even to detest him boldly in these very respects; this is not love, this is a derision; to love in some respects, to loathe in other respects, the loathing, being implied in friendship as an effect of relief, this is without a doubt a love of friendship, but it is at most to assure the friend of his distinguished consideration; friendship is a love accompanied by circumstantial restrictions that motivate it and justify it by limiting it. To love conditionally, with certain precisions and discriminations, is this not to subalternize love? Let us go so far as to say that the moral paradox is virtually implied in the rationalist idea of that which is universally human. The man who is the moral subject of the *rights of man* and of the *duties of man* is not a man qua this or that, in a word the man *insofar as,* but purely and simply a man, a man without another precision or specification; a man without *quatenus.* But first, the man who is representative of the duties of man is essentially the bearer of the moral law and of values in general, responsible for these values and for this law—which is something that should not surprise us, since duty, by itself, speaks only of efforts and ordeals, of austerity and privations. I am affected not only by my professional obligations and by assignments that the schedule and the calendar serve to restrict in time but by an infinite and always unfinished task; and this task, which is indeterminate and without any time limit, lasts as long as one's life and may require the sacrifice of this life. Assistance to a man in danger has implications for me not *qua* professor, firefighter, or lifeguard, or as a representative of a particular social category, that of rescuers: it is incumbent upon me because I am a man and because the drowning person is a man like me. Such are the most urgent and most imperative duties. Before jumping into the water, I do not seek to verify if the man in danger is my coreligionist or even my colleague, if he is from my tribe, if he belongs to the same club or to the same clan as me . . . No! I go immediately to the man in danger of dying because we have here, he and I, the same essence and the same origin. The one who asks *why* and the one who considers himself obliged to explain *because of* this or that are as pitiful as each other when they quibble about whether to give or not give assistance to beings who are in danger. I will not allow the man at risk of death to drown under the pretext that a miserable prosopolepsia, a criminal pettiness, dissuades me from giving him aid and assistance!—And in the same way: the militant for the rights of man does not become bogged down in specifying the social and political categories involved in his struggle. The man in the rights of man is not the man *insofar as;* in other words, the rights of this man are not the rights of a man considered as a citizen, voter, or taxpayer, or as a passenger, as a tenant, as a telephone service subscriber, or as a user of public transport—and neither is it the addition of all these partitive rights that would compose, in its unity, the rights of man. In general, the rights of man are not the privileges that one more or less closed human group claims with respect to another human group . . . And are these even rights? The "right" to live, the "right" to exist and breathe, the "right" to freedom are such obvious, elementary rights that they have no taste, or flavor; they go without saying, and I owe you no particular recognition for the gift that you think you give me by conceding them to me. Here is a paradoxical and by that very fact eminently moral eccentricity!

I am at the very least one of these "others" in favor of whom one calls for justice and right. I do not constitute an exception to common law, even if it favors me! Must justice be justice only when it is at my expense? My rights come back to me as a result of duties to others? This would be worse than a derisory bit of luck, this would be an absurdity! I do not admit to being personally excluded from the legal and moral community that extends to all moral subjects. I as well, after all, am a representative of the great human community. There is no reason (in the rational sense) to excommunicate me. But it is indeed necessary to talk here of a mystery . . . This shocking inequality that reason refuses to admit, well, moral pessimism makes it possible: my neighbor has all the rights over me and these rights are for me as good as duties, without my being able myself to prevail over them, or myself being able to deduce directly from them my own rights and my own latitude for acting; if your rights sketch my duties in relief, then the opposite is far from being true, and the proposal is far from being reversible; your duties are not automatically my rights; at least, it is not up to me to apply such a rule to myself. Such is, thus, the double paradoxology that governs the rights and duties of man.

This love that loves the *hominity* of the man—and loves it on account of love, not on account of reason—, that loves mankind as one loves someone, that incomprehensibly loves the person-in-general, that loves the mankind that is personified in the person and in the person broadened to the dimensions of humanity, this love is obviously paradoxical. As there do not exist on the planet other moral subjects than men, a philanthropic love is necessarily an ecumenical love; and if there were in the cosmos other inhabited planets than the terrestrial globe, and on these planets other beings endowed with reason than men, then the philanthropy would extend to them, and I would begin to love them fraternally. Every community, by withdrawing into itself, can become a clan among other clans, a tribe among other tribes. But the human "community" is by its very definition a superlative: this community is the most enormous that can be conceived, and it offers the maximal opening to love, which is that of universality: for it is omnilateral and coextensive with humankind. And there is only one single humankind! The law of all-or-nothing is valid here. Universalism is only truly universal on condition of not admitting of the least exception. There is no other exception than the except-me, the unjustifiable exception at my expense, the impenetrable mystery of sacrifice! This is simultaneously the scandal of theodicy and the insoluble aporia of anthropodicy. That exception mysteriously confirms the universality it should logically contradict. Save for the unique, the paradoxical, and the irrational exception of the first person, universalism does not tolerate any exception, and that by its very definition: for if there is an exception in so-called absolute universality, then it is the case that it is not, that it has never been, universal. One single, one extremely small exception, just one and not more than one suffices to open the first breach in universality: the minuscule exception is, indeed, the breach by which racist discrimination creeps in insidiously at first, then sweeps in irresistibly; the slightly opened fissure allows the torrent of heinous racism to pass through. It is thus a priori and without needing to enumerate particular cases that moral universalism excludes all discrimination, says "no" in advance to every nascent distinction, to every velleity for discrimination; the most fugitive of exceptions in this respect is condemned as absurd and against nature; it is a grave insult to man, a moral menace for all men. Even for beings who apparently are convinced of the equal dignity, brotherhood, and co-citizenship of all humans, it sometimes happens that an imperceptible nuance of disdain, an impalpable difference in treatment comes to light; a difference that is as shocking as it is imponderable, and that is all the more offensive given that it is expressed in measured terms. A certain condescension that is barely perceptible in language or in manners sometimes expresses an infinitesimal racism that is much more perfidious and venomous than crude racism; racial discrimination will quickly degenerate into racist segregation. The smallest reservation, an almost invisible restriction, the briefest of hesitations, or, conversely, a slightly affected amiability, a suspect eagerness, or I-know-not-what-kind of exaggerated thoughtfulness arouses in us an inexplicable uneasiness; these condescending people are undoubtedly poorly cured racists . . . And we wish to respond to them: what use is this one-upmanship? Do not tire yourself out; do not go out of your way; nothing replaces what is natural and what is spontaneous.

The unconditional preferability for others with respect to me is summed up in a first paradox that is also the first appearance of disinterestedness: abnegation has neither cause nor rational motivation. But the because belongs so intimately to the mechanism of thought and explanation that it reappears, in one form or another, to restore a reassuring equilibrium, to offer compensation, a legality, or a comprehensible meaning to the gratuitous moments of the heart; the decision in favor of sacrifice does not for long remain unmotivated, nonreciprocal, and arbitrary. Irresistibly, our incurable rationalism, or rather our need for intelligibility, restores the causal link that would justify, or at least would explain, love without causes: as long as our language renounces with difficulty the category of causality! 1st: Some would perhaps prefer a "philadelphia" founded on consanguinity and a vaguely motivated solidarity to an indeterminate and, on balance, unmotivated philanthropy; I would love other men *because* they are my "congeners"; because they are my brothers or cousins in humanity. This biological or generic kinship would thus be the reason for loving! Here you have a reason that gives the appearance of a pretext . . . A symbolic and metaphysical reason. One says: it is the call of blood that speaks to me in the distress of my fellow man, of my creaturely brothers and sisters . . . But this blood is not the blood of so-called superior races, it is the blood of human lives in general, this is the blood that flows in the arteries of all men. No! such a love owes nothing to the sanguine formula. 2nd: But causality reappears more subtly still, under a new guise, to exercise its rights: we would love *even if* the person who is loved is not worth it, *even though* he is not worth it, and *precisely because* he is not worth it, and *above all because* he is not worth it! However, a concessive causality is still a causality, and the even-though is a mere backward because. Here we are referred back to the cynical challenge. Deliberately to love the most abominable rogues for the sole reason that they do not merit it, specifically to prefer the roguishness of rogues, to prefer the most repulsive of beings by virtue of a systematic predilection, a Nazi executioner for example, would be at best a defiant escalation and more likely a shameful perversity. 3rd: Can we say, at least, I love the other because he is not me although being wholly like me? because he is like me without being me? because he is my similar-other? With respect to the other, the even-though and the because coincide! This dialectical and reflexive interpretation of the ambiguous relations between identity and difference might explain what is inexplicable in altruism. But why love? Again, the *because* is too much. 4th: To live for the other, whoever this other may be, and uniquely because he is the other—indeed, one can say it when it is decidedly impossible to avoid the because . . . For etiology has a rough life! It is disinterestedness that consequently becomes a motivation . . . the motivation of unmotivated altruism and the interest of a disinterested love; and it is ultimately gratuitousness that has become the spring of an unusual kind of etiology! In other words: it is the absence of a cause here that is, itself, the cause . . . We can call this absence of a cause the Other [*l'Autre*], a so to speak anonymous name that implies an infinite postponement, an opening on to the future and the incognito: the cause would be the inexplicable fact of alterity, or at least the naked alterity of the other. But it remains understood that alterity is not by itself a reason for loving; it is not a reason; it is even less a motive! The fact of the other can just as well be for me a reason to dread or even to hate. After all, does there not exist a "disinterested" hatred? At the extreme level of gratuitousness, there undoubtedly is nothing but pure love.

We must conclude: the first person soars up toward the other with a thoughtful, spontaneous impetus that, far from allowing itself to be magnetized by an antecedent value, itself founds this value, and does so independent of any utilitarian or social consideration, of any rational motive, of any objectively founded motive: it is indeed love itself that is the founder; for it is the surging source of all legality. Why this love of the one for the other? Yes, why? Because it is the one, because it is the other; because it is her, because it is me. Because . . . because . . . This stubborn 'because' is obviously not a reason, or a causal relation in which the cause and the effect, being quite distinct from each other, are logically and chronologically articulated with each other. Here, one better understands how the 'because' refers to itself, how causality bends back on to itself, how the cause repeats itself in the effect: the circular relation of the effect-cause to the cause-effect is, if not a tautology, then at least a circle eventually reduced to a point; earlier theology gave the name *causa sui,* cause-of-itself, to this point and considered it the central mystery of divine creation. For it is by this *aseity* itself that love is divine.—The *quatenus* (insofar as) of which we speak here is circular like causal reciprocity. The man who is for the rights of man and who is for the duties of man, the man of philanthropic love is a man beyond *quatenuses;* he only possesses his dignity as a man qua a privilege specially conferred on his merit or as an honor given as a reward for services rendered: the honors that underline the distinction, similar in that regard to every discrimination, result from prosopolepsia; and the "honors," too, are granted (or refused) according to the prosopolepsia: but the "honor" of being a man is only honorific in a manner of speaking; this honor excludes all prosopolepsia, and no one can refuse this honor to another without destroying himself and without becoming again a beast. Is it doxical, that is, in conformity with common sense, to love one's neighbor inasmuch as he is this or that, and to love him all the more when his merits are greater, when his records of service weigh more heavily; but it is paradoxical to love him without taking into account his titles or his merits. The paradox is to love the man not inasmuch as this or that, because of this or because of that, Jew or Greek, but inasmuch as nothing at all or rather without any inasmuch, or, which amounts to the same thing, of loving the man insofar as he is a man. As the *causa sui,* beyond which one cannot climb, its circularity announces here the ultimate recourse and the supreme instance. To love man without any *quatenus* is to love tout court and absolutely, to love *period.*

When two men, strangers to each other and unknown to one another, meet in the immense solitude of a desert or in the eternal silence of the mountains, these two forlorn men look at each other and greet each other; they interact without needing to be presented to one another; they shake each other's hand without any other form of protocol. They are alone in an unfriendly environment, but they already know each other even though they have never seen each other; they exchange an initial word and the wind, the rocks, and elementary nature return the echo of this word. This word is already in itself a welcome. Such is the word that the solitary traveler, lost in the night, addresses to another solitary traveler: such is the word that beyond any petty prosopolepsia the man addresses to another man on the road of life. In an inhuman world, this salutation testifies to the fraternity of two faces and will celebrate the encounter of the two gazes.

3. To Live for the Other so as to Die of It. Love, Gift, and Duty. Beyond Every "Hactenus."

To-live-for-you *implicitly alludes,* in an indirect manner, to the possibility of death. But to live-for-you-so-as-to-die-of-it *explicitly gives preference* to mortal sacrifice and death proper. It is an undertaking that engages us, theoretically, up to the absolute. This second paradox brings into play the degree of love. To live so as to die of it would obviously have no meaning if the living being were eternal in his ontological constitution, if he were a priori incapable of dying (which is absurd) and, therefore, condemned to obligatory immortality: he would thus live for his brothers without effort, without merit, and without risks, and he would devote himself to them body and soul as easily as he breathes: abnegation would be a function of life neither more nor less than the circulation of blood in the arteries; sacrifice would be an act as simple as saying hello, good evening, and good night! The words "sacrifice," "heroism," "courage," and "virtue" would no longer have meaning . . . Unless the torture of perpetual life, incomprehensibly, is itself this death, this eternity of torment, this damnation in the noon light, this hell! "I die of not dying," said Saint Theresa. We would say thus, like Émilie Makropoulos, the heroine of Čapek and Janaček, condemned to perpetual life by the elixir from her father: "You others are lucky, you are going to die." Indeed, man is a weak and vulnerable being, in whom death can enter by all the interstices of the organism, seeping into the smallest pore of tissues . . . This precarity of human life is called finitude. And it is the disproportion between the finitude of the being and the immensity of the duty that explains the second paradox. In death there is a dimension that escapes us and will always escape us. This aporia refers us to the mysterious, insoluble contradiction that opposes thought to death: thought is justified in being *against* [*a raison* contre] death since it is aware of it, but death gets the *better of* [*a raison* de] thought since it annihilates the *thinking being*. A thinking-mortal being, mortal qua being a being, immortal on account of thinking, is it not itself a sort of inviable hybrid, an incarnate paradox? Thought, in a certain measure, encompasses death, but the opaque nothingness of death encompasses the thinking being in its night. How does one explain this contradictory reciprocity? And likewise, duty, value, and moral action do not give preference to definitive annihilation, they do not have the concepts, not even the language, to account for this nonbeing; they are acquainted only with the plenitude and the infinite continuation of being beyond death. And yet the agent, that is, the subject of the action, is preposterously mortal!—How can a finite being, one limited in time and in its powers, assume an infinite duty? This enormous task is a priori an impossible task, a burden that human shoulders cannot support. No, this is not a truly serious and realistic program for men.—And along the same lines, how can a finite being love with an infinite love? We would respond: by throwing all his efforts into living . . . The one who loves undividedly, who loves intensely, enduringly, and tirelessly perhaps loves madly, but not infinitely: for he is only a man! And if he becomes crazy with love, it is because his heart is too small or too narrow for an infinite intoxication. Are the resources of the lover not limited? One can die of love, die of loving . . . The one who loves infinitely meets up with death on the way. Love is strong like death: that is, it is simultaneously stronger and weaker—especially weaker . . . since, when all is said and done, the lover will not survive. The ambiguity leans toward the side of misery . . . And finally: how can a finite being infinitely give of himself? God, yes. He can do it. In some way, that is his definition according to Plotinus: the One, that is, the Absolute, gives without changing: what it has given, it still has—and this is a paradox; the more it gives, the wealthier it is—and this is a miracle; a fairy tale! Its generosity is inextinguishable. It is thus beyond the alternative: that is to say, it takes no notice of any pettiness, any penury, any stinginess. As Jean-Louis Chrétien has subtly shown, this paradoxology has meaning in the *Enneads* and in Christianity.[4] In any event, man is not God: what he has given, he no longer has; what he has given has diminished: his reckless profligacies have to be drawn or withheld from his assets, subtracted from his credit, deducted from his riches. The finite being, subject to the sad laws of misery and a merciless arithmetic, knows that he can count neither on an eternal youth nor on the infinite renewal of his wealth. He should resign himself to rationing; in anguish he watches over the gradual exhaustion of his resources, the lamentable depletion of his vital forces.

Yet in the heart of man, there is a moral ambition that protests wildly and desperately against the obviousness of weakness and finitude. Mistrusting every verisimilitude, the moral agent does not hesitate to declare that to will is to be able. Is this a paradox or the expectation of a miracle that makes the impossible possible? The imperative for infinite sacrifice and for absolute disinterestedness does not in principle (that is, theoretically) acknowledge any limit or admit of any restriction. In formulating the first paradox (to live for others but without dying of it) we said that the paradoxical nature of this paradox consists in the exclusion of any 'because,' of any causality or motivation; philanthropic disinterestedness turns its back on partiality and looks down on prosopolepsia as much as on folklore; its sole object is the austere nakedness of the human; in opposition to closed love, which takes pleasure in the tiny garden of its small parish or in its minuscule fraternity, philosophical disinterestedness is essentially open love. The second disinterested-ness is disinterested above all with respect to the being itself of the subject. Hence, the agonizing and even bloody ordeal that we call sacrifice. Sacrifice is not merely a renunciation of this or that, sacrifice is the extraction of all being from the totality of one's being. To say yes to nonbeing is an incon-ceivable decision that the will assumes ecstatically in some manner. To the first ecstasy by which the I would open up to the limits of the universe, let us oppose the second one, by which the soul painfully comes off the hinges of its being-proper. The generosity of the first disinterestedness was that of an ecumenical heart who welcomes all men without de-manding their passport and who says to them, Everyone en-ter, there is space for everyone in my dwelling,—and who does not even know the usage of the conjunction *quatenus.* And as for heartrending disinterestedness, it is rather un-aware of the adverb *hactenus,* the one that signifies 'until here but not beyond'; *up to this point,* but no farther.

4. All or Nothing (Option), from All to All (Conversion), the All for All (Sacrifice). With the Entirety of One's Soul.

Circumstantial determinations—degree or "percentage," in-tensity, duration, posology, and chronology—to which the adverb *hactenus* refers, these determinations and categories are no longer valid if it is a matter of morality; they no lon-ger need either to be specified or stipulated: quite the con-trary, such a stipulation would instead be offensive or deri-sory from the instant the categorical imperative of duty or the imprescriptible demand of love is in question. We were saying: Man is a finite being on whom is incumbent an infinite duty and who loves his neighbor with an infinite love. Let us show how the moral man, in obeying this radical imperative, engages the *all-or-nothing,* is converted *from all to all,* and goes *for broke.* The law of the all or nothing, according to Stoicism, governs the realm of virtues, which are present in each one of them, and it governs the wisdom itself that reigns over this realm. The extremist law of the all-or-nothing has as an immediate consequence the equality of offenses, which is, in Cicero's *Paradoxa,* the sixth of the six Stoic "paradoxes": *isa ta katorthomata.* A peccadillo is a great sin, and, conversely, a venial offense and a mortal offense are the same; the one who has come closest to the target and the one who is farthest away from it have both missed the target: there is no middle ground; both of them are in the same boat! An entire extravagant arithmetic, disparaging moral progress, plays with the intransigence of the all-or-nothing: the relations of big and small, of more or less are reversed, upended; the categories of space, of time, and of quantity are turned upside down. But the paradox of the equality of offenses, just like what is "counterintuitive" in the Beatitudes in the Gospel, can also have an intentional meaning: for in the world of intentions, of duty and of love, this paradox, far from being a game, is the daily truth of our real-life experiences. And first, the great simplistic and simplifying law of the all-or-nothing renders the gradations of the more-or-less futile and null and void. As long as it is about tasks and jobs and their remuneration, the little and the much can be weighed, measured, compared, and ranked; but with respect to this movement of the heart, to this undivided impetus that we call intention, the little and the much prove to be equivalent or, instead, indifferent. The principle of all-or-nothing, in subalternizing quantity, only attaches importance to intentional quality; for it, it is take it or leave it! It does not have the time to weigh or estimate motives, it does not worry about counting the drops, the granules, and the centigrams. It does not get into specifics! It shows itself to be magnificently negligent with regard to posology. This is not a grocer but a nobleman. He clings to approximations and to the essential, main options. Is not the magnetizing intention always whole and complete? Always indivisible? The principle of all-or-nothing wants only to know if the heart is there or the heart is not there. *Ama, et fac quod vis.* Likewise, there is always an element of Manichaeanism in the extremism of the all-or-nothing. Here it is the inherent purity of the intentional movement that is in question. Fénelon, a phenomenologist before his time, does not compromise on this point: pure love is without any admixture of self-interest, or it does not exist; the purest purity of this maximum love necessarily is an absolute superlative about which one can wonder if a man in general, a carnal, deep, and sensual being, is capable of feeling while in this world: just as a speck of dust suffices, according to the *Philebus,* to turn a maximum whiteness gray, so one milligram of sordid mercenariness, a very small calculation of egoism, a hint of self-interest, or an infinitesimal ulterior motive suffices to tarnish this transparency and this disinterestedness; of pure love, there remains nothing—nothing but an unspeakable admixture—: for the blending of pure and impure is obviously impure; in one fell swoop, one drop of hypocrisy has made a poison out of this drink.—Man, thus, only has the choice between a wholly loving love and hypocrisy; between a fully good will and duplicity. The off-course, average man has lost the golden mean. One single air bubble in the block of transparent crystal whose name is love, one single imperfection, a minuscule opacity in this transparency, a shadow of self-love in this light, the slightest fold or the slightest complication in the simplicity, the smallest duplicity in this simplicity—and the so-called love is no longer sincere (*sine cera*), that is, of pure quality. Having just emerged from simplicity, the average man immediately becomes bogged down in duplicity. For a tiny impurity is already a great, a mortal impurity . . . The slightest reservation about these matters, or the most fleeting restriction, casts a serious doubt on the sincerity of the feeling: is not an obsession with distinctions already a camouflage for a suspect reticence and the alibi for a bad will or a broken will? These petty matters and these subtleties convey the caution of an amateur rather than the impetuses of an impassioned lover. Partitive and partial love loves at the fringes of one's soul just as verbal and superficial promises promise from the edge of one's lips . . . Loving intransigence itself is characteristic of duty as well as of love: love and duty—they do not admit of any restrictive condition either of time or place; or of degree or of time limit. By law or theoretically, that is, without regard to the question of knowing whether this is possible, love and duty only know but one single degree: the superlative; one single size: the maximum; one single philosophy: maximalism; and one single tendency: extremism.

This commitment of the entire person in love or in sacrifice is accomplished in the still more striking form of initiation or conversion: the imperative of the all-or-nothing thus becomes a conversion of all-to-all. As a basic principle and when it comes down to it, the Good sums up the superlative requirement of duty just as the beloved embodies the extreme imperative, the absolutist imperative, of love; and the other values themselves have value only in relation to the beloved; without him, nothing is worth it. That which is infinitely demanding demands that we love it with all our hearts, not with a divided heart, or with a quarter of one's heart, or with a single auricle, or with one ventricle. And can one even speak of a relation of the lover to the absolute? The idea of a relation implies a viewing angle, that is, the unilaterality of the pure *quatenus* or of the *hactenus*. The conversion of the entire soul, preached by Plato in the seventh book of the *Republic* and then by Plotinus, evokes an identification of types more than it institutes a unilateral or partitive relation; the Gospel itself confirms the remark so often uttered in Deuteronomy, which it considers the first commandment of the entire Law. Bergson renews the meaning of it when he recognizes in the paradox of free will this nonrelative relation of consciousness to itself. The prisoner turns toward the light of the sun, not merely his gaze or merely his head, but his entire body; and he does not merely turn it a few degrees or from an acute angle, like a partisan who differs slightly from other partisans, but he makes an about-face and a half turn, and he heads in the diametrically opposite direction: this is a radical turn; and it does not only pretend, like a braggart who believes himself to be at the theater, cries "bravo," and "more!" and then, having saluted the immortal truths with a tip of the hat, remains immobile, stuck in place like a post,—but joining the gesture to intention, he arises for good, and sure enough marches toward daylight to go meet dangers and anticipate the truth; he is not content to say that he will do it, indefinitely or to the second power, but he does it purely, simply, and immediately. Likewise, the man impassioned by truth is converted to this truth by a conversion (*epistrophe*) that is a radical reversal [*inversion*], or better yet, an interchanging [*interversion*] of all to all, which is thus accession to a *vita nuova:* he does not touch this new life with a hasty and negligent kiss, but he adopts it and embraces it as one embraces one's spouse. For such is the difference between the hurried dilettante and the impassioned lover. The released captive is converted to the Good not with a small portion of his mind, such as, for example, cognition, or a fortiori with a tiny portion [*portion-cule*] of this portion, like reason, but with all his soul, *sun holei tei psychei,*[5] with the entire expanse of his knowledge, with all the strength of his power, all the effort of his willing, all the fibers of his sensitivity. In a word, with the entirety of one's soul and with the entirety of one's being. *"With the entirety of the soul,"* such are the Platonic words with which Gabriel Ferrières ends the book dedicated to his brother Jean Cavaillès, "philosopher and soldier."

The moral paradox is still more acute if one translates it into the categories of quantity and temporality. The principle of all-or-nothing and the depreciation of scalar progress were, for the Stoics, but one single paradox. Being an issue of material needs, the will staggers, measures out, and divides up its effort according to the circumstances, the physical possibilities, and the timetable: half-measures, part-time work, compromises, and distinctions—here is its daily bread: one task follows another in the daily schedule; instances of work easily lend themselves to intermittence and periodicity; for they are always quantifiable; productivity, in such cases, is the only end and economy is the only law. But all these concepts become derisive when it is an issue of moral obligation. However, they suffice for those people whom Kierkegaard called Sunday morning Christians . . . Once per week, isn't this a most reasonable periodicity and a promise of stability for conformist complacency? But as it happens, the gratifications that bring a steady, happy medium to the good conscience that is very contented and conformist, such gratifications emit a strong odor of hypocrisy, that is, of mildew: and they no longer have any more relation to virtue than regimented physical training has to asceticism. When the man of duty is the man of a demarcated, timed, and administrative obligation, one can conceive that he decrees, Enough of that! Up to this point, but not beyond! For having passed a certain limit, the man of such a duty is no longer indebted, and the person responsible no longer has responsibility; because of its rigidity or, at the very least, because of its stringency, closed obligation can seem to be compatible with such a division. But moral duty is not compatible, and love even less so! Our neighbor wants to be loved the most enduringly, the most faithfully, the most intensely as possible, as much as the resources and the strength of the lover permit; and even beyond these resources and this strength! A love that plans in advance its own loving undertakings and its loving progress, that loves the beloved beginning from such and such a degree and up to a certain point (!), in other words, that ceases to love beyond this point, such a love pretends to love, and as a result loves no one: the latter is a soul that is tepid and of little faith. How does one describe the hurried lover who, having a date with his beloved this evening, announces in advance, I will wait for my beloved until six o'clock this evening, but no longer? The one who, in living in the eternal present of his love looks at things as of now from the outside and, willingly, gives preference to his own disaffection, such a person is not a sincere lover.—The passionate lover, situated at the heart of this eternal present *of which the center is every-*

where and the circumference is nowhere, would rather wait for the end of the world, if he had to, and even beyond the end of time if he could. Infinite is his patience. He does not know what a time limit is. He does not look at the stopwatch, this passionate lover. Love counts neither the pennies nor the minutes; it neither is stingy nor haggles. Tolstoy knows it, as does Kierkegaard: to be a Sunday Christian—on Sunday morning from eleven o'clock to noon—, this is the only ambition of the bourgeois people in the parish. But Leo Tolstoy has not abandoned becoming a Christian of Christian *life,* that is, a Christian of *Christian continuity* . . . Let not only the holidays be blessed and sanctified, but also all the work days and every hour of every day, and each minute of each hour and each instant of every minute; let the entirety of life in its fullness and in the most humble details of its duration be a perpetual festival; let temporality be entirely festive in its everydayness and all the way to the infinitely smallest of daily meals and even into the voids of sleep! In opposition to Aristotle, Tolstoy willingly admitted a sanctification of nocturnal unconsciousness and childlike innocence. But a continuous celebration is exhausting and satisfaction in every instant is chimerical; and Tolstoy's despair is all the more profound. Tolstoy does not rely upon the methods of the *Philokalia*[6] in order to accept in his heart the continuity and the serenity of an uninterrupted prayer.

Extremism is systematic by profession, but love and duty are extreme by vocation. Professional extremism becomes established conventionally in its excessivenesses, as if it traded in them, but extreme love itself looks to the horizon, and even beyond (*epekeina*) the horizon, to the infinite . . . And Plato for his part says that the Good not only makes the knowledge of knowable things present (*pareinai*) to us, but in addition it makes the knowable things be (*proseinai*) by conferring being to them and, along with being, the essence of the being (*to einai te kai ten ousian*), the Good itself being, by its moral dignity and its creative power, infinitely beyond essence (*epekeina tes ousias presbiai, kai dunamei huperechontos*).[7] Demonic hyperbole, cries out Glaucon in the sixth book of the *Republic* by invoking Apollo, the god of the sun. But this exclamation is not only humorous, since Plato establishes in the same book 6 the analogical correspondence of the sun and the Good, of light and of truth: at least on this point Plato barely takes part in the condemnation of what is excessive (*hubris*), a condemnation that constitutes the unanimity of Greek tragedy, of gnomic poetry, and of Greek wisdom in general: but the mediocre excessiveness of the tyrants has nothing in common with the divine Platonic hyperbole . . . In that, Plato would himself be the first of the Neoplatonists, or rather of the Ultraplatonists, since he refers us, like Plotinus,[8] to a superessential transcendence (*huperontos autos*); and Plotinus says again: the Good is more than beautiful (*huperkalos*), and it rules in the intelligible world beyond the most excellent things (*epekeina ton ariston basileuon en toi noetoi*).[9] In trying to express the inexpressible, Pseudo-Dionysius's negative theology will borrow the paradoxical path of contradiction and speak to us of the *dark ray* of the divine super-essence, and even (here the contradiction is coupled with poetic incoherence) allows us to glimpse the more than luminous Darkness of silence. This is how Nicholas of Cusa, the theorist of learned ignorance, proposes the coincidence of contraries to us: the identity of the Maximum and the Minimum is thus incomprehensibly comprehended!

Between the finitude of a power limited by death and the unfathomable infinity of moral duty or love, the paradoxical contradiction is sharpened to the paroxysm of the absurd and the untenable. It is thus in the course of temporality and in the final stage of this course that the infinite vocation of man encounters the opaque wall of death and finitude. Moral duty imposes on us a task that is both exhausting and inexhaustible, duty requires an indefatigable tension and will that are commensurate with an effort that is always recommenced and always unfinished. Duty, as such, does not make exceptions for death. There is between *duty* and *power* a disproportion that *willing* madly seeks to offset: moral existence, by virtue of this infinite disparity itself, will always be controversial. Religions, too, manage to adapt the obligations and the practices of their faithful to a schedule. *Hactenus!* were we saying, in speaking the language of a conscience that uses its resources and powers sparingly. Up to this point, but no farther! That is what the wise and prudent manager decides about closed duty. *Hactenus,* indeed, belongs to the vocabulary of trading firms and to merchants busy with bartering. The conscientious worker, to reassure himself, pretends not to see any difference between the duty that is infinite and the jobs that one can plan or increase gradually. But duty is not a job. Here it is necessary to choose between all or nothing. Even more, the duty that falls on me in the name of timeless values does not take death into account, that is, the obstacle par excellence: for death, at first glance, bears some resemblance to a physical and literally indifferent contingency; death, a natural contingency, cuts short, over time and without any explanation, the infinite purpose of the moral will; and on the other hand, duty, an ideal exigency, rightfully disregards this blind limitation that death in fact imposes on our vocation: duty gives us work for eternity! Its role is not to put us on guard against the danger of exhaustion and the peril of death! Indeed, if moral legislation, if moral values are eternal, then how are the bearers of these values, how is the subject of this law mortal? Let us, however, note that death itself is not a simple, empirical accident, a fortuitous *impedimentum;* death is our fate [*destin*]; . . . a fate that does not destine [*destine*] us to anything, that destines us to an I know not what kind of unknowable; we think that we glimpse it by calling it destiny [*destinée*]. Death is a mystery, our mysterious fate: the incomprehensible collision of an infinite duty and an absurd death undoubtedly plays some kind of role in the sublimity of sacrifice.

But if the *hactenus* is already sordid and petty when it is the law of conscience that is always concerned with planning its own labor and always inclined to go on strike and haggle over its effort, then the *hactenus* is all the more of a farce when love applies it to itself . . . A pitiful farce . . . Or better yet: the *hactenus* is an excuse and a pretext of bad faith. This *up to this point* is in fact a spatial sophism. Love— the one, naturally, that is a "Gypsy child"[10]—has spontaneity as its sole law; spontaneity and inexhaustible generosity; and, oddly associated with this generosity, insatiable desire. Just as being does not analytically imply the cessation of being (for there is no reason outside of violence for being to cease being!), so the fact of disliking, itself too, is never directly implied in love; pure love does not find in itself or by itself the reason for falling out of love: it finds this reason in extrinsic factors. Let us, however, note: there is a big difference between the continuation of being and an impetus of love: being is *tenacious,* but love is *vivacious.* Or, more simply: being is inexterminable; the nihilization of being-in-general is nonsense and a contradiction, and it is absurd to claim to conceive of it; being, because it is atemporal, does not imply, but on the contrary, a priori and logically excludes the negativity of nonbeing and death; being, in order to persevere in its being, that is, in order to "conserve itself," does not have need of any effort: the principle of identity suffices for it; to nothingness, it statically opposes both its indestructible plenitude in action and its impregnable inertia: for being, in its "tautousia," asks only to continue to be. There, where there is being, there is no place for nonbeing; thus what is absurd about the contradiction requires this . . . But it is, if not contradictory, then at least against nature that a sincere love envisions in cold blood its future disaffection: this repudiation is not so much an absurdity as a scandal! Turned toward the plenitude of vital positivity, toward the affirmation and the perpetuation of life, love protests violently, desperately, against what renounces it; love clings with all its strength to existence; for its dynamism says no to every limit; being rejects the negation named nonbeing, but love passionately *refuses* the nihilizing hatred. It does not want to die. So it hops up and down with impatience. Love braves death, out of defiance, to the point of getting out in front of its own loss. Or, more precisely, love rebels against the scandal of death and against the threat that death places on the loved being, but the impetus of love is not in fact impetuous enough to go beyond death. Love is stronger than death, but death is stronger than love: love and death are thus not as strong as each other—for they would then be in equilibrium and would neutralize each other reciprocally—, but stronger than each other—which is contradictory and brings about an unstable and shattered, dramatic and literally insoluble situation; not, strictly speaking, a dialectical situation but rather a kind of incomprehensible reciproc-

ity; a convulsive and tense alternation; an impassioned conflict brought to the paroxysm of the tension: the lover dies of
love, but love triumphs in succumbing. Love and death have
a tug of war and fight over our torn up and breathless flesh.
Love does not possess the magical power of tearing away
the beloved from the talons of death, but above all it does
not immunize the lover against either exhaustion or even
simple fatigue. Its almighty power is, thus, metaphorical
enough. Love is simultaneously stronger than and weaker
than death. Which of the two will have the final word? And
is there even a final word? Perhaps the last word is infinitely
the penultimate one . . . Poets and mystics sometimes go
no farther than this interrogation, which also is an expectation and which points at a far horizon. Certainly, the fact
of finitude is there, and sooner or later this fact will make
the lethal future [*avenir*] come to pass [*advenir*]. But the ever-
possible postponement of death and the vagueness of the
fateful date seem to keep the door of survival and the course
of love, if not eternally open, at the very least indefinitely
ajar. *Mors certa, Hora incerta:* such is the formula of the ajar-
ness. The *Quod* is implacable, but the *Quando* remains half-
opened; and this humble permissibility is sufficient so that
love acts *as if* the necessity of dying were itself not certain:
the vagueness of the date rubs off on the quoddity. Love innocently uses this ambiguity and the semi-indetermination
that results from it. Does not the possibility of a postponement sine die authorize the craziest of expectations? Nothing is wagered or consummated, provided that the day and
the hour remain in suspense.

Duty and love are thus, at least in this respect, analogous and comparable: they always want more than they
want, they always want something else. And one is tempted

to say, since nothing satisfies them: They do not know what they want.

Let us now apply to duty and above all to love the paradoxology of the divine hyperbole. A love that would decide in advance to "cut its losses," whatever may come to pass, is not love: this love is a sordid calculation and a repulsive caricature. Who can say, Enough already, or, That is sufficient? The currency of love, in contrast, is, Never enough! "Stop" . . . But by what right, if you will? Love has never itself said if it agreed to stop, nor when it is necessary to stop, at what moment, at what hour, at what point; and why at this moment rather than any other, and starting with what degree of fervor it is preferable to interrupt the loving crescendo. Stop? But it is necessary *never* to stop! Even to breathe, even to survive . . . To stop loving is a crime. Love is unaware of the two words *ananke stenai,* —two words that would be, out of the mouth of a loving person, words of abdication; it does not expressly acknowledge the necessity of stopping, it does not even make an exception for it. Even if it is quite necessary, in fact, sooner or later (and by turning away one's eyes) to end by stopping, the anticipated and universal determination of a maximum for the hurried man is an indicator of bad will: a clandestine complacency toward defect; a capitulation. The witness and the spectator, the sociologist, the responsible educator, or the therapist undoubtedly have the right and even the duty of preaching "moderation," to the extent that they are outsiders with respect to the conflict of duties; but to the extent in which I myself am engaged in a clear conflict, in which I myself and personally am the moral agent, I must not usurp the perspective of the referee.

Saint Augustine said that the only measure of love is to love without measure; better still, it is the absence of measure that is itself the measure. Applied to love, the *meden agan* of Solon and Theognis is a mockery; rather, one must say, Never enough, *never too much!* always more! Whatever sages and gnomics may think, the word "excess" does not have a meaning when it is an issue of love: like love, the moral imperative overflows indefinitely from its current literality. The excess could not, thus, become the object of a prohibition when it is an issue of love. And this is why the phobia of an "immoderate" love already implies an injurious restriction, a derisory miserliness, a type of parochial sordidness. Beginning from the moment at which love must be measured out in doses, it is no longer an anhypothetical imperative, but a conditional prescription: it is no longer the moral law, but like medications that are given by prescription, it depends on its posology. With regard to love, the question of "how many drops" does not have a meaning, and quantitative precisions in general are completely futile. Saint Symeon, the New Theologian already mentioned, says about prayer what we are saying about love: "Do not get it into your head that you have gone beyond the measure of fatigue, and that you can subtract from prayer . . ."[11] Here the words 'fatigue,' 'excess,' and 'extravagance' are no longer relevant: love leaves them to petit bourgeois timidity; it is not scared of going beyond the measure or of crossing a limit; the limit recedes progressively in the face of its impetus [*élan*]. The loving *impetus* [*impetus*] does not want to hear anything about the auditor who, when the opportunity arises, would make up for his overruns; its only law is the more-and-more, which exalts itself and intoxicates itself on its own, like a holy fury; its only law is the frenetic crescendo and the accelerando, and the precipitando that leads up to vertigo and, in the end, risks blowing up everything.

In fact, the more-and-more is not able to become infinitely distended, since infinite love, with its infinite abnegation, necessarily has as its subject a finite being: well before having attained the supreme limit of abnegation love's being is already nihilized; death, which is the ultimate term of mortification, has sacrificed the lover, and with the lover the love itself. To speak the paradoxical language of the First Epistle to the Corinthians: the wisdom of the world is but folly beside God and vice versa: *to moron tou theou sophoteron ton anthropon estin.*[12] This is obviously not a response! Does such a chiasmus have the value of an explanation? In the *Phaedrus,*[13] Plato speaks of a madness of love: *manian gar tina ephesamen einai ton erota.* And he also says this:[14] the greatest of all goods comes to us thanks to delirium, the delirium that is given to us with a divine gift; *nun de ta megista ton agathon hemin gignetai dia manias theiai mentoi dosei didomenes.* But he does not explain with any precision in what way extreme love is a delirious love, or why this love loves, literally, *madly:* why one can truly be *mad with love.* Yes, why? Because love carries within itself its own negation; love, at the extreme limit, contradicts itself. Such is the sublime absurdity of sacrifice, like the lack of rationale in that which is heroic: sacrifice nihilizes every problem, including the very one that poses it. Like Tristan's love for Isolde and the love of Isolde for Tristan, the loving passion is affirmed to the point of desiring its own nothingness. Isn't this the height and the fine tip of a paradox? For one can die of love! For one can love so as to die of it, it is the internal contradiction that is insane, indeed even absurd, and in certain cases sublime. Quite simply, it is the unfathomable mystery of love—a mystery that is as unfathomable as it is insoluble. An altruistic goodwill and love both require that we live for others up to our last breath and up to the final expiration of our respiration, up to the last drop of our blood and up to the last globule of this last drop, up to the last systole and up to the last diastole! Such is the vertigo of love at the point of going over into the void, the vertigo of wildly frantic love at the edge of nonbeing. The last breath is a breath after which there are no other breaths. But just as despair harbors a mercenary hope if it still counts on a future, so sacrifice is suspect if it sacrifices an entire life up to the last breath—merely the second to last one—while expecting a last breath. Between the penultimate instant and the ultimate instant, if they distinguish themselves from each other in a noticeable way or succeed one another, the ego has time to regain its assurance; the least bit of life revives all one's projects, encourages all the calculations, and justifies all the speculations and all the ulterior motives. The one who expressly wants to preserve his last globule has chosen the hither and says no to sacrifice. It is enough that a shameful calculus has subtly grazed the goodwill: the goodwill has changed itself into its opposite. It is enough that an imperceptible reticence, that a barely whispered distinction, that a timid velleity of postponement—and already the disinterested will, which interest proper has tempted, has become impure and weak. A goodwill that is absolutely good holds nothing back in reserve; its acceptance of sacrifice is *100 percent* clear and sincere. But a will that is *almost* good is only a velleity: here the approximation that is the *almost* reveals to us, in place of a great goodwill, a weak and pathetic will worth three pennies; worse still: it reveals to us a clandestine bad will hidden within the flanks of the good one, a bad will that is the subwill of the good one, which is the secret malevolence of the exoteric benevolence . . . Unless the bad will itself is simply hiding a nonwilling [*nolonté*]! The ambitious person has found again his guarantee!

5. The Three Exponents of the Conscience. Debate or Coincidence of Interest and Duty: The Irreplaceable Surgeon; Duties Toward Loved Ones.

In seeking out the omni-absent omnipresence of morality, we discover it in the form of the three exponents of conscience. On this side of every exponent is only simple and undivided vegetative instinct: the pre-egoistic instinct does not even suspect the possibility of an altruistic splitting in two, is not yet welded to itself; it has never before contested the obviousness of pleasure. No conscience, then, a fortiori, no crisis of conscience! The first conscience beyond this unconsciousness [*inconscience*] is in some way a supernatural reflection: it repudiates things obvious to the senses: to *re*nounce here does not have the sense of repetition but rather a *reflexive* sense; beyond the I, which does not even have a consciousness of itself, it takes an interest in the existence of the other, which is an object of love; at the horizon of raw being it discovers what is before-being [*devant-être*], which is the gratuitous task of the moral man; this task is called duty. The first conscience becomes aware of this paradoxical fact, that things obvious to the senses do not at all *go without saying*. As concerns the second conscience, it has second thoughts [*se ravise*] . . . Such is "cynicism"! A "reflection" to the second power and a paradox on top of a paradox, cynicism professes and assumes, expressly and scandalously, this adhesion to the trivial obviousness that idealism renounced . . . There is something provocative in this manner of openly assuming the egoism and the *philein* of philautia! Better still: the egoism of the ego is not only professed as such but also claimed as a right; around his ego, the cynic cynically reconstitutes a type of derisory axiology and (if one can say it) an entire table of values with its categorical imperative, its first emergency, and its subordinate imperatives. Me first and above all! I prefer myself to all the rest, and I proclaim it out loud! My own pleasure, an object that not long ago had a naive adherence, has itself become my duty and my religion—not because the positivity of this pleasure would be relatively rational or in any way beneficent, but simply because it is pleasure. Concerted adherence takes over from naive adherence. Out of defiance! And to finish, here is the second change of one's mind, which is a reversal of the reversal and which brings us back to our point of departure: with the conscience paying attention to its own delicateness, cynicism itself can emerge as a hypocrisy or as a snobbism or as a type of complacency. And neither is there a reason for stopping there: nothing in turn prevents a fourth conscience from going farther than the third one, and *sic in infinitum;* each conscience finds outside itself a surconscience [*surconscience*] that is its conscience, and each surconscience a super-conscience [*super-conscience*] that, in turn, is the conscience of the surconscience: the splitting in two and along with the splitting in two the historical alternation of *sometimes . . . sometimes* [*tantôt . . . tantôt*] do not, thus, have an end.

One can conceive of privileged situations in which the aporia is resolved in advance, resolved even before having caused a problem: there is indeed a conscience but not a crisis of conscience. And for example, an irreplaceable surgeon has the good fortune of telling himself (even if his hidden motives are not entirely disinterested): I devote myself to all of humanity; I am forbidden from unnecessarily putting at risk the irreplaceable person who I am by blindly wasting my precious competencies, or from indiscriminately squandering my eminent capacities. Better yet, I literally do not have the "right" to do that! The duty of the great surgeon, if he is the only one who can do thus-and-such a delicate operation for which he is a specialist, would rather only be to dedicate himself wisely, by managing as much as is possible, his inestimable aptitudes. What luck! A modestly limited altruism, a very knowing devotion: such, then, is the duty of a doctor when he is a specialist of the rarest of specialties. It is a question not of the madness of sacrifice but quite simply of good management and wise economics. The only rule, in similar cases, is the interest of the greatest number. It is philanthropy itself that dictates to us a rationally justified egoism, that sparingly prescribes solutions to us. And it is not a pointless play on words to say that rationing, for finite beings, is a rational solution. Our duties toward the human races are best reconciled with our possibilities. There is nothing to object to in this timely reasoning that is common sense itself. Does not utilitarianism rest on a prudent management of our finitude? We were speaking of a privileged situation! Privileged in what respect? In that it does not imply any crisis of conscience, no collision of incompatible duties or a conflict, and no conflict of contradictory obligations. Is the insoluble aporia resolved, given all that? Strictly speaking, there is no conciliatory mediation: the contradiction is forthwith eluded, or, better yet, it is nihilized in advance, reduced to the state of a pseudo-problem; barely have the alternative and the dilemma that follows from it started to appear . . . and they have already gone bad. The problem will not even have had time to be posed. The irreplaceable specialist sparingly manages his irreplaceable competence, and works by that very fact for the human race! If that is a solution, then it is necessary to admit that the solution is entirely nondialectical—let us say more: this is an unexpected bit of luck, a miraculous windfall. The one who has found the means to be altruistic via egoism or, vice versa, who has obtained permission to think about himself in the name of disinterestedness and to live for himself in the name of philanthropy, such a person simultaneously accrues all the advantages; in him is fulfilled the providential coincidence whose name is Harmony; the philosophy of optimism has been conceived in his honor and to justify his good luck. The right to the self-fulfillment and to the conservation of his being-proper has, in some ways, become his duty. Happy, one thousand times happy, is the benefactor, who, in working for himself, works *at the same time* for humanity! He wants for nothing! The blessed benefactor [*bienheureux bienfaiteur*] knows neither the remorse nor the scruples of bad conscience; the renunciation of his being-proper [*être-propre*] will be spared him; he is spared heartrending options, sacrifice, and tragedy; he is exempt from paying the tax called the alternative. He is at peace with himself.

The coincidence of right and duty does not have the same meaning depending on whether it is a question of the duties of an irreplaceable doctor or the duties toward loved ones. In the first case, the consciousness of having certain rights can conceal an egoistic sub-intention, a clandestine and even sometimes unmentionable ulterior motive that is hidden at the very bottom of one's heart of hearts: the secret motivation is, thus, a philautia camouflaged by honorable scruples . . . The irreplaceable practitioner does not provide his irreplaceable service any the less: there is an official motivation there and nice little reasons that would justify it are not lacking: condemned to hypocrisy by the subterranean machinations of egoism, this glorious motivation is thus far from being a simple pretext or a sophism of circumstance . . . Far from it! However suspect it may be, the duty that one invokes is perfectly legitimate; this duty is perhaps a semblance, but the semblance is rationally founded.—And, conversely, with respect to those close to me, I am not only the irreplaceable technician, the greatest genius over whose services everyone fights, I am the one to whom the most tender connections of love unite particularly dear beings; the latter themselves have need of my life in order to survive; not that I hypocritically borrow their viewpoint and apply to myself the language of altruism by using, in place of others, the discourse of others: it is spontaneously and with all my soul that I want their good fortune; there is no longer room here to distinguish between the heart of hearts that whispers quietly and a duty that one loudly professes; there is nothing but my sincere and passionate interest for others; and this disinterested interest is so eloquent that it inspires in me not only my absolute devotion to the second person, to the person of love, but paradoxically the very limitation of this devotion and the suspension of my efforts, indeed, the apparent negation made necessary by finitude; this contradiction does not come from an ulterior motive, it is not a ruse that would permit us to keep our rights in reserve—not at all and quite the contrary! It is the heroic seriousness of a sincere love that orders me to will, with the good fortune of the beloved, the means for this willing. So delicate is my solicitude . . . Here, still, the intimate interpenetration of infinite love and of the desire to live or survive a priori set aside every crisis of conscience; immediately, without trickery or sophisms, without any reasoning, the obligation to live that is incumbent on me by virtue of the duty of assistance is analytically contained in this love and in this assistance. It is love that imperiously orders me to preserve my being-proper and to stay alive; it is love itself that implores me to live out of love for the beloved. And conversely, it is instead the despair of the suicidal person, who, under the appearance of courage, is tempted by desertion, by cowardliness, and by abandoning his post—ultimately, by egoism. Not only does the candidate for nothingness literally not have the right to nihilize himself, he does not have the taste for it either, and cannot bear the thought of it, provided he imagines the distress of his own people. My passionate will to live for my own people, to provide them with aid, never to abandon them, to devote myself body and soul to their happiness and to their safety is strong enough in all circumstances to restrain me in the joy of existing. And as for the ineffable gentleness of living, as for the permission to become acquainted again with the light of day, it is enough that we have not expressly asked for all those blessings: continuing to live is a grace that is made for us, a gift that is given to us over and above—and that is the most beautiful of all gifts.

6. The Happy Medium.

To love or to be? To love while renouncing being, just like the one who accepts being entirely love, or to wallow in the thickness of being while renouncing love? This insoluble dilemma, if it does not allow of any logical solution, leaves us, however, several ways out. In order to make possible that which is impossible, in order to break away from the alternative to which its lived contradiction reduces it and in which its internal paradox confines it, the simultaneously moral and finite, the finite-moral being has in particular four alibis at its disposal: first, the *happy medium,* which is above all a trick and does not directly imply ambiguity, but rather that which is a mixture and an approximation; second, the stationary tête-à-tête that is stuck in place on account of the *mutual neutralization* of love and death, of duty and being, a tête-à-tête that in the end leaves the final word to death itself, that is not a way out but is, on the contrary, a blockade, and that is a means of evading every solution; third, ascetic sublimation, which searches out a response to the question of "how far" not in an approximation but in the infinitesimal and in the *almost-nothing;* and finally, an *alternative beating* that one could compare to a vibrating phenomenon. Among these four alibis, the first one, whether it is rational or approximative and hesitant sometimes resembles a solution. The second one, love locked in place by being, being sacrificed in place to love, the one and the other simultaneously, is the contrary of a solution since it continues with the blockade, that is, the general immobilization. The third one alone is a true way out, but not stealthily: it is an escape into the infinite. The fourth one is, if one can say it, an escape in place.

The first alibi is offered to release us from the vertiginous option that an alternative without an exit imposes upon us: from afar, neutrality can appear to be a combination; from afar and broadly speaking, "neither the one, nor the other" (*neutrum*), that is, indifference on one hand and "the one and the other" on the other seem to be almost indistinguishable, or at least amount to the same thing . . . After the agonizing alternative of the all-or-nothing, optimism starts to hope again: there still are perhaps beautiful days and a beautiful future for that which one calls the happy medium. Optimism thus claims to be stabilized in the optimum of a happy medium situated halfway between being and nonbeing. To reduce the disproportion between our physical resources, which are limited, and the moral exigency, which is infinite, will it be necessary to stick with the idea of a medium devotion, perhaps even of a medium heroism? A heroism that is equally distant from the two extremes! Now, there is a turn of phrase that is as ingenious as it is absurd! To calculate this happy medium, to determine quantitatively that which is equidistant, to measure out doses of an amalgam, or to mix pleasure and wisdom, as the *Philebus* would propose to us, here are, by all appearances, various ways of solving an insoluble problem. By comparing the philosophy of the *golden mean* with moral maximalism, we were obliged to admit that if this golden mean, in the measure in which it is "just," that is, normative, is itself a type of maximum, then "maximalism," in turn, never radically tears itself away from the field of finitude and of intermediarity. Aristotle, the theorist of middleness [*médiété*] and of the golden mean (*mesotes*), aims at the center: for the spirit of finesse is not lacking in him. But the happy medium is still farther away from the extremes and extremism than the golden mean [*juste milieu*], since it is not even *just!* Neither just, nor particularly keen . . . Good [*bonne*] or bad, the happy medium [*bonne moyenne*] is always medium—medium, or, rather, average! The happy medium, which has adapted to that which is impure and to compromises, never really succeeds in the major breakthrough that would permit it definitively to transcend this world of relativity and mediocrity. The very idea of a "posological" compromise between pleasure and mere exigency implies the fundamental finitude of duty: the question of *how much* (*poson*) supposes, indeed, that egoistic enjoyment and infinite duty are comparable and commensurable and, in all honesty, fundamentally homogeneous; on the same plane and of the same order; easily viewed on the same scale. For they are both supposed to be quantifiable. A few drops of altruism very sparingly in the ocean of egoism so as to compromise the mixture . . . or, indeed, if we want to be more honest, and consequently more normative, a small amount of being, a small amount of love, as much of the one as the other! Mix them with care. It should be noted, it is true, that after all that, the symbiosis of the soul and the body, too, is a complex of discordant and even contradictory tendencies, and that this combination is, however, lived as a simple thing, that this double life is one and the same life, and that this cacophony, despite its dissonances, is incomprehensibly perceived in a unique harmony . . . But this would be to forget the point at which this psychosomatic contradiction, which is so paradoxically viable, is, when all is said and done, inviable [*inviable*]—inviable and unbearable [*invivable*]; unbearable and at the same time preposterously viable! Despite the ambivalence, or rather because of it, those things that are incompatible remain fundamentally incompatible: sooner or later, death will cruelly lay bare the basic fragility of this unstable stability. This tense, agonizing, and dramatic situation resembles that of two spouses who can live neither together nor separately, neither the one nor the other, nor the one without the other, and who push each other away by attracting each other; they have a choice only between two forms of misfortune. Isn't this a *passionate* situation? A situation that is never governed by a contract, and that is thus not exactly relaxed. Even more does the same thing apply from the moral point of view, if it is true that morality, by its very definition, excludes all neutrality. Neither with nor without. Neither the one nor the other! Every pact in these matters is deceit, every combination a deception and a false pretense. "So then, because thou art lukewarm (*chliaros*), and neither cold nor hot, I will spue thee out of my mouth."[15] Isn't a lukewarmness that is exclusive of every conflict a simple indifference, a cloying adiaphoria? It is on condition of being torn apart and unbearable that the symbiosis is experienced!

7. Mutual Neutralization.

Is it necessary to think that duty and being fight each other to a draw as do love and death, that is, outside all dialectical mediation? A tie game and an insoluble "isosthenia," such is the perspective the second way out offers us. The relationships of duty and love to being seem to be paradoxically analogous to their relationships to death. Duty, because it is in the service of values, infinitely surpasses the limits of being; death, in many cases, could emerge as a news item, as an anecdotal detail, as a physical accident that scratches or harasses or traumatizes the body, but that apparently does not concern axiology in any way; value, one will claim, is indifferent to these derisory contingencies. However, it is self-evident that the vocation of the moral being is to bring into being that which is before-being [*devant-être*] and to this end to preserve itself in being: the actual accomplishment, in this particular case the historical advent of a value, is itself the elementary raison d'être of what is before-being.

The philosophy of duty would be a simple comedy if it were a discourse about duty considered in the absolute by forgetting the being of this having-to-be [*devoir-être*]: once it is put into parentheses, we would now have to deal only with a hollow duty, with a duty in itself, and one that does not even know *what* it must become. The important thing, the only one that counts, is the response to the question What do I need to achieve? In other words, What must I bring into being? For the moral being has as its vocation to bring into being that which is not yet given, to bring into being that which is before-being; the before-being is not destined to remain a phantasmal before-being until the end of days: the before-being is made for one day being accomplished here on earth. And so value is, indeed, the *raison d'être* of being, since without value being would not even merit existing, would not have the right to existence, since without value being would not be worth the trouble of being lived; without value, the being would only be what it is . . . Life is worth nothing without reasons for living; but what are reasons for living without a hope of life, without a life that at least is potential and future? But in turn, being is no less the raison d'être of the *having-to-be,* a raison d'être that is not rational or notional, a raison d'être that is not juridical or ideal but vital. This stipulation of actuality itself indicates a duty, the most important of all duties: if it is not, strictly speaking, axiological or normative, it is nevertheless drastic without being transparent, for it expresses the exigency of an advent. And conversely: someone's accidental death on the street corner is a stupid mishap devoid of any normative meaning, a blind chance, as "traffic" accidents sometime are; and yet this absurd accident alludes to a mystery that sanctifies it: it compels us to meditate on the mystery of destiny.

By virtue of the same impenetrable reciprocity: love goes infinitely beyond the polarity of being and nonbeing—and yet being is the fundamental condition of love . . . which is the fulfillment of it; and, vice versa, mad love, in spite of hyperboles, does not have the power to go beyond death. To love so as to die of it can have two meanings, one sublime, the other trivial, and one of these two meanings is to the other what for Plato the Aphrodite Urania is compared to the Aphrodite of the Crossroads. In the sublime meaning, the nonbeing of love, airborne like oxygen, is rather super-being than nonbeing: this nonbeing that is super-being is paradoxically, incomprehensibly a life; a life beyond being; a life more immense than the starry sky of hope. And this life, in its intensity, is the affirmative life par excellence. Love-qua-passion, transfigured by death if one believes the lyric poets and mystics about it, would find its accomplishment at the heart of that which is suprasensible: glorified, purified by death, condensed to the extreme, being is volatilized in the inferno of tragedy; on the inside, the being is transformed into light.

—But on the plane of physical and prosaic reality, the being, inasmuch as it is compact, massive, and earthy, is itself a type of death: the being in the ontic sense is living on borrowed time . . . A life that is a death! With this paradoxical reversal, with this hyperbolic absurdity, one can recognize the language of the *Phaedo; The Imitation of Christ* uses the same language. During its life, the being is simultaneously weighed down and hounded by the potential of death that it carries within itself and that is its "organ-obstacle." The Song of Songs tells us: "love is strong as death."[16] Note that it does not say: love is stronger than death; for that would imply that love has the power to render us immortal . . . Love is stronger than death, at least pneumatically and in a figurative sense and as a manner of speaking, but death is literally and figuratively stronger than love . . . Love and death are both stronger than each other! In fact, vanquisher and vanquished, stronger and weaker do not have the same meaning in the one and the other case, they do not have the same simple, definitive, univocal, and unilateral meaning that they have in war or in the conflicts of empirical forces; victory in one camp and, due to the alternative, defeat for the other camp . . . In explaining the extrinsic ambiguity, we encountered the paradox of an *absurd reciprocity of being-within,* a paradox that scandalously and so arrogantly took exception with the principle of identity. We called it the paradox of the encompassing-encompassed. For this very reciprocity is a contradiction that destroys itself. How can a moral "axiomatic system" have a value for thought and legislate in its place if it is owing to thought that it takes on a meaning? And in the same way, how can thought be the thought of a thinking-mortal being if it is owing to this thought that we think death and immortality? In a word, how can someone simultaneously be inside and outside: outside of time so as to think it, and inside while aging? Indeed, one can do it. Plotinus brilliantly understood that this paradox is itself the response since it is the formulation pure and simple of the trans-spatial mystery.

What about love, then? Love (and with it, duty) is simultaneously weaker and stronger than death: weaker, but not to the point of throwing itself into its arms, stronger, but not infinitely. One is tempted to invoke, as is the usage in similar cases, a sort of "dialectical" debate in which love and death would excite each other *over and over:* love is threatened by death, and the more it is threatened and attacked

by the lash of danger, the more impassioned it is. Such is
the paradoxical auction that emerges in the complex that is
ambivalence; the danger of death greatly increases the fervor of love, the fervor itself, as a repercussion, makes the
danger more acute and death more inevitable and, in any
case, imminent, since the lover can die of love and since
this love can also destroy itself. The chiasmus of love and
death, complicated by a zigzagging relation, will make it easier to understand how the loving being thus bounces from
love to death and then vice versa, from death to love. This bizarre mutuality does not cease to heighten the bidding. Will
we have to consider the thickness of being and ultimately
death itself as the organ-obstacle of love?—As for the conciliatory synthesis, which is in this case the interpenetration of
love and being, being above all a speculative commodity or
quite simply an alibi that refers us back to the philosophy of
the happy medium and the good conscience, there only remains, or so it seems, to make do with the idea of the pure
and simple tête-à-tête: being and duty, being and love clash
with each other, and mutually hold each other in respect,
stare each other down menacingly: no dialectical shift or
any transitive influx that would set the contradictories in relation comes to pass. Nothing happens. A blocked situation!
This sort of equilibrium brings no solution to the insoluble
isosthenia of love and being, offers no exit from the stag-
nant situation . . . Or rather, yes! there is an exit, an exit that
is the contrary of a solution; this exit is death itself. We were
saying that death and love, each outdoing the other over and
over, are infinitely stronger than each other. Infinitely? But
no! Not infinitely. This is obviously false. Admittedly, the human being regains strength in loving and regains, thanks to
love, a vital plenitude, a new youth; but love pushes back

the date of death only to a certain limit: the *hora incerta* is an undetermined maximum, and yet the meta-empirical fact that there is a maximum ("maximality") is in itself unsurpassable. Love does not eternally immunize us against death. And even if love were the stronger, it would not be in the same manner as death, neither on the same plane, nor in the same sense, and especially not in the same moment. Love, starting from its first impetus, can indeed be the stronger one,—almost the strongest: but it will fatally succumb to the sad truth of old age, to the incontestable obviousness of decline, and finally to the invincible, almighty power of death; the iron laws of being are inexorable. Love, even if it slows down aging, does not exempt us from dying: the living survive, but all in all, vitality recedes, and its defensive strategy is established each time on a smaller front by reducing its claims. And above all, in order to love one must be. This condition, which strongly resembles a self-evident truth [*verité de La Palice*], is obviously the most general and the most necessary of all conditions. If there no longer is a loving being, no longer a substantial subject, will there still be love? Love without someone for loving? A love without a loving subject? A troubled love? While waiting to be able to decide how love *is fulfilled* in death, let us at least remember that love itself *leads to* death since one can die of love! Madly, paradoxically, love itself tends toward its own nonbeing. Stronger to start out, and at the end of the day weaker: such is love; it is the irreversible time of life that bursts the unbearable contradiction of the vanquisher-vanquished and that shows (without explaining why) how the knife of fate [*destin*] slices up in full flight the hope of an infinite destiny [*destinée*]. Simply put, blind fate cuts short a destiny that is open. In the measure in which love prevails over the beginning and death prevails over the end, one cannot consider them symmetrical or even asymmetrical: symmetry and asymmetry are indeed spatial structures, and those structures would have meaning only if the beginning and the end were given together; but when the beginning is given, the end does not yet exist, and when the end is given, it is the beginning, a posthumous solemnity, that no longer exists: the not-yet and the still-more are indeed moments of an irreversible time, essentially incompatible and incommensurable moments: to claim that the second one is the reverse of the first is to project two successive time periods into the order of coexistence and simultaneity . . . Suffice it to say, continuing on this track, that birth is a death right side out and that death is a birth in reverse! A love that is stronger than death and a death weaker than love, now here are two metaphorical ways of speaking; but the omnipotence of death, if one considers only the prosaic empirical world, is apparently the literal truth. And not only does the last time decide once and for all, and not only is the last time the only one that counts, but when this last time is death, one single time suffices, one single time, one fell swoop, one single tangency . . . and everything is finished in an instant and forever! The first time will then and *already* be the last, the last time was the first *anew:* first and last in eternity and for all eternity; not only ultimate but "primultimate"; not only definitive, but "semelfactive." Every repetition is useless here, nay even contradictory; for the very idea that one can die two times is, in itself, absurd.

The tête-à-tête of love and death, of duty and death, excluding every genuine reciprocity, thus corners us in an impasse. The *more-and-more* thus ceases to appear as a sign of vitality and a passionate crescendo; it is only a symptom of fever and a frenetic auction; it comes up against, as a last resort, in a final analysis, the barrier of death; this is the supreme failure, the final tumble into nothingness. Death inevitably has the last word, the concluding remarks—indeed!—the final words that incomprehensibly close our mouths and gag us for eternity. Death hushes in one fell swoop the words of love and the imperatives of duty! And forever. Death, period! Then (but can one say "then"?), then silence and blackness, and at the end of a certain time, forgetting. As for the rest . . . what remains? The echo itself apparently is death . . . The posthumous memory is submerged by the ocean of the lack of understanding and by the sand of indifference. Would the dying vibration of the pause in which the living being seemed to survive also be death?

8. Up to the Almost-Nothing. The Least Being.

Since the moral option can neither be formulated by the static philosophy of the happy medium nor even resolved by the sharp aim of the golden mean, nor eluded by mutual neutralization, let us at least examine ascetic extremism, which goes *until* the end of mortification. For such is indeed the problem: up to what point can the man of abnegation and ecstatic altruism push the exhaustion of his being-proper, at the risk of himself being absorbed into nonbeing, and, as a result, of annihilating altruism itself at the same time as the altruist? How does one go, at great risk to one's life, *up to* the extreme edge of the *almost*-nothing, all the while taking care not to cross the irreversible boundary that separates this almost-nothing from the nothing? The asymptotic approach to the boundary, past which the loving being would vanish into love, and thanks to which the lover would coincide ecstatically with the beloved via a unitive fusion without having the time to relive in him this mysterious and silent approach, this furtive approach does not at all resemble the static and trivial approximately of the happy medium. The happy medium knows nothing about the spirit of *finesse* . . . It only knows arithmetic! More simply, it would undoubtedly be advisable to distinguish two modalities of the *almost:* the *approximately,* with which common sense contents itself, and infinite *approximation;* the latter is the continual approach of a spirit that is always closer to the goal and at the same time also always far away! In contrast to the rough and obtuse hit-or-miss procedure of druggists, the former approach is above all a movement of the spirit of finesse: lighter and more imperceptible than the shadow of a shadow, the spirit of finesse is a keen spirit, a spirit that is *on-the-brink-of;* it is moral in secret as if by infinitesimal fluxions. The almost-nonexistent that is still existent, the existent that is already almost nonexistent takes refuge by means of love in minimal or infinitesimal existence, that is, in the existence that is the least existence possible; the lover makes himself small, the smallest possible, to the point of disappearing, and thus risks no longer existing at all . . . For this is a risk to be run! *Ascesis* is thus not an easy thing! When the existent person, by dint of loving humility, is at the point of becoming entirely nonexistent or at least *almost* nonexistent, or at least *barely* existent, the problem of asceticism is going to vanish into thin air at the same time; and catharsis will no longer have a raison d'être: the existent person is therefore in the middle of sublimation! If it were not a question of morality but rather of virtuosity, one would say that the third means of escape requires a tour de force or more exactly a considerable dexterity [*tour d'adresse*]. This game with the danger of death is an acrobatic game. Just as intuition comes closest to a burning reality and then, *at the point of* being consumed by it, withdraws and stands back, so the lover who is mad with love, at the point of sacrificing himself, pulls himself together and gives in to a type of infinitesimal egoism and succeeds in surviving. The lover who *almost* died for his beloved does not preserve a memory from the far off shore, since he never drew alongside it, but instead a muddled reminiscence, since he at least grazed the nearer shoreline. Abnegation in some way tends asymptotically toward the zero of nonbeing: this zero is the limit of renunciations, and abnegation becomes indistinguishable from nihilization pure and simple as soon as the fateful tangency occurs. The last instant, because it is the limit of the human and the supra-human, is indeed always ambiguous; in the amphiboly of ultimacy, being and love correspond to the acute paroxysm of incandescence. This paroxysm is the thunderous flash of sacrifice. *Usque ad mortem; heos thanatou;*[17] up until death, but on this side of it; up until death, but beyond. Those are the two *up-untils* that are confused in one single instant but between which love hesitates when it is at the point of making the mortal leap. Up until death, death being excluded; or, still: up until the last instant, with the exception of this last instant itself—the last instant being the next-to-last rather than the last, and even the antepenultimate rather than the penultimate; it is in retrospect and in the future perfect that the last breath turns out to have been the last from the fact that there will no longer be any others after that one! Better still: the last instant is more extreme than supreme; the abnegation of this altruist-acrobat is a quasi-abnegation, an abnegation that holds back something, an abnegation that keeps in its possession an ulterior motive, a small chance of surviving; the person who lacks hope hopes that Providence has somewhere secretly set up an invisible net for catching the survivor of the perilous leap, and this hope is as intangible as the net itself; he perhaps speculates on the miracle of the last chance: at the very moment of toppling into the void, he imagines glory . . . almost posthumous, which would come back to him if he escapes alive. Will we dare say that in the sincerest sacrifice there sometimes is a type of imperceptible cheating (which is so excusable!) and one that resembles a wholly pneumatic hope . . . The person lacking hope, in short, resembles an intrepid acrobat whose performance makes our hearts flutter, but he is neither a martyr nor a hero: for that he lacks the minuscule interval of time, the supplement of infinitesimal endurance that has made a sacrifice of his devotion; he lacks being able actually to cross the threshold of death. The devotion to others is thus a devotion on this side of death, an intra-vital devotion, and the will that takes it on remains within immanence. Yet a devotion that extends to the totality of existence by excluding the supreme gift, that is, by excluding the gift of one's own life from the donation, this devotion limit can be called *that which is serious,* and it remains, in some way, secular. Even if "total" (almost total!), the devotion is still a partitive gift, a gift that gives something while retaining something else; its gesture is all in all efferent and afferent—or better still: what it gives is defined with respect to what it keeps; as with affirmation in relation to refusal, the empirical gift gives the effect of relief.

But a genuinely total gift, a gift that "would not give" this or that, such and such a determinate possession, one that would much rather be a gift of all of one's being-proper, offered by the being itself, a gift that literally would be a gift-of-oneself, how could that be conceived? The last instant is extreme, like the previous one, and it coincides with it, but it is additionally the supreme article; the desperate decision that accepts it is not so much *serious* as *passionate;* contradiction inhabits it. The devotion that devotes itself body and soul up to and including death is called sacrifice. Sacrifice is an abnegation that renounces everything and accepts every hardship, including death. It is here that the monstrous, the implacable, the absurd logic of abnegation lies in wait for us, so as to harass us with its scruples and its remorse. As long as there remains in you a drop of blood and a breath of life, you must pass on this drop and this breath into the dying life of your brother so as to reanimate him. But what if this drop is the last one? The same question continues to haunt us: up to what point *can, should* the altruist go in the rarefaction of his being-proper? The finitude of power blindly cuts short the infinity of duty. Morally, I must go on infinitely; there is no moral reason to stop. Will the sophism of *acervus ruens* be our last recourse? But physically, it is indeed necessary to stop before death occurs. At what moment should one stop? And why at that moment rather than any other? Timid people and the overly sensitive will stop earlier than is necessary; the one who stops too soon, with too comfortable a margin, and who is imperceptibly and invisibly pressed to be done with it, is not a sincere altruist; the martyr who stops too late, that is, beyond (*epekeina*), the martyr who is carried away by his spell has already sunken into the night of the "demonic hyperbole" and of the wholly-other-order. Between the two, the border is a wavering and infinitely ambiguous line: between the two, the extreme good will, mad with love, plays a tight game; for the tension is acute. Likewise, we were saying that the good will is passionate: it goes as far as is possible; better yet, the closest possible to its own nonbeing, inasmuch as its strength permits it and up to the limit of its strength, and, yet on this side of the limit, but not with the express intention of remaining on this side: and it does all this without our being able to respond in a universal manner to the question *Up to what point?* Its survival is thus a type of grace, or rather a miraculous chance.—In asceticism's responses to the question of *up to what point,* the borderline victory of love evokes a far-off glory or better yet a mystical horizon: we think that we glimpse this horizon at the end of an infinite exhaustion of being-proper—an exhaustion or rather a sublimation that leads to the mystery of what is impalpable; existence in outline form, by dint of fading into the almost-nothing, ends up by disappearing; the pianissimo is but a whisper, and then it dies in silence; love, by dint of loving, spiritualizes our ontic substance to the extreme; the being, by virtue of love, makes itself more and more transparent; the lover in his entirety becomes love. The preponderance of duty over being has, as well, a pneumatic sense, just like the victory of love. Sublimation leads not to nothingness but to hope.

9. The Oscillatory Beating.

For want of being able to hold together being and love under the form of the happy medium, there remained for us the blockade of the stationary equilibrium (with stagnation and death as the sole exit) . . . provided that a blockade is a way out! And when all is said and done, our last (next-to-last) exit was a flight up to the point of the almost-nothing. This is the penultimate solution! The man who takes refuge in infinitesimal existence gets close to it with an infinite approach that is regular or not, rectilinear or not, but always progressive and goal oriented; and this approach can last until the end of days! From this approach, let us finally distinguish the fourth way out: evasion in place. A flight toward the horizon or a flight in place (if one dares say that), they both find the solution in movement and in temporality; this evasive or cinematic solution permits us to escape being torn apart; but movement toward the infinite goes somewhere: somewhere, indeed, into that which is unfinished [*quelque part, certes, dans l'inachevé*],[18] but somewhere all the same: it is a movement that advances, that therefore has a vocation and a horizon; whereas movement in place itself goes nowhere. This movement in place is a movement of shuttling back and forth, a going out and back, a going and coming back that goes from the one to the other and comes back from the other to the one, and at high speed: for the movement is so rapid that it evokes, when worse comes to worst, the image of a vibration. Inasmuch as the round trip, by virtue of its alternative rhythm, implies a trip back, it excludes the loving flight, the mystical flight into the ecstasy of the almost-nothing; it is fulfilled in immanence. The *alternative* of love without being and being without love adopts, in time, the rhythm of a hurried *alternation*. As this alternation, as a whole, is equivalent to a cycle, one does not know from which end to begin, or at which end to finish. But as it is indeed necessary to begin from somewhere, let us take love without being as a point of departure: at every instant, lightly touching nonbeing, the lover is at the point of being annihilated; but at that very moment in which he dissolves into the ecstasy of his loving nonexistence, at the moment in which, via unitive identity, he becomes other than himself, at the moment in which the lover loses himself in the beloved, at that very minute, the lover is at the point of deepening, of filling out; he becomes stout and thickens, the lover, that is. The almost-nothing, which indeed very narrowly missed no longer being anything and disappearing into the anonymity of a cosmogonic love, impalpable like ether, such is how it regains its strength: the risk it runs, henceforth, is no longer the risk of loving perdition but that of adipose degeneration; the monster that threatens it is called gentrification. At the finish of this process, there indeed no longer is anything but being without love. From this point on, the process is turned upside down, and the point of arrival of the preceding one becomes the point of departure of the subsequent one: the movement that brings us back from being without love and that is threatened with suffocation to a love without being is the same process of volatilization and ascetic rarefaction of which we were speaking in describing the third way out: being reanimated and already sublimated by the breath of love, in turn, becomes an almost-nothing—no longer the initial almost-nothing that initiated condensation and degeneration, but the terminal almost-nothing that announces the glory of pneumatic love. Because it is simultaneously being and love, ontic egoism and gift of self, the *loving-being* never has a long-term stay in either the land of egoity or the land of abnegation: it is in the instant that love-without-being veers into being stripped of love, degenerates, and becomes gentrified; and vice versa, it is again in a single instant that the grace of love grazes us with a touch or, better yet, with an infinitely light tangency; and those two instants are one simple and same instant, a single disappearing appearance, considered sometimes as a disappearance and sometimes as an appearance, according to the perspective that one chooses; and as the first almost-nothing initiates no irremediable decadence, the second one announces no lasting conversion. Everything happens furtively and as in a flash of lightning, in this instant-spark that is either a primultimate flickering or the emergence of the almost-nothing; immediately after or before the fifty-ninth second of the fifty-ninth minute of the eleventh hour (here, before and after amount to the same thing, coincide in one same point), the glimmer of love has extinguished-united, has disappeared-appeared into the thickness of being. It speaks volumes about the supreme instability, the extreme fragility of the superlative that, in the language of Fénelon, we call pure love. Pure love is only pure in the duration of an instant, that is, outside all duration; the instant before it was still impure; a second later it will already and again be impure. We were attempting to explain the *paradox of mutual neutralization,* that of love by death and that of death by love, and, continuing on this path, the *paradox of absurd reciprocity;* in this double paradox one recognizes, without too much trouble, the *mystery of aseity:* the loving-being is *causa sui* qua love, and effect of itself qua being. Such is the absurd contradiction that explains what is inexplicable about movement and free will. Isn't this vicious circle liberating? Here again, Bergson would be our guide. Liberation is perhaps at the finish of the fourth escape, but certainly not of the second one; for the second one, as we will remember, is blocked by death, and as such it is undoubtedly a way out of misery and subterfuge; it is not an infinite escape . . . : in the vibration of duration, it is the entirety of temporal continuity that is infinitely renewed from every instant to the subsequent instant by the development of circular causality. Petrarch, from "Triumph" to "Triumph," leads us up to the sixth one, the only one that never misleads, that does not betray any hope, the only one that after the Judgment will bring us eternal glory: after the wholly relative and provisional victories of finitude, those of love and death, of time and temporal glories, here is the victory of victories, the ultimate and supreme victory, the sovereign victory that is the frame of reference for all the others. But as for us here below, we do not ask for so much. We would instead say, There is never a definitive victory, never a victory that is unilaterally victorious, as in war; there is nothing perpetual except the very alternation of victory and defeat; and there are, thus, only instantaneous victories, ones that punctuate an eternal undulation and an eternal circularity. These instantaneous victories are just as much a repeated miracle. After all, isn't it life itself that is this continued miracle? Miraculously fished out, and at the last moment, in the nonbeing of love, miraculously revived, or protected, by a rescue *in extremis,* from the suffocation of a being without love and without oxygen, the loving-being is a continual, miraculous survivor, a survivor at each instant and at each fraction of a second. Two contrary tropisms struggle against each other in the heart of the loving-being: first the temptation of a sedentary lifestyle, of a quite contented good conscience, and of good sleep: this is the part of being without love. And then, of the qualities that are defaults and that bourgeois morality condemns: this is the part of the love without being. And this part is at the origin of all that is ambivalent, ambiguous, and passionate in us; to believe Plato's Diotima about this, Eros receives this heritage simultaneously, from Penia, his mother, inasmuch as she is a vagabond and a beggar, and from Poros, his father inasmuch as he is an emeritus hunter, an indefatigable marcher (*ites*),[19] and an intrepid adventurer. The loving-being is threatened at every instant by one or the other of these two deaths, by one or the other of the two asphyxias that lie in wait for it: sometimes, for lack of being, it dies of exhaustion, sometimes for lack of love it dies of repletion; it is continually at the point of losing half of itself.

The one-upmanship with no way out of love and of death makes us think of a zigzag: but this one-upmanship peters out. The alternating beating that exempts us from responding with yes or no, of willing either the one or the other and of choosing one of the two things, in turn delineates like a saw-toothed graph: the vibrating alternation blunts and softens the sharp alternative. Prevented by its finitude from going all the way in whatever it may be and notably up until the extremes, and refusing, however, to slumber in the quietude of the happy medium, the moral will oscillates from the physical to the spiritual: this is apparently all it can do. The two obstacles off which it alternatively rebounds, the two limits against which it butts up, the two extremes that, in the end, send it back and forth adapt as it were to the amplitude of its oscillation.

The metaphorical, and therefore to some extent glamorized, character of this representation is undoubtedly something suspicious: an analogy does not necessarily imply taking a moral stand. Unless fleeing in place is "taking a stand" . . . ! A way out, a perpetual avoidance—just so, here is what one calls a back-and-forth! Incapable of settling down, one would say that the moral will is pursued and so to speak hunted down by the incompatibility of the two contradictories that each of them pushes back toward its opposite; the so-called moral will is always elsewhere, sometimes here, sometimes there, here when one believes it to be farther away, and, when all is said and done, nowhere and everywhere, the two together. *Ubique-nusquam!* But if the vibratory movement, clouding the trails, blurring every finality as well as intentionality in general, were itself the only way out, then we would rightfully respond: one can only erase the alternative by eliminating moral life entirely; this latter "solution" is rather an illusion of the psychological order, a way of numbing the conscience: with the reaction time and the delay ascribable to inertia slowing down the formation of images, the previous impression staying on in the subsequent one and the subsequent one rubbing off on the previous ones; the very rapidity of their succession yields the change and favors the impression of continuity and the illusion of accumulation. However, we have not transcended the alternative! Isn't this pseudo-continuity an effect of vertigo? All things vibrate, dance, and whirl, as the world whirls around the dervish and at the same time as he does . . . This fusion of images carried away by the movement, a fusion that is supposed to resolve moral dilemmas, is undoubtedly an impressionistic illusion, a more or less honest trick, and maybe even—who knows?—an evasion. The synthesis of colors dissolved into whiteness has at least a physical reality that is lacking in the phantasmatic synthesis of a good and an evil mashed together and confused, by the effect of speed, in the vortex of qualities. The approximately that characterizes the static happy medium and the approximately that results from the cinematic blending thus finish by being confused. Bergson, denouncing the cinematographic illusion, the generator of sophisms and pseudo-problems, has undoubtedly criticized the fluctuating wills, wills that are incapable of being fixed, wills that come and go like the "shuttlecock" between two rackets. Bergson was pleading, in all circumstances, for "nominalist" rigor and the universal particularity that is lived in the concrete and determinate existence of what is perceived. The vibratory movement does not blunt, does not erase, the qualitative polarity of the good and bad intention; although that polarity is never Manichaean, the acute option still shows through the fuzziness of ambiguity; through the infinitesimal fluxions, a will asserts itself again, and this will chooses its camp without ambiguity: the will was a spirit of finesse, and the spirit of finesse is still a will. Such is undoubtedly the brilliant paradox of Bergsonism, a paradox of which the paradoxology is due to the impossibility of rationally expressing a mystery: at the very depths of the discontinuous continuity and unambiguous ambiguity it is indeed the mystery of temporality that hides itself. The oscillation between love and being, between duty and being is thus neither a simple passing fancy nor the mark of a versatile amateurism. Narrow are the straits in which it is necessary for us to navigate between love without being and being without love. The halting pace of the loving being in this strait in which the contradictories send it back and forth from one to the other sometimes ends in a terrifying trembling in place: more often, perhaps, it will allow us to foresee the beating palpitations of a tender heart. Music expresses it with a tremolo. This trembling, nostalgic vibration, which is passionate as a lamentation, testifies to a tragic tearing apart that does not have the right to be idle; this tearing bleeds in us in the agonic and panting contradictions of the deaths of love.

10. To Fit the Most Love Possible into the Least Possible Being.

The unambiguous ambiguity of moral exigency is thus four times ambiguous: 1st: because it is halfway between extremes, because it is simultaneously the one and the other, and because it is at the same time neither the one nor the other; 2nd: because the infinite demand of duty and the imprescriptible rights of existence mutually neutralize each other and remain at the point of death in the equilibrium of the marasmus; 3rd: because in its infinite ambiguity, the opaque being, consumed by the fire of love and set ablaze by its light, becomes more and more diaphanous and that ad infinitum, without, however, ceasing to exist; and 4th: because in the end the will, torn apart by the two demands, vertiginously oscillates between the one and the other. And in the end, it is the very ambiguity of the four ambiguities that makes the inconsistent consistencies, the obviousness that is so unobvious, so deceiving and yet indestructible and infinitely renewing, of the moral imperative. A modus vivendi is established between the moral agent and this inner misery that is the incorruptible incompatibility of being and love. But it is not enough to determine the moral condition of this modus vivendi: what still remains to be explained is that which is inexplicable, the metaphysical foundation of the alternative and the raison d'être of this malediction. A fortiori, it is not enough to explain how the *Homo duplex,* that is, the *loving-being,* can be wholly transformed into love, can itself become entirely love (on condition that it can), if one does not determine the weight, the range, and the limits of the obstacle that is anti-love. The moral being is manifestly a being and, what is more, the moral being is moral on account of I know not what intangible, invisible, and secret intention that is formulated nocturnally in its heart of hearts. But does the very transparency of this heart of hearts allow us to isolate an opaque, irreducible, incompressible element, which it is quite necessary to accept just as one accepts a necessary evil, and which is a fatal consequence of our finitude? This *least evil* would be, according to the form it dons, a *logical minimum,* an *ontic minimum,* an *ethical minimum.* In the moral alternative, it is love for others that is the positive pole and the object of a vocation. Is it necessary to repeat again that the ambition of love is, by right, unlimited? Indeed, the moral being is a lame being whose power is finite and whose duty is infinite. Without playing a game of words: his ends are infinite and his means are modest. In order to elevate itself to the sublime ends of disinterestedness, the altruistic will must with effort climb the sheer path of the medium by fighting against gravity and against its natural inertia. For it carries on its shoulders the heavy burden of naturality. This laborious itinerary is called mediation. Ascension and moral progress thus can be neither continuous nor regular nor direct; they are neutralized and offset, and even beyond, by relapses and retreats. Up to this point, confronting being and that which is before-being, being and love, we got no farther than a complication of the first degree, which is also a one-way complication: just as the ego is the compact or massive nucleus of egoistic retraction, so being is the innate, opaque, and impenetrable part of the loving-being; the more this nucleus of our destinal gravity is proven to be massive and dense, the more the being is difficult to manage and to transfigure; the more the nucleus is opaque, and the more the ray of light with difficulty traverses the screen that this being without love and without duty places in its path. It can be said that this irreducible residue, impermeable to loving influence, is called Evil: this would be a deposit, a remainder, or better still, a simple scrap; it would not have any function of any sort . . . The more there is being, the less there is love: love and being are inversely proportional to each other. But when, if worse comes to worst, there is no longer anything but being without love, when there is no longer anything but being in the pure state, then there is not even being in general, at least not of being worthy of this name; there is nothing but a monster and a repulsive caricature; there is nothing but an unformed, impure, unspeakable being; a cadaver. And vice versa, the extremes come together: if a being absolutely deprived of love is not even a being, then a love without being is not even a love; the third escape pointed out the danger to us: a love that takes refuge in nonbeing or at least goes to the point of almost-nothing, this love, sublime as it may be, risks no longer loving at all. Are we therefore sent back to the median zone, which is that of bourgeois comfort and security? No, there is no medium zone, there is no golden mean. But there is an unstable and hazy boundary line on which is established, by dint of trial and error, by touch-ups and infinitesimal approximations, this relation of maximum to minimum in which Leibniz's optimism would find the optimum point. The determination of this point and the outline of it result from a debate: the spirit of finesse determines it. Indeed, we have the right to say: the less there is being, the more there is love; but on the other hand, as there remains only an apparition of love when there is almost no more being, and no more love at all when there is no being at all, we can limit ourselves to saying: *the most love possible for the least possible being* . . . with the understanding that in order to love we must resign ourselves to being! So it is that we recommend (for want of something better): the fewest words possible for the most meaning possible; the least of lost space and the least of lost time possible for the most soul possible. And always, of course, *as much as is possible! Quam maxime, quam minime* (*hoson dunaton*). The most possible: this relative superlative in the maximum of the maximalism authored by fate, taking into consideration the circumstances and the physical or historical conditions; this is the supreme (relatively supreme!) recourse . . . The most possible with the least expenditure of being: such is our refrain.

What all this implies in all cases is modesty, humility, and sobriety, extreme spiritual density, and at the same time, the horror of conceit and showing off. And more generally, in the language of ends and means, like small investors: a man who is a man, that is, a perpetually finite being, has to expend in means the minimum that is strictly necessary for its end, if he sincerely wants to realize this end; no more, no less; such is its *necessary evil*. To expend less by skimping on the means, like small investors, would be to cast doubt on the real intention of succeeding, would be to confuse foolishly the passionate good will for the end with the hoarding of fanatics and collectors, who, being happy to live in the daily grind of the common, finish by forgetting the end of which the means are the means; hypnotized by the anguish of the "expenditures," they do not reflect upon the seriousness of their project, that is, on the function of the mediation. But to expend too much by throwing the means out the window so as to dazzle passersby while infinitely wasting resources that are necessarily finite by living, like an ostentatious man, in luxury and conceit, this would be a false generosity and another, particularly insidious, form of bad faith. There are thus two opposite forms of bad will, two Machiavellian ways of searching out the obstacle: a petty will that is velleity and that desires the end without the means, and a will that dreams of suffocating and of forgetting the end under the sumptuous eiderdown of the means; both desire the end separated from the means that would make it possible. This does not mean that there is a sensible economy halfway between thrifty people and prodigal ones, as Aristotle would suggest to us: one could, therefore, imagine a good administrator who quietly goes mad and squanders his riches judiciously; good faith would be halfway between two opposite forms of bad faith: the sordid hypocrisy of misers and the superabundant and redundant superfluity of bluffers. What a beautiful symmetry! The one who blossoms in the satisfaction of simultaneously accumulating all the advantages is undoubtedly the most Machiavellian of all . . . so to which saint should one devote oneself, or with which faith should one identify? Orphaned good faith, abandoned at the side of the road, feels overcome with despair. Well, there is nothing about which to despair! Provided that we renounce measuring to the millimeter the shortest route or verifying both sides of zero, that is, of diaphanous innocence, the equidistance of the two opposite hypocrisies, provided that we renounce weighing to the milligram the weight of conversely egoistic motives, innocent goodwill rediscovers spontaneously and infallibly the *via recta* of the shortest path. This is the goodwill that Leibniz calls "consequent": this will, far from willing by principle and Platonically, wills the end and the means that will make it possible, wills the end and the means jointly, wills the one with the others in a single, indivisible, and organic act of willing; this passionate will is the only will that is integrally good, and one can no longer distinguish it from love. For loving inspiration is an eloquent as well as persuasive counselor: it knows in all cases what it has to do and does not need precision scales to assure itself of this.

3
The Least Evil and the Tragic Side of the Contradiction

1. Impetus and the Trampoline. Rebound. The Effect of Relief. The Positivity of Negation.

Up to this point, the inverse relation between being and love has appeared to us as a relatively simple complication; a complication without an exponent. Men are perfectly adapted to this complication. What proves this is, in the vertical dimension, the most common paradox of everyday experience and mechanics: to descend provisionally so as to come back up, to fall down so as to ascend higher, faster, and with a more powerful takeoff. Such is the law of antigravity, which resembles a levitation but which is not, however, a miracle. The loving-being seems to rebound off the trampoline of the antithesis or more exactly, to use Diotima's words, takes off, in the process of ascension, from lower levels (*epanabasmoi*), which the sixth book of the *Republic* calls "hypotheses" (*hupotheseis*),[1] so as then, from level to level or from hypothesis to hypothesis, to work its way up to the anhypothetical principle of all things (*mechri tou anupothetou*). For this very reason, the key word of Plato's dialectic is *horme,* impetus [*élan*]. Free fall certainly has neither impetus nor intention, but the engineer is capable of salvaging it, of artificially redirecting it toward the heights by using the

cunning of machinery and technical measures; the trampoline, the lever, the seesaw effect are the simplest instruments of this ingeniousness. *Epibaseis kai hormai,* as at the
end of the sixth book of the *Republic* for Plato, or *epibathra,*
as in the treatise on the Beautiful for Plotinus.[2] When it is an
issue of dialectical flight, the movement toward the depths
gives a more energetic impulse and a more powerful spring
to the impetus toward the heights: the two movements, *although* being in opposite directions, or rather, *precisely because* they are in opposite directions! form a single action
that is amphibolic and that responds to the same intention.
The least surprising paradox is here expressed in its most
contrary form! To a certain extent, the upward movement
was potentially implied in the opposite movement that paradoxically invites us to take off from a stepping stone and put
pressure on the lower rung . . . And yet the downward movement is not potentially contained or analytically included in
the upward movement, since, at least on the face of it, it denies it, disrupts it, and even contradicts it; and it does not
confirm it either, since, at least on the face of it, it invali-
dates it; strictly speaking, it does not even make up for it,
nor is it deducted from its upward force. Recoil and gravity
were the paradoxical conditions of the impetus they seemed
to deny, but the impetus, to soar skyward or to fly, to tear
oneself away from inertia and the fall, needs, furthermore,
a supplement of force. The dynamism and the elasticity are
shown, in spite of everything and by an almost immediate
reading that is barely an interpretation, in the appearance
itself. Does the impetus, at the point of soaring skyward, the
impetus, ready to leap, gathered up into itself, holding its
breath, the heart beating, the impetus concentrated in a sort
of meditation that is void of all thought and outstretched to-

ward an imminent future that is void of any present, still adhere to matter and muscles, or has it already taken flight? One thing is certain: it only hangs on to the body by a thread, but in spite of this delicate thread, it is solidly fastened to immanence; it sinks its roots to the depths of our naturality; invisible, it hides at the center of this matter that carries it and propels it. The impetus is inseparable from the matter from which it is born: the matter holds it back, weighs it down, and hinders it, but at the same time and *in this way* serves it as a fulcrum point or foil. The body is thus simultaneously the worry of the impetus and the foundation of its confidence. We could perhaps be allowed to call this mixture of worry and confidence the Serious [*le Sérieux*].

The rebound, the effect of relief, the positivity of negation—these are only metaphors or manners of speaking: metaphors and manners of speaking only transform the moral problem of the least evil into another language. The ball that bounces on the spot and falls back instantly seems to say no to gravity, but this refusal has no intention, except, indirectly, for the intention of the player who wants to win his match; and above all, this refusal did not last more than an instant; this refusal without any consequences or repercussions is the exact opposite of a miracle; this leap has nothing supernatural about it. And on the other hand, the champion, taking his impetus from the trampoline, does not see beyond the immediate success: it is enough for him to win an instantaneous victory, to beat a short-lived record. The rebound is entirely impetus, but it lacks sustainability! And conversely: the effect of relief, such as a pithy scene, seems to immortalize or perpetuate a contrast, but at first glance there is no impetus. Antigravity, which constitutes all the elasticity of the impetus, is indeed comparable to an effect of relief. But only comparable! However, the effect of relief is precisely an *effect,* in this particular case, a "stereoscopic" effect, an optical contrast that is immobilized in space, which becomes more pronounced thanks to that which is clear-obscure and in the antithesis of rays of sunshine and shadows; even the Manichaean opposition of Good and Evil, of light and darkness, is still a static opposition: the periodicity of these vicissitudes as well as the regular alternation of day and night in the end turns into a tête-à-tête—a tête-à-tête in which the two symmetrical and pre-given principles are compared to one another. Isn't such an alternative an aesthetic category rather than a moral option? But above all, the effect of relief, insofar as it sometimes has something sensational in it, is essentially a spectacle, an exemplary and often normative spectacle, a spectacle for spectators who are dazzled and filled with wonder. The mere presence of a third party, the indiscreet intrusion of a witness, and a fortiori the gaze of spectators, reinforced by binoculars, condemn innocence to relegation. Innocence is sent into exile. Or, better yet, innocence, banned on the spot, itself begins to pose for the gallery; starting with the effect, everything becomes theater and stage production; the exhibition degenerates into ostentation and counterfeiting. The spectators applaud the timeless spectacle of Manichaeanism.

Negation itself is, in its own way, an effect of relief, owing to the pedagogical and often even polemical function that falls to it: for example, it rectifies an error . . . But the impetus is thus so brief, so condensed, so immediate that one barely senses it. It is no coincidence that a dialectic of negation is highlighted by Bergson in *Creative Evolution.* On two occasions, and while considering these problems outside every systematic dogmatism, Bergson explains the paradoxical, ambiguous, and even contradictory relation of "spiritual energy" to matter: as it concerns the vital impetus [*élan vital*] and beginning with the visual system. The vital impetus, rebounding on the trampoline of matter, makes the sheaf of divergent species gush out in all directions, and transcends the disjunction of the One and the Many. The "march toward vision," canalized by the optical nerve and by the visual system in general, is simultaneously limited and made possible: a field, a range, so many determinations that are, after all, negations and without which sight, paradoxically, would not be perceptive; it is by taking our inspiration from Bergson and his disconcerting intuitions that we can make sense of the nonsense of the organ-obstacle. So how do things now stand for negation? Bergson tells us that negation is a "judgment of a judgment," or as we prefer to say, a judgment with an exponent, a judgment to the second power. An absurdly affirmative proposition is implied in the negation, but it is rejected immediately: it was an allusion, barely an insinuation; however, the indirect form of this negative affirmation, which has connections to the language of modesty, projects onto the truth a more striking light, a more abrupt lighting. Isn't the shadow of negation itself an effect of relief? So it is that our refusals indirectly are telltale signs of our options. Nevertheless, as we were indicating when we were passing from negation to moral refusal, the *no* [*non*] of the refusal has a greater passionate charge, a "negative positivity" more intense than the purely formal and logical *not* [*ne . . . pas*] of negation, for the latter denies without refusing; negation *says not* [*ne pas*], but the monosyllable of refusal rejects and vomits, period; absolutely and without restrictions, without specifying either the delay or the degree or the *inasmuch* (*quatenus*). If the refusal is often aggressive to

the point of being confused with a belligerent act, if the refusal is a dramatic and militant taking of a stand and sometimes a historic event that has happened once and for all,
then negation, even if it is tacitly polemical, always maintains a speculative, Platonic, and in some way notional character. Every negation is, in its own way and indirectly, a type
of vague determination; an undetermined determination. It
is at the limit of all negations, and consequently ad infinitum, as in negative theology, that the equivocal determination, defined by the refusal, would become univocal . . . almost univocal!

The impetus that lifts us up above ourselves, toward the
forgetting of ourselves, toward abnegation, toward altruism,
and toward love necessarily gets support from being-proper
so as to transcend it. Such is the first degree, or better, the
first exponent of the complication; or still more precisely:
such is the complication to the second power, the one that
is, like a judgment of a judgment, a complication of simplicity. Here the negativity of the negation is not a mere grammatical jumble, the budding of a cumbersome rhetoric that
shows off and takes the place of meaning, like the circum-
locutions of those known as the "Précieuses"; here my body
is at the origin of the drama! The body, weighed down by its
egoism, its gluttony, and its instincts, is not a dispensable
burden, the occasion of a futile chore with which love would
willingly be laden, whereas it could have spared itself it. If
naturality were this gratuitous and altogether extra-vital
surcharge for the loving-being, then asceticism, which rids
it of it, would be an expeditious, slightly frivolous, and almost amusing task. How *does one be rid of it?* This disdainful
word, *apallattesthai,* appears quite often in the *Phaedo.* How
does one set the moral bird free so that it flies swiftly away

toward the heights? Or with other examples: it would suffice to throw overboard the entire bundle along with everything it contains—concupiscence, greed, self-love, vanity—without taking any inventory or making a selection, be it what it may; one would not even take the time to open it, one would not even give oneself the trouble of undoing the bow . . . Good riddance! Good-bye worries! The traveler without baggage, rid not only of his worldly goods but also of his very being itself, would truly be imponderable and aerial, light as love is. But this ablation of all being hurts! Is this even an ablation? The ablation is always partitive: it subtracts something and leaves the rest. The one who is *jointly* [*indivisément*] soul and body, and who not only is deprived of his worldly goods and his properties, but is mutilated in his flesh, this person suffers and bleeds; but, the loving-being who is indivisibly [*indivisiblement*] being and love, and who is not only separated from his flesh, but who is incomprehensibly deprived of his total being . . . by what name will we call his suffering? This chimera is called angelism; but one could just as well call it extremism or purism. Well, the chimera does not aspire to the serious. In this world of relativity, of commonness, of intermediarity, in which are combined, for the mixed beings that we are, all the conditions of life, the inert and blind weight can at the same time serve as ballast: it is the same weight, but it provides the necessary impetus to permit us to climb. Let us show how this paradox can be applied to moral ambiguity. The ego of egoism is the heavy stone that altruism has to lift; the being of the loving-being is the weighty millstone that love has to drag around and that strains the "levitation" of the impetus. But this is really a quite simple matter, and almost too simple to express. If there were no heavy stone, there would not be any altruism in general; if there were no insurmountable mountains to be moved, there would not be any faith; and if there were no weighty millstone, there would not be any love. Without this millstone, which makes us groan out of lassitude and weep out of despondence, love and hope would have long ago deserted the valleys of terrestrial existence. Kant already said it: in the void of the vacuum the dove crashes down . . . And, likewise: if the world is void of atmosphere, of every obstacle to be surmounted, of every problem to be resolved, then love becomes a thin mist that dissipates and vanishes into space. Love, fragile like a bird, yet infinitely more, would not be able to live without the pressure of obstacles that prevent it from breathing and loving. The organ-obstacle, well, there it is.

2. One After the Other. Mediation. Pain.

Rebound and impetus, the effect of relief, the positivity of negation . . . What does all this mean? If our analyses resulted in the application of concepts like mediation or the least evil to the moral problem, then we would obviously have bypassed the problem. Nothing in what is conceptual or dialectical either concerns or appeases moral disquiet. As concerns a moral tearing apart, the powers of conciliatory and healing synthesis remain without effect. Philautia, naturality, or, as we were saying at the time of the controversy of "pure love," concupiscence divert us away from altruism, while in some respects these condition it, sometimes even exalting disinterested love. So be it! In discursive mediation, there is the principle of temporality, which sorts out everything. Contradictories refuse to coexist, and one is not even able to unite them together in one thought: they fight among themselves, like incompatible spouses, to the point where one has nihilized the other. But they can succeed one another! The one first, then the other; or still: sometimes the one, sometimes the other . . . Man is perfectly adapted to this regimen. Such is the slyness of time! Alternation, as well as rectilinear temporality, by diluting the contradiction allows for avoiding blockages and total immobilization. Everything is a question of timing: sensuality drags us downward at a given moment, love tears us away from this gravity at another moment . . . Were we ourselves not talking about *escape mechanisms?* As concerns the elasticity of the instantaneous spring of love, it owes its explosive energy to those two irresistible forces that meet each other and at the same time repel each other: the being of the ego pulls downward, love, impatient to take off, projected onto its trampoline, catapulted by the very resistance of instinct, leads us toward others [*autrui*]. Not only does time resolve the contradiction, but it is the continued solution to it. To outflank the contradiction of the unsolvable dilemma, thereafter going with the tangent of succession, and thus escaping the cul-de-sac—these, in particular, are the tricks of war and these tricks herald oblique and ingenuous sagacity rather than the head-on courage of sacrifice and death. Gracián, intending his aphorisms to be used by courtiers and diplomats, could have written a manual of escape . . . if escape did not itself require the courage to confront as much as and more than the art of prevaricating. In any event, patience, prudence, and precaution are the virtues most often recommended by the subtle Jesuit to the courtier and even to the warrior: first, patience, because it is the art of waiting judiciously and, in a word, the *temporalization* that best uses the machine of time. The iron law of fate, *mora,* concedes to us the delay. The one who makes use of the delay, who dives into the delay, has already exited from the impasse; he will perhaps see the end of winter. Allow us to cite the admirable 55th maxim of the *Oracle Manual:* "We must traverse the large career of time before we come to the center of occasion. A rational temporizing ripens secrets and resolutions. The crutch of time does more business than the Club of Hercules [Hercule]. God himself when he punishes us, makes use not of the rod but of the season . . . Fortune rewards with interest those who have the patience to wait for her."[3] Benito Pelegrin, who has proposed for us a new classification of the Aphorisms,[4] is not wrong to begin with the theme "of the end and of the means" and then to group in the proper place the maxims that are related to the set of problems of adaptation and opportunism. It is true that in this ataxic and disjointed world that is the world of universal belligerence, humans are not able to gain access to ideal harmony all at once: however, in spite of conflicts and being torn apart, in spite of the antithesis, the balance sheet of the mediation proves to be positive as a whole. Mediation, all in all, at least goes somewhere. Mediation is not an amorphous and invertebrate temporality that would go adrift: it is, on the contrary, expressly well ordered, articulated, and even structured for the purpose of a specific end. It differentiates itself in that regard from naked temporality, which, itself, goes nowhere, if not up to death, up to the end of time, or up to the universal marasmus. Depending on whether one envisions mediation under its exoteric aspects or in its esoteric meaning—in other words, whether one considers the accumulated obstacles and the lost time, or whether one envisions the general meaning of mediation—, one feels driven to pessimism or encouraged to pursue the path of optimism. *Barricades block the street and pave the way,* is what you could read on the walls of the Latin Quarter in 1968; this path is certainly not a rectilinear expressway linking one point to another . . . And in a different place, on a poster bearing the signature of Cremonini, in which one distinguishes an inextricable tangled mass of scrap iron, of paving stones, of overturned cars and heaped-up debris, of insolent words spread out: "Against forbidden directions: the roads of what is possible."[5] This insuperable chaos is perhaps a promise and a hope: this pessimism, in the final analysis, is optimistic. In the single word 'mediation' a reassuring finality is already implied: the means are an allusion to the end, and they are only means in comparison to the latter; they summon the end, they point it out with a finger; like indicator arrows, they indicate the correct direction, the direction *toward.* There is thus no reason to be filled with wonder if the pilgrim of mediation commits himself to starting off on the right foot, with gusto, in a good mood and with a good conscience, on this rocky road on which he stumbles with each step. Something to be done, a defined effort to be accomplished, a defined itinerary to be traversed: the conditions of the vocation and the good conscience are combined here. The benediction of the final term—which, however, does not yet exist—retroactively spreads to everything that precedes it or readies it. Bergson would perhaps call such a propagation the retrograde march of direction. The end justifies the means . . . But, in turn, the means were already normative: they presage the end and make guesses about it. And more generally: the "least evil" itself, in the order of what is relative, is still optimistic . . . Relatively optimistic! It is thus not by accident that Leibniz's *Theodicy* makes such a use of the concept. The evil of being is an evil, but (the accent here is on the adjective), it is the *least;* the smallest possible, taking into account the circumstances and the incompatibles or inconsistent things; precisely in the meaning in which the broken line, in a given medium (a refringent medium), is still relatively the shortest path, the shortest possible line; the refraction of the light thus demonstrates that the solutions of the divine economy are relatively the best. In the absence of excellence or perfection, the "least evil" proposes to us negatively, indirectly, and almost timidly—and we were going to say, modestly—the best for which we could hope. And likewise: temporal succession cannot make the contradiction null and void, but *at least* (still and always the concessive relativity of the least evil!) it makes it viable and free flowing, it "makes it pass"; it postpones the crisis, the rejection, the deflagration. Time is, in many circumstances, the least evil . . . provided that one is able to associate excellence, or at least exemplarity, with the modesty of a least evil that has renounced every claim. Time expresses our adaptation to this world of misery. The resigning interjection *alas!* gives way in the heart of a man for a concessive *despite* in which resignation took comfort.

It is necessary to admit, however, that the pilgrim of the moral adventure does not advance in the light, he walks in the night without knowing where he is going, always on the brink of losing faith, of giving up, of abandoning everything . . . The moral "adventure" is not a sport or even an adventure, let alone a dangerous adventure! That would be too easy! That would be good fun! The adventurer of this adventure is not an alpinist who measures with pride the path already traversed and the height already attained, and neither is he the happy companion who sings along the way . . .

Moral anxiety is a bitter anxiety; it never turns around to contemplate the panorama of its own performances; innocence does not listen to fairy tales of sanctifying work: it remains forsaken and orphaned in its unremitting and unrewarded effort.

Is it necessary to think that pain, it if comes to complicate the effort at mediation, will make our innocence more innocent? Pain is, in general, obligatory innocence. A man who sincerely suffers, with his body and his soul, ordinarily barely thinks about his great, daily theatrical representation, and forgets, at least momentarily, to pose for the gallery of his admirers. This means that the pain that one truly suffers, if it is a necessary evil, is of a less convincing necessity than every other form of least evil or mediation. One resigns oneself to it with more difficulty. Or one never adapts to it completely.—Is this to say that pain is necessarily hell? that there is no sincere suffering outside the malediction of despair? Generally, the man beleaguered by the torments of suffering has nothing more pressing than restoring in front of himself a very humble future, a finality, a small reason for hope, as vague as it may be, an incredible teleology, and a reassuring direction. Recycled pain, skimmed over in the great synopses of the dialectician, becomes an *ordeal.* The ascesis of the *Gorgias,* as everyone knows, already prescribed burning-cutting, *kaiein-temnein,* that is, a philosophical cautery and a philosophical lancet. Surgical pain is an acute and nagging pain since it burns and wounds; but its instruments are not instruments of torture: like the arrows of love of which Saint John of the Cross speaks, it has, in a manner of speaking, purifying and redemptive powers. This ambivalence is recognizable in the accounts consecrated to the death of Socrates: the hemlock that the executioner brings to the sage is not a sweet beverage; but in its own way this poison is a medication; the bitter potion is also a remedy: it will serve to loosen the links between the soul and the body, and thus to heal this type of original affliction that is the psychosomatic symbiosis. Pain is admittedly a lived and irreducible event that is added to the mediation and that, as such, is of an irrational essence. However, pain itself is salvageable as an ordeal or a *moment,* that is, as a link in a necessary and beneficial sequence; in a word, as a necessary evil. Starting with the day on which one becomes aware of this capacity for redemption, it is not too difficult to "provide oneself with a justification." This present in which there is pain, which seems eternal and absolute, will consist of only one time; in the illumination of super-consciousness, pain is nothing but an episode and a slight, supplementary detour on the path of mediation; pain is part of the general process called healing. Hell is the inconceivable place of eternal suffering, infinite and monstrous suffering that is ethically unjust and unmerited, that is, thus, beyond every punishment and which touches the damned; and it is in purgatory that the tradition has located the provisional phase, not for the damned but for the condemned, those condemned to the temporary pain of the punishment. It tells us, this small suffering that is portioned out and adjusted: wait and accept your suffering with patience, since nothing is definitively lost. The mediating [*médiatrice*] synthesis, the medicating [*médicatrice*] pain, the delay, in the end retain their cicatrizing and therapeutic virtues. In the world of action, the *never-again* is nonsense; for, interrupting the continuation and the sequence of causes and effects, it would lead to an absurd void.

The apophatic philosophy of the moral paradox is never finished with its negations. Mediation, we were saying, is not

at all paradoxological: the quasi-rational function of mediating temporality is precisely to separate one contradictory
from the others; the contradictories, transformed into successive moments in the fluidity of becoming, take turns instead of tearing each other apart; they will appear, one after
the other, each in its time and at its hour, and this is the most
elegant, the most ingenious, and the most peaceful of solutions. The antagonism is circumvented! Since the *Homo duplex* is undoubtedly double and in a manner of speaking amphibious, he will be able alternatively to devote himself to
his body and to the care of his soul. The alternation is really
a regimen: a regularity of the rhythm, equity, and simplicity of periodism, everything facilitates for man the adaptation to this exemplary vicissitude. Happy is the man of good
conscience! He devotes his workdays to the tasks of a well-
understood egoism, and his Sundays and holidays to pious
works and to the poor; this happy conscience reigns over a
harmoniously arranged time in which two successive sched-
ules are booked, one for exercises for the body, the other
for charity. The means are able temporarily to belie the end,
to suspend its advent, to send it off on vacation; from the
moment it concerns a discursive succession, the contradiction is diffused; the collision has become inoffensive. We
will have a conscience at rest. But one can wonder if a conscience at rest, and one that has eliminated every anguish,
every moral anxiety, is, on the contrary, not already spoiled
by complacency . . . On the other hand, a love for others,
in principle, does not admit of partitioning. Let us remember what was said about the totalitarianism, the extremism,
the maximalism of moral exigency: the idea of holding back
for oneself and only for oneself, and for one's own personal
perfection, and under the pretext of equality, half the labor

and the time and the ascetic exercises supposedly necessary for the moral amelioration of the human race, such an idea is itself derisory. What am I saying?—the simple inclination of diverting, for the benefit of my salvation and my immortal soul, an infinitesimal instant of my moral zeal is a fraud lined with an intolerable hypocrisy. Abnegation vomits these temporal amenities; it does not support the sordidness of an economy that is too ingenious; it does not desire to follow in the same "grid" upon muscular awakening and upon the dietary quarter of an hour; it wants the entire space; it wants the totality of our time and our life . . . Intolerant superlativity, the *nec plus ultra,* here is its credo and its law! The words of Plato and of the Scriptures that are mentioned so often, *sun holei tei psychei, en holei tei kardíai sou, ex holes tes suneseos kai ex holes tes ischuos,* [6] end up back at themselves under my pen; whether it is about strength, intellection, or love, one single haunting word ceaselessly returns like a refrain in the exhortations: the word *holon.* With all your strength, with all your comprehension, with all your heart. And even with all your thought, *en holei tei dianoiai sou* [7]—as if it were also important that thought about the other and the tender concern for the other indefatigably reappeared in the smallest detours of reasoning and mediation, as if it were necessary that that one same loyal worry inhabited all the comings and goings of discursive and dialectical thought. In a word that says it all: *with all one's soul!* All everywhere and all the time. This word, in one fell swoop and in one go, disparages every program, sweeps away every schedule, subalternizes measuring and posology. Categories are scrapped. *All or nothing!* After that, everything has been said.

Deciphering the mediation, its detours and tricks, its sudden turns and pretenses, if one is expecting illumination of the moral problem, can only be the opportunity for the greatest misunderstandings and the most bitter deceptions. Not that love, in order to arrive at its ends and manage its affairs properly, must hatch plots, erect machines, and put together strategies: the idea of tricks of love and of a masked love, of a protean love, an expert in disguises and costumes, always in the middle of plotting some new expedient, *aei tinas plekon mechanas,*[8] already belonged to the myth of Platonic Eros. Poros, as we know, is the name that Diotima gives to the father of Eros; and *Poros* signifies *passage* and *path of communication.* Hence, one can conclude that mediation does not have secrets for a love capable of infiltrating the craftiest schemes, of slipping into the most complex situations, of setting each being into relation with all beings. But a love that is too ingenious and a bit scheming is still more foreign to true love than the mediation itself. It is that love, the son of Poros, is above all a possessive and attention-seeking love; its goal is the conquest of a woman, the ambition to please her; it does not for this purpose retreat in the face of the most suspect machinations. The seducer is in his own way a virtuoso, a virtuoso, as Jean Maurel would say, of fraudulent flings and schemes of all sorts. The deceitful strategy of Eros sometimes resembles that of irony, and it makes use of the same weapons: understatement, oeillades, innumerable varieties of allusion and simulation; love pretends to stand back so as better to come closer, as an athlete retreats to gain impetus . . . and also as the strong wish to appear weak! Love is expressed *a contrario.* Is this ruse not the ABC of amorous paradoxology? Doesn't the amorous person feign indifference? Maneuvering is the ordinary game and the trivial tactic of coquetry; it does not speak the mysterious language of love: it speaks a hermetic language that is relatively easy to interpret and, accordingly, plain for all to see because it sends us uniformly back to the ego and philautia. To decipher the code of the love-trickster, it is necessary to consent to the delights of hermeneutics and rhetoric. To level off the provisional obstacles placed along the dialectical chain, an average sagacity suffices. But passionate love is not an artisanal, industrious, instrumental mediation for the purpose of an extrinsic end. Neither is such a love a painful trial undertaken for the purpose of beautiful revenge. Such a love does not speak a more or less transparent esoteric or allegorical language that would entail decryption. All the details that one could provide about these paths and means are futile as well as indifferent alibis. What an out-and-out hunter this Eros, in truth, is!

3. The One with the Other: Ambivalence.
Of Two Intentions, One.

Mediation would have at least made intelligible, thanks to becoming, the modus vivendi of the contradictories . . . but by making their acute conflict fluid; by cushioning their collision. Yet is there a case in which contradictories are given together, *uno eodemque tempore?* Is this case the *ambivalence* of sentiments? Dismissed are both the courteous alternation and the convenient vicissitude! We are almost touching the most critical point of the paradox. What is going to happen? Contradictories are not given alternately, that is, *one after the other,* one first, then the other, but simultaneously, that is, *one with the other:* not only in contemporaneity or synchrony, like juxtaposed and parallel experiences, but in intimate symbiosis. Beyond, there would be nothing but the *coincidentia oppositorum,* the miraculous identification of contradictories. The complexes that result from certain alloys and from certain mixtures are rather psychological curiosities: they do not necessarily make crises of conscience. The sentiments conclude among themselves bizarre alliances and unusual pacts, whose sui generis affective tonality varies infinitely, according to what dominates in the amalgamation and the associated components.

But the somewhat Manichaean duality of the good and bad intention, of altruism and egoism determines in this slightly aesthetic plurality a type of summary reclassification and an acute simplification. To continue, loving hatred is not a hatred, or even a mixture of love and hatred: loving hatred is a love, a passionate variety of love, a love embittered by failure; the unrequited love [*dépit amoureux*] is not a frustration [*dépit*], but another variety of love, a love excited by deception and perverted by rebuffs. This ambiguity is falsely ambiguous . . . Better still, the latter ambiguity is profoundly unambiguous! True *ambi*valence is not a mixture in the plural, nor is it a complex of sentiments: the true ambivalence is that of man, simultaneously single and double, *simplex-duplex,* but ripped *in two (ambo),* torn between two incompatible values that each pull it in their own direction. It is thus necessary to distinguish very carefully the innumerable plurality of choice and the duality of intentions. The aestheticizing conscience, which is psychological and pluralistic, experiments with infinitely mixing and combining the colors on the palette, the sounds and qualitative nuances of their timbres in a musical synthesis; to the lover of painting and to the dilettante, it offers as a spectacle the spectrum of multicolored qualities, in other words, polychromy; it chooses from an amusing and picturesque diversity of colors and tones, as it chooses from an amiable variety of flavors and smells, after having compared the specimens exposed to the display and the samples of the collection offered to its gaze. The comparison of the more and the less, the assessment of the scalar degrees are the elements of this permanent comparative that presides over daily empirical choice. The amateur, having to resolve the empirical problem of choice, elects his preferred color, his preferred song, and his object of predilection from each genre.

But in the choice that we call the *option,* there are on the whole two possibilities offered to our free will [*libre arbitre*], as with the couples of contraries (*suzugiai*) in Pythagoreanism. Choice, according to Leibniz, animated by the teleological principle of the "best," always implies the comparative to some degree, and it is thus preferential; but it can also be reduced to a decision, to an, if not blind, then at least arbitrary wager, when it motivates itself by its own aseity: man, in this case, oscillates between two exigencies, between two solutions, or as we were saying, between a value and a counter-value that contradicts this value. There are only two possibilities: and not one more! It is not worth it to count! Nor does Prodicus's Heracles himself need to count: there are only two contradictory solutions, the Good and the Bad; if there had just been a third solution, then on Prodicus's interpretation Heracles [Héraclès] would no longer have been a hero, but rather an amateur. *It is one or the other:* such is the great polarity of the all or nothing, of the yes or no, of being and nonbeing that is incumbent upon us and that fills us with anguish. Abnegation or the idolatry of the me: such is the steep, vertiginous choice that it is necessary for us to accept and that we call option; in black or in white: that is the effect of austere, well-defined, simplistic relief to which the amusements of polychromy and polymorphism will be reduced; there no longer is multicolored variegation, there is only antithesis without a middle term. The two composites are in fact two directions that turn their backs on each other; *hodos ano, hodos kato:* it is one and the same path, says Heraclitus; but this unique path, one can take in one direction or take in the opposite direction, toward the top or toward the bottom; climb or descend. Even the words "right side out" [*à l'endroit*] and "backward" [*à rebours*] are spatial metaphors rather than temporal experiences; however, they have an intentional and qualitative signification. In the two opposite options, there are indeed two intentions that are opposed. Is it either one or the other? But first and foremost: *it is either one or the other!* For it is the alternative of the intentions that explains and inspires the alternative options. The option in the option, the only one that is important, the only decisive one, for it alone decides everything at the core of the heart of hearts, this is the intention. An intention to go somewhere and a nascent movement, toward the heights or toward the depths, toward the right or toward the left, toward the front or toward the back, the intention indicates the *sense* [*sens*]: the sense as signification, the sense as direction. The intention, is it not, it too, a type of movement, a *movement* toward . . . ? Do we not say: a good movement, a bad movement—and especially a *first movement?* One cannot blend the good movement and the bad, or combine I know not what unnamable, intermediary amalgamation with them: for there is no intermediary, no *tertium quid!* Revelation is right to say: "Damned are the lukewarm!"[9] These movements of the soul imply judgments of value; and on the other hand, they are very secret shakings of the conscience . . . Prodicus's apologist shows us Heracles at the intersection of intentions: does he go down the rocky trail of virtue or the road of easy pleasures? Two divergent paths and even two modes of life for which bi-willing will make either the one or the other exist by accepting it. The alternative of intentions, as Bergson has well understood, is not a true bifurcation, since we bring it into being only after the fact or retrospectively, and, in a manner of speaking, in the future perfect, in the very act by which we espouse one of the two options.

With every intermediary being excluded between the good movement and the bad, one passes from the one to the other (or reciprocally) in one fell swoop and almost without noticing it by an imperceptible conversion: a milligram more or less, a millimeter left or right, a second too soon or too late—and all is lost (. . . or won!). But first, all is impure with respect to the purest pure love, with respect to the candor and to the immaculate whiteness of innocence! The asepsis is total, that is, 100 percent, or it is not at all. Is the mixture of the pure and the impure not already impure, impure itself and for a long time, impure from the outset, impure since the beginning? A drop of impurity, claimed Stoic paradoxology about the "total mixture," would rightfully be sufficient to taint the ocean as a whole; and, likewise, a grain of egoism, one single almost microscopic granule, can make suspect the most regal of offerings; for generosity is not divided up—and more than that, an impalpable ulterior motive will have been sufficient. And less than that: the ulterior motive of an ulterior motive, the shadow of a shadow, a suspicion of complacency, an imponderable hypocrisy . . . the smallest mental reservation that comes to be betrayed in some revelatory lapse—and the good movement has become a bad movement and the good intention is instantly corrupted down to its roots: the fragile and very fugitive virtue that is barely grazed by a diabolical ulterior motive, by the smell of mold and sulfur, shrivels and instantly veers from all to all. This decay is the form that the principle of the excluded middle takes in the world of intentions!— Simply put, the real problem for the moral man is not the innumerable plurality of complexes but the abrupt duality of intentions: this disjunction (the alternative!) urgently and personally calls to us, looking us in the eyes: which of the two (*utrum*)? the one or the other? and it calls again: *an . . . annon?* One cannot simultaneously go forward and go back; no synthesis is possible between the assault and the escape; the univocal clarity of courage does not admit of any middle term, of any subterfuge: for every recourse, it leaves the poltroon only with the permission to be changed into a statue or shamefully to disappear into the ground.

4. The One in the Other: The Paradoxology of the Organ-Obstacle. The Eye and Vision According to Bergson. The Although Is the Spring of the Because.

And here now is the paroxysm of the contradiction and the nonsense, the most acute point of the paradox: here the contradictions neither occur *one after the other,* according to a determined chronological priority, as in the sequence of mediation, nor coexist *one with the other,* as in ambivalence, but they are *one in the other.* Doesn't the absurd reciprocity of being-in make the contradiction more scandalous, and even more inextricable? We were suggesting, beginning with Bergson and *Creative Evolution,* what one will allow us to call a *paradoxology of the organ-obstacle:* the sensory apparatus is inseparably organ and obstacle, simultaneously instrument and impediment. How should one understand this organ-obstacle? Is this to say that the organ-obstacle is an organ on one end and an obstacle on the other end? Or again, that the same factor is indeed the two of them, but not at the same moment—that it is sometimes the one and sometimes the other, alternatively, instrument by day and impediment by night? Is it that the organ and the obstacle alternate according to the alternation of even and odd dates? Or, in the end, does this mean that the organ-obstacle is indeed organ and obstacle at the same time, but not from the same point of view, or in the same sense, that it is an organ from a certain point of view and an obstacle under some different relation? No, none of that! This would be to desire to save the principle of identity at any price and to save it at the price of a ridiculous truism.—The hybrid is organ and obstacle at the same instant, from the same point of view, in all its extension, as in all its understanding, therefore, independent of any *quatenus*! For example, the ego is physically the fundamental and permanent obstacle that turns me away from others, and at the same time, and *by that very fact,* it is the fundamental condition of altruism. Our distinctions, relaxing the tension of the contradictions, would immediately normalize the paralogism . . . Without a doubt! But here we are referred back again to the most discursive of mediations! It is in all their scope, and in their essence itself, that vision and hearing are simultaneously hindered and made possible: they are made possible by and in the very fact of the impediment! Is that not the height of it all? a challenge, a type of provocation? And yet, when one has understood this, one has understood all there was to be understood. Georg Simmel[10] recognized this inconvenience, this happy negation, this valid narrowness in works of culture, dance, and poetry as well as in the life of organisms; he called it "Tragedy" because this contradiction apparently is a poverty and this poverty, in turn, is *by that very fact,* and *paradoxically,* the condition of all fecundity: the condition and the ransom, as one would have it, according to whether one prefers the optimistic or pessimistic version! Against all logic, the although only makes the because more complicated; the despite, by reinforcing causality, is inexplicably only *one more reason!* The poverty in this is the providential inconvenience and the welcome narrowness, just as heaviness is the condition, the inconvenient condition, of the grace that surmounts it! If the paradox is the professed contradiction, then the organ-obstacle is that which is irrational insofar as it has become viable thanks to movement. In the indivision of the organ-obstacle, the coincidence of contradictories is neither diluted by a mediation nor softened by the ambiguity of an ambivalence but is carefully concealed and rendered invisible. The organ is not simply an organ, in a unilateral and univocal manner: such as it appears, no doubt, in the primary and physical obviousness of experience; a tool of work, a musical instrument, a weapon of war, the organ is that thanks to which the action and the work (*ergon*) are possible, and thus it is entirely positivity: the balance sheet of the organ-obstacle, if one focuses on profits and losses, appears "globally positive"! The accent will be on the optimism. But that which exoterically is positivity can *also* be revealed esoterically, in an analysis and for reflection, and, moreover, for reasoning, as a negation and invisibly as a partitive limitation. Platonic supernaturalism has made the reversal of what is obvious familiar to us: appearance, which is obviousness itself in the physical order of the empirical, is eminently debatable in the order of the meta-empirical and the metaphysical. But conversely, the obstacle, in turn, is not unilaterally an obstacle, a simple obstacle whose unique and absurd function would be to obstruct; for if the eyes hinder vision and that's that, then it is necessary to conclude: man would see a lot better without eyes! A glorious vision, an angelic vision, one that nothing hinders is not an infinitely clairvoyant vision, but rather a blind vision: blind because it is unfettered, blind because it is "adialectical." That which is without obstacle is, by that very fact, without an organ (*aneu organou*). *An effective vision is an inconvenienced vision* or, as Bergson very lucidly explained it, a "canalized" vision,[11] with the optical nerve being, in a manner of speaking, the symbol of this "canalization." Using Bergson's language, we ourselves were saying, Canalization expresses the two things simultaneously: vital impetus [*élan vital*]—in this particular case the march toward vision—and the resistance that limits this march by guiding it, by determining its direction and the force of its impetus. More specifically, everything happens as if vision "were choosing" a *field* and a *range* without which it would remain undetermined, that is, blind; everything happens as if hearing carved out for itself a certain sector on the scale or from the gamut, a sector on this side but beyond which there would be only silence. In all cases, it is the limited permission, accompanied by obstacles and circumscribed by vetoes, that makes the action possible. He who is everyone is no one; he who is everywhere is nowhere. To be someone and somewhere, it is necessary to renounce universality and omnipresence. Let us recall in this case: the effect of relief, to which negation owes its energy, did not go unnoticed by either Bergson or Schelling . . . Narrowness is in some way the tacit condition of every true personal presence.

Having arrived at this point, perhaps we must provisionally conclude (for every conclusion here is provisional):

the organ-obstacle of love and of the moral will is infinitely aporetic and disconcerting to infinity, one never goes all the way to the end and to the extreme tip of the good will, but neither does one touch the extreme base of the bad one: the latter is unfathomable just as the former is unreachable; the moral will and the witness that judges it endlessly oscillate between the two poles with an alternative beating that is similar enough to the one we were describing as being the fourth way out. Allow us to auscultate this vibration more carefully, this beating of an unsettled heart. The organ-obstacle is an obstacle from its depths to its summit, as we will confirm by uncovering the infinitesimal motives of complacency; and, conversely, the organ-obstacle is an organ not only on account of the positive means it uses to give us relations to the world, but indirectly on account of the very limitation of these means: for every negation is a determination. It is not sufficient to say that the power of the moral will is relegated to an intermediate zone: the will can do what it can *despite* the obstacle and by that very fact *thanks* to it! Isn't there a kind of metaphysical perversity in expressing it as such in a language that is so violently contrary to all good sense? The *although* would be one of the paradoxical springs of the *because:* better still, the concessive, and consequently indirect, element would be more efficient and more decisive than simple causality!

5. This Beating of an Unsettled Heart. A Mediation Imprisoned Within a Structure.

And yet this frozen, congealed, petrified contradiction that we call the organ-obstacle does not have a moral charac-

ter: these two words that are united into one word do not respond to a moral set of problems. Even more than mediation,
the organ-obstacle is subtracted from becoming: mediation
oriented toward an end; at least the end fictitiously follows
from the means; the organ-obstacle itself does not acknowledge time; one is tempted to say that the organ-obstacle is a
mediation immobilized, imprisoned within a structure; the-
sis and antithesis are given together and as such completely
chosen, already measured out, and in the same package.
Bergson, in underlining the contrast between the marvel-
ous complexity of the eye and the miraculous simplicity of
vision, found, to put it simply, a very striking language that
evokes the anti-teleology of Schopenhauer:[12] all it needs is
for the eyes to be opened and vision takes place: this happens without any problem! Mediation (assuming that one
can use such language here) is collected as a whole in the
functioning of the organ. Stemming from the inseparable
interpenetration of inhibiting forces and positive forces, the
organ-obstacle is not only a factor of inertia and a decelerat-
ing element, it is still the point of insertion of consciousness
and of life into the world. A disconcerting and irrational al-
loy above all! A conspiracy that is impossible to thwart! The
instrument and the impediment, far from contradicting or
paralyzing one another, cooperate in action to achieve this
structure that is simultaneously stable and unstable, but, in
any case, primarily viable, which we call the finite being.
For the organ-obstacle is a perfectly domesticated monster.
The normal regimen of this being is the perfect adaptation
to the status of being "amphibious": it neither lives two occasions simultaneously, nor on two parallel planes; it does not
feel itself to be double; or, to be more precise, it does not feel
anything, it does not perceive anything: in a normal state,

the complex of soul-body lives its psychosomatic existence in a simple and undivided experience that is the very truth of the immediate. *Soma, sema.* This orphic paradox is a beautiful metaphor that is aggravated by a play on words. But the "incarnate" man does not feel incarcerated. The ingenuous soul does not feel himself in prison in his own body. Strictly speaking, an ingenuous and healthy soul does not even feel himself *in* his body: he lives his corporeal existence naively without asking himself any questions. Isn't feeling ill at ease or cramped in the corset of the body a symptom of neurosis? At best, it is a retrospective reflection, accompanied by a metaphor, on the nature of the psychosomatic *vinculum.* Unless it is just a lot of grandiose rhetoric . . . This is even more true of being in general in the measure in which the fact of being is perfectly abstract and imperceptible: the man who is double and simple, *duplex-simplex,* does not directly perceive in his normal state the heaviness and the inertia of his being-proper, no more than the average man perceives the heaviness of the atmosphere. One sometimes speaks of the weight of being, of the difficulty of being, as if naked being, *Esse nudum,* were able to be heavy or light, more or less heavy: but 'being' is the most general, the most indeterminate, the most empty and insipid and nondescript of all the verbs, the most technical, too, and it signifies, by that very fact, the most elementary and the most neutral of all signifieds. Being without qualities represents, as it were, degree zero of the relation and of the feeling. If one sticks with metaphors, it would undoubtedly be preferable to speak of a tare or, better, of a gravity without weight, of a meta-empirical and destinal malediction: this tare that, without having anything in common with original sin, would a priori encumber the finite being, one can neither escape it nor concretely feel the anguish of this millstone.

6. The Pinprick of the Splinter, the Burn of the Ember, the Bite of Remorse. Scruple.

But the invisible and imperceptible tare sometimes becomes painful: this is the case when the organ-obstacle begins to squeal and limp from the effect of pain and sickness. Sickness is the malfunctioning of the organ-obstacle. Normally, vision is the simplest thing in the world: simple like hello; it is enough just to lift one's eyelids . . . and before one has had the time to pronounce the two monosyllables *Fiat Lux,* light already illuminates everything around us. But when a tiny ember lodges itself in the cornea, the thing that is the simplest in the world and the easiest becomes the most difficult: in an instant everything becomes an obstacle, in an instant the exercise of the most natural function creates a problem; the contradiction that was latent in the organ-obstacle has become an intolerable inconvenience and an impediment to living. Sickness and pain problematize that which was not made for posing a problem. Good-bye adaptation! The *it-goes-without-saying* of vegetative existence no longer goes without saying! The continuation of the being, of the being pure and simple, did not require any particular effort, was not subject to any technical condition, did not imply a concrete worry of any sort: but the difficulty of living can require an effort—and what an effort!—and imply innumerable worries; and what's more, in certain pathological cases, the difficulty of breathing is a cause of anguish and oppression and calls for an urgent intervention. The functions of a healthy body are in general accomplished with the most comprehensive insensitivity, and Schopenhauer undoubtedly is right to consider feeling an infinitesimal degree of suffering. If perfect happiness [*bonheur*] has no history, then it is still more true that happy [*heureuse*] health is blessed [*bienheureuse*], especially in overall anesthesia and overall analgesia. Let us take one step farther: just as the happy equilibrium of the organ-obstacle is at the mercy of a splinter in one's flesh or an ember in one's eye, so the happy harmony of a good conscience in which wholesome pleasures are in harmony with good works, such a blessed consonance is at the mercy of an infinitesimal dissonance. Here what responds to the pinprick of the splinter, the burn of the ember, is the bite of remorse. Nevertheless, the analogy, if it aids comprehension, is only an analogy: it suggests without explaining. Remorse, a moral and thus in its own way supernatural malaise, is of a wholly other order from the pain of organs, just as a gratuitous scruple is of a wholly other order from egoistic worry. Scruple and worry are two forms of aporia . . . But the preoccupied aporia, which drives away euphoria, is first formed starting from the ember and around self-interest when the latter is harmed; it breeds simple regret. And the scrupulous aporia, which is at the origin of bad conscience, is formed around a guilty freedom and starting from a ridiculed value.

In the presence of the double structure called organ-obstacle, the action is stripped of its natural function, which is the solution of a problem or the reconciliation of contradictories. But the moral problematization destabilizes the perfect, reciprocal adaptation of the "soul" to the "body," not by force, as does sickness, but gratuitously, for nothing, and apparently without any reason. For example: we feel I know not what kind of absurd scruple about enjoying a perfectly innocent pleasure, we feel I know not what kind of insurmountable repugnance about accepting a sum of money that is unquestionably owed to us: a secret voice whispers and *murmurs repeatedly* within us that softly commands us to refuse this money, to waive this convenience. It undoubtedly is nothing more than a vague malaise or an inexplicable modesty. What is completely made and completely given in the symbiosis no longer goes without saying; the sacrosanct obviousness of my own pleasure and the untouchable legitimacy of my interests are no longer the center of the world; my personal glory has ceased to be for myself the Law and the prophets. The presence of others, which a regimen of good health, of good temper, and of a well-contented good conscience had put between parentheses, such a presence reorganizes around itself the entire universe of values; my neighbor is henceforth my unique duty, my permanent worry, and sometimes even my remorse. Gone is our serenity. Between a suffocating, bestial egoism that would take up all the space in the ego and an angelic sublimity in which sacrifice, by dint of being natural, would no longer cost anything and would not even have any meaning, there is space for an intermediary zone: that of human suffering and moral anxiety. A zone of instability and tension in which passionate disturbances reign. This is the world of the man who is torn apart, tortured, and bloodied; the ego and love each pull from its own end and leave us gasping for breath in our moral confusion. Unamuno, meditating on Pascal and the "Mystery of Jesus," speaks of an *agonic* anguish. *Agon* or war: two forces in battle, two forces that contradict each other. But the agony of which Unamuno speaks, which he claims to have recognized in El Greco's *Crucifixion,* is not simply a duel in which two antagonistic forces battling with each other clash: this agony is not a unique contest, even less a debate in which egoism and love size each other up. In fact, the confrontation is inside love, interior to this love itself. For anti-love is not only the contradictory condition of love, as the paradox of the organ-obstacle proposed to us, it is also the constitutional ingredient of it; the ego is a fundamental component of altruism . . . and, conversely, an altruism suffocated by the ego is itself driven to barricade itself jealously in the enclosure of philautia. The two, all in all, amount to the same thing and are true together: being, like anti-love, is never nihilized, and it dozes in total disinterestedness; forgotten egoism only sleeps with one eye open. But altruism, in turn, is the permanent remorse of the ego: man is never completely egoistic, as La Rochefoucauld claims to demonstrate. However, he is also not capable of ecstatically tearing himself away from himself, or of himself becoming entirely the other person in his entirety, as Fénelon prescribes. All in all, he remains in the middle, sometimes on the verge of sinking into his being-proper without love, sometimes on the verge of evaporating into love and nonbeing. It is sometimes said: the core remained good, the core remained healthy. But it could also be said on another occasion: man is fundamentally wicked. And besides, does the moral intention have a core? Isn't that rather unfathomable? Into the moving sands of the intention, one sinks infinitely!—But here the unstable situation of the *loving-being* appears as a situation that is intrinsically disrupted [*contrariée*], and even contradictory [*contradictoire*], like an *almost* impossible situation or, more simply, like a tragedy in the sense that Georg Simmel has given to the word. There is indeed an insoluble antagonism, an irreducible antagonism, between love and the condition sine qua non of love, a contradiction that is so derisory that it would easily be able to appear as nonsense, and which is hidden in the very heart of the moral problem: the contradiction indeed is literally *in adjecto*—such that it does not even leave to the moral problem the time to be posed, or to the good conscience the delay necessary for choosing; goodwill finds itself nose to nose with the dilemma that paralyzes it in place. This is a reason for being discouraged! But just as ultimately the absurd coincides with irony, there is also something about which to laugh. Egoism refutes love by definition, and yet at the same time love supposes or even vitally presupposes the ego that is derisorily, paradoxically, contradictorily its vital condition. The enamored ego rebounds on the trampoline of its egoity. An incomprehensible challenge among all the challenges! What impedes loving is precisely that which kindles the fervor of love, or even quite simply that which makes love possible . . .

7. Anti-Love (Ontic Minimum), the Organ-Obstacle of Love. To Love It Is Necessary to Be (and It Would Be Necessary Not to Be!), to Sacrifice Oneself It Is Necessary to Live, to Give It Is Necessary to Have.

The lover, even if he in fact ceases a little too early to dedicate himself to the beloved, if he capitulates or resigns more quickly than is necessary, if he does not wait to die of love, if he guesses what will become of his own attenuation, this overly busy lover does not by right admit of, does not a priori and in advance recognize any limitation to this infinite love . . . For as we have shown, one can die of love: for lack of *being fulfilled in* death, love can at least *culminate in* death; madly, paradoxically, love itself tends toward its own nonbeing! This stipulation that irrationally burdens love is called finitude; but it is just as much fatal *servitude* that weighs down love. Servitude says no, yet insofar as it is finitude, it simultaneously says yes and no, affirms in refusing (or in renouncing), posits personal existence by circumscribing it and putting up with the limit of it, which is death. Indeed, the servitude of love or, in a single word, matter, is not only the inherent contradiction of a nonbeing that ultimately *negates* [*nie*] love, it is still, and reciprocally, the derision of a being that *abnegates* [*renie*] it . . . by pretending to posit it—of a being that it is nevertheless necessary to preserve. Alas! twice alas! Here the sometimes partial or provisional abnegation [*reniement*] would be rather ironic. This is indeed the height of derision: the obstacle, par excellence, the fundamental obstacle is precisely being itself! And the obstacle of obstacles is, as if intentionally, the condition of conditions. Isn't there here something about which to laugh? Being is not a sin that one would have committed some beautiful morning, since this is a pregiven given and a type of a priori. For you and me, this a priori has never begun, has never happened. But this a priori is the servitude of love, the *ontic minimum* that tolerates and presupposes, so as to survive, the *ethical maximum;* or, conversely, this is the tare drawn from the spontaneous impetus of love, the coefficient of inertia of this impetus. But the strict ontic minimum is still so much more minimal (if one dares to say it) than the vital minimum! Alongside the ontic minimum, the vital minimum is almost a luxury! The ontic minimum is "100 percent" irreducible, and no asceticism would be able to climb back on this side (beyond?) without becoming flattened in the nothingness. If abnegation [*abnegation*] does not cease in the nihilization of the loving-being in time, how will we distinguish abnegation from pure and simple negation, that is, from the negation that with a single act simultaneously suppresses both the problem and the bearer of the problem? In principle, abnegation prescribes to loving love [*amour aimant*] to give of itself, to devote itself body and soul to beloved love [*amour aimé*], which is the second person of love; the first person of love should lose himself [*se perdre*] with total perdition in the second. To live for others, such is, to the letter, the impossible commandment. To live for others? But my heart beats for me and my blood flows for me; it is for me alone that I breathe; and it is only in myself that I suffer. This is all the more reason that the ontic minimum, which so to speak is the material base and the naked substantiality of the ego, represents the irreducible element of every ipseity. The vital minimum indeed is the condition of my subsistence, of my persistence, and of my consistency, nay, even of my existence; but the ontic minimum is the condition of my *being;* of my being tout court; of my being in general; and it is the absolutely elementary condition, the condition of all conditions, since it conditions all the others. To be: here is the prerequisite par excellence (*kat' exochen*), not in an a priori formal and epistemological sense but precisely in the sense of an ontological presupposition. The verb 'to be,' we were saying, is the fundamental, the most general, the most indeterminate, the emptiest, and therefore the least technical verb, since it requires neither an effort nor an apprenticeship nor a specialization of any sort: for to be, one only has to be! Improvisation suffices. Above all, the fact of being is without any taste, without any flavor, without any psychological qualities, and it is therefore exclusive of sensuality. The nonbeing of death a fortiori and in one fell swoop settles in the most radical and the most expeditious manner all the undertakings of an active life, without it being necessary either to enumerate or to detail or to cancel the meetings one by one! And conversely, the stipulation of being is the condition without which (*sine qua non* . . .) all the other conditions are inefficacious and without potency, but one that, by itself alone, is a simple, purely negative permission, and that thus is a necessary but insufficient condition. Whatever one does, and almost by definition, being seems to preexist doing: that is what the logic of ontology requires; or at least such is La Palice's great truth, such is the substantialist truism, which, by virtue of an incurable vicious circle, refers us back to the most abstract of truths and teaches us nothing about anything . . . Whether it is for loving or for fighting or for bowling, the prerequisite of prerequisites in all cases is to exist. If one does not begin there, then nothing will begin. In the first place, in order to love, it is necessary to be! This indeed is the least of presuppositions, and it is the presupposition of presuppositions implied in all the others. Second: in order to "sacrifice oneself," it is still necessary to live. So that I am able to "sacrifice myself," in courtesy, allow me one little thing, one last breath of life, some crumbs of existence, an almost nothing; allow me my humble minimum that is barely ontic, that is almost meontic, so as to allow me to make an offering to someone; there is nothing to sacrifice when one has nothing to lose. Independent even of the moral decision of sacrifice, it is death in general that borrows its seriousness from the ontic presupposition. To die it is first necessary to live: for what does not live does not die. For example: the Caucasus does not live, thus the Caucasus does not die; such is the case for mineral things. What lives a vegetative existence barely dies, very late and very slowly. What lives slowly and as if on the back burner will often have its flame die out gradually: and there you have the lot of an average existence, of an existence that flows halfway between living and dying, and that is never either truly living or entirely dead. In contrast, the man who lives intensely will die passionately, and sometimes heroically: this is the fate of brief lives, and it is also the fate of heroes whose dramatic existence is constantly threatened, constantly recaptured, and ultimately lost again. Lost forever! Up to the moment at which the supreme minute becomes immanent, the hero and the poet will have, with their brief existence, with their terrifying adventure, an inspired relationship that they live with all their soul and all their being. Third, in order to give, it is necessary to have; if one possesses nothing, the gift that one makes is but a tall story, a bad joke. To give what one does not have is the specialty of charlatans, of conjurers, and of crooks . . . Or rather not! Why speak such a vulgar language, with such vulgar thoughts? To give what one does not have is a miracle. It is the miracle of the genius creator and of men who are exceptionally generous. Love itself does not burden itself either with the principle of non-contradiction or with the principle of conservation: it incomprehensibly gives what it does not have, and it creates this not only for giving it, but *in the giving of it,* and in the miraculous act of donation itself; and therefore it is inexhaustible and unlimited. Jean-Louis Chrétien reminds us about the Good in Plotinus, and we have remembered it with him. The Good gives what it does not have, and, conversely, one can add: what it has given, it still has.[13] Or, as Seneca writes: *Hoc habeo quod dedi*—what I have given, inexplicably, I still possess. I still possess it even though I have not kept it, even though I have not preserved it hypocritically or under another form, even though I have given it sincerely, without dishonesty or an interested ulterior motive, or a mercenary trick, and, consequently, without hope of return. The creator does not need to hoard, or to economize: savings and treasures, he renews them himself by squandering them. Such is the generosity of nature during springtime! The creator does not need *to have* so as *to give* and, reciprocally, he does not impoverish himself in giving, and neither does he have a need to go out of himself to give of himself. Long is the list of paradoxes of place and quantity that Plotinus enumerates with the fixed intention of causing a scandal, of challenging the logic of petty people and the arithmetic of the underpaid. What a wonder! the more I give, the more I possess . . . From which nest eggs, from which strongbox does the indigent billionaire take these treasures he throws out the window? But the gifts of daily humble love are not as sublime as the "miracle of the roses,"[14] or as inexhaustible as the benedictions of Providence or the verve of nature in springtime! They sometimes asymptotically approach being confused with the gratuitous gifts of charity, but they only touch this limit fugitively, with an impalpable and infinitely light tangency. Indigent love is laboriously, painfully drawn from resources that are not infinitely renewed. A gift measured in terms of human possibilities always implies something partitive; a gift, by the very fact that it is a gift, is relative to some kind of frame of reference; a gift always makes more or less of a reference to something else that one does not give, that one provisionally prefers to hold in reserve; the partitive gift skimps a bit, or else it *changes its mind*. What am I saying? in the very gesture of the offering, into this efferent gesture of an outstretched hand, and outstretched not for receiving and begging but for giving, one was already squeezing a nascent retraction, a barely suggested virtual reflux; in the gesture of offering there is already the gesture of holding back or giving up that, like a distant resistance, imperceptibly neutralizes the donorly spontaneity. We call this secondary effect of reflux *changing one's mind.* This almost imperceptible reflux is the secret reticence that darkens our most generous resolutions. Changing one's mind is the shadow of finitude projected onto altruism by an egoism still on the lookout! For the as-for-oneself is always on guard . . . In the very secondarity of such an aftereffect, one still recognizes the alternative, which is the effect of relief that dramatizes every human generosity, that makes every sacrifice agonizing and passionate. In the lighting of the partitive gift, an infinite gift, a total gift, would especially be a figure of rhetoric: not a donation of this or that, of such and such a worldly good (a gift package, for example), but a donation of being itself and completely, a donation of oneself by oneself; this hyperbolical and transcendent gift strongly runs the risk of being something nonsensical . . . or a beautiful metaphor. It does not matter: man is capable of conceiving of this divine gift, which elevates him above himself and the principle of identity. The improvising man *becomes a zither player by playing the zither.* Aristotle understood this present participle of the contemporaneity and the extemporaneity in which one glimpses the drastic and magic virtue of the creative gift: the apprentice who has suddenly become master and self-cause in the grace of an instant assumes the problem to be resolved and breaks the accursed circle; he says goodbye to the destitute alternative of giving-keeping, cuts the Gordian knot, and accepts the adventure of the gift without compensation.

To love, it is necessary to be. And to love truly, it would be necessary not to be. To love it is necessary to be, but to be it is first of all necessary to love; for the one who does not love is a mere phantom. And likewise, in order to do, it is necessary by definition to be. But above all: to be, truly, intensely, and passionately, it is necessary before anything, to do, to act, and to create! What solution will we find for this insoluble contradiction? what way out of this impasse? The condition of existence contradicts the vocation; and, vice versa, the vocation—loving, creating, giving, fighting—paradoxically has for a condition its own contradiction: having, which is the negation of giving, being, which is the negation of love. The tragedy of the dilemma brings into play an extremist logic for which despair would be the consequence; this despair is not only a psychological sentiment that would admit of gradations and shadings and whose components would be measured out or combined according to a learned posology: it is a limit case; what is tragic in this case has as its essence the extreme and passionate tension of the impossible-necessary, the solution to which, theoretically, would be death . . . if death were a "solution"! The desperate person can say, like Saint Teresa, although in a wholly different sense: "I die of not dying," since in the two cases, whether he succumbs or survives, he is condemned to death. He has the choice, if one can say so, only between two forms of nothing: the nothing of love-without-being and the nothing of the being absolutely deprived of love; for although two "nothings" are one single and same nothing, the nothing of pure love-without-being and the nothing of being-without-love are absolutely indiscernible from one another. Besides, the impossible-necessary, because it excludes any middle term, is expressed with the double veto *neither with, neither without,* which sums up what is tragic about the insoluble situation for a being who is cruelly tortured. Must we consider the loving-being in terms of an entity of fits and starts that would sometimes be being-without-love and sometimes love-without-being, alternately? The irreversibility of death forbids us from allowing for this absurd idea of two alternating phases . . . Taking it that way, it would perhaps be more philosophical to appeal to the metaphor of a vibratory beating, according to the meaning we gave this beating in speaking of the "fourth acrobatic act." *To live for you, so as to die of it,* we were saying, such a heroic absurdity, such an unbearable contradiction, is lived in the instant like a continued death that itself is the shadow of a continued resurrection, that itself is the reversal and the negative of this resurrection. The beating dilutes in some manner the exclusivism and the dilemma of incompatibles that refuse to coexist. But in fact, the vibration evades and slows down the inevitable failure to which the option drives us in the end; for when it comes down to it, we must choose one of the two things: either die by dint of living for others [*autrui*] . . . and renounce all ways of living for others by indirectly renouncing living, just by resigning from life; or to live by renouncing the devotion of oneself body and soul to living by fraudulently and clandestinely holding back a little something, to live by cheating; the indigent person who will not be able to sacrifice himself all the way removes and smuggles out something of himself, or he surreptitiously sets this something aside, be it only with the intention of regaining his strength and of preserving a father for his own children, a husband to his spouse, a soldier for the city . . . How could we not forgive hunger strikers who cheat a little on their fasting with the sole intention of being able to fast longer? The ethics of the Russian revolutionaries turned a blind eye to this pious

contraband, to these tiny clandestine discrepancies with respect to the letter of the fast in circumstances in which what
is important is not the religious purity of the penitence but
the pragmatic efficiency, the moral exemplarity, and, to be
completely honest, the seriousness of the militant demon-
stration . . . And what is important is not to make a bet or to
best a record in sports but to fight for a cause. Also, it is necessary to know how to give in to time, just before the point
of death: heroism would thus be to give up martyrdom and
great suffering. When one has gone through the ordeal of
acute pain without hope, it is commendable, ingenious, and
extremely moral to play a good trick on one's enemy and to
feed oneself in secret. It is thus abnegation itself that imperiously demands of every man to survive so that a sacrifice is not a suicide. It is abnegation itself that advises us:
live a little and from time to time, if you want to live for others [autres]! In this case, the diversion, far from being an
unmentionable case of cheating, is, quite the opposite, the
most sacred of duties.—In every moral imperative, and notably in the requirement of altruism, starting from the instant
in which it is pushed to the extreme and carried to the absolute, there is a nascent absurdity or a "demonic hyperbole,"
as states, but not without humor, the sixth book of the *Republic:* for the Good does not have an essence but is beyond
essence *epekeina tes ousias:*[15] and we know that Plotinus's
hyper-Platonism will go beyond the heaven of essences and
the intelligible, not with humor, but for good. By the way, in
the *Phaedrus,* doesn't Plato speak of a delirium of love? Our
finitude as moral creatures, confronted with infinity, with
the immensity of duty, the disproportion and the disequilib-
rium that ensue, all this sufficiently explains the misery and
impotence of the moral solutions; and when one invokes fin-

itude, it is necessary to comprehend not only the brevity of life in general and the possibility of dying at any instant, but also the paucity of our vital resources and the fundamental fragility of every human existence. This is why we are sometimes devoted to petty thefts, to small ruses, to small dishonesties, and to the pitiful sophisms of hypocrisy.

8. The Obstacle and the Fact of the Obstacle (Radical Origin). Why in General It Was Necessary That . . .

We can say, It is being that creates an obstacle to duty and to love . . . Anything can be said! But this insane paradox is not easily supported, even when one takes the pious precaution of baptizing the organ-obstacle obstacle [*l'obstacle organ-obstacle*]. Is such a euphemism serious? A euphemism is, to the letter, a verbalism. Let us nevertheless understand that this internal denial is the very condition of the moral vocation and the guarantor of its dignity. Under whatever form, the uprooting called sacrifice implies a bloody tearing and pain; and this pain would in general not be able either to be cut back or eluded. This irrecuperable pain is not an extrinsic and "exemptible" inconvenience that one could elude or cut back on without grave consequence: even after healing, the tearing leaves a trace that is simultaneously the ransom and the signature of the alternative. Or better still, every trace will be erased, but the *trace of the trace,* the trace "with an exponent," will not be erased: this trace is indelible, just as the sickness of that which is irreversible is incurable. And along the same lines: *Mors certa, Hora incerta.* It is never necessary to die on such and such a date, of such and such a sickness; but the *fact of* death, the necessity of dying in general, sooner or later, in one manner or another, is absolutely unavoidable and tolerates no exception. No pain, taken alone, is essential, incurable, or sacrosanct: for example, childbirth without pain does not provoke the anger of God: but painfulness, that is, the *fact of* suffering in general, sooner or later, in one form or another, is unavoidable. The cause of such and such a suffering can be eliminated: that is how one removes, by excision, a splinter lodged in the skin. But the *fact of* pain in general, the mere fact that suffering is possible on this earth, who will cure that? And *why in general was it necessary for* the loving-being to be sick with the sickness of being? For being is the sickness that will make him die: the sickness of sicknesses and the sickness of healthy people . . . Schopenhauer perhaps would have said to us that the positivity of feeling and the negativity of suffering are the recto and verso of one same finitude. But on that basis, sophisms keep watch over the one who is not capable of understanding the paradoxical correlation of the organ and the obstacle. If being is the incurable sickness of the loving-being, one would be able to cure the latter only by a pure and simple suppression of his being . . . But that is a bad joke! Yet nonbeing obviously is, and that a fortiori, the radical and simultaneous cure of all sicknesses, of the most serious sicknesses as well as scratches: for one cannot have all the misfortunes simultaneously; and death, in one fell swoop, rids us of all the other misfortunes. Will it be necessary for us to think that death is a cure? or only a solution? If one dissociates oneself from such absurdities, then it is preferable fully to accept the contradiction, the insoluble contradiction that is simultaneously malediction and benediction and that is our intrinsic misery. Or, using a different terminology, the contradiction and the alternative that flow from it do not represent the weight of a fate with which we would accidentally be laden: for nothing therefore prevents us from unloading the burden without tragedy, without a dilemma, without any tearing, and to ascend with one step toward the "religious and holy truth."[16] The cause of the slowness would instead be the tare, and not even the tare, but the *fact of* the tare that derisorily weighs down our impetus. But can one stick with this unambiguous idealism that is cleverly coupled with an obstacle?

9. Being Without Loving, Loving Without Being. The Interaction of a Minimal Egoism and a Maximal Altruism. The Afferent Countereffect of the Efferent Impetus.

First, to exist: *that is the least of things!* This physical and massive minimum is the fundamental opacity without which the sacrifice would not have anything to sacrifice; so there is disinterestedness; a minimum of self-interest is necessary, for lack of which renunciation would be void of meaning, for lack of which the sacrifice would be a pretend sacrifice, a simple figure of speech. Here again, we come up against the unavoidable internal contradiction that constitutes the entire parodoxy of morality: an elementary egoism, inherent in being-proper, is the minimal, and in a manner of speaking the vital, condition of altruism. This condition is by definition reduced to a verbal abstraction, one without an intentional soul and without life: it is necessary for the verb 'to love' to have a subject in general, a logico-grammatical subject in the nominative . . . A negative, abstract, and purely formal condition. Can one at least say, It is the being, the loving-being, that is the foundation of love? For to love, it is first necessary to be. And that by definition. Monsieur de La Palice, whose oracles we listen to so often, could not say better. But this foundation is entirely conceptual and indeterminate: a logico-grammatical subject in the nominative is not yet a lover! Indeed, if there is love, then there is necessarily someone in general who appears to or claims to love, or who has a vocation of loving . . . But this someone can do something entirely different from loving: for example, he eats well, he digests, he breathes, etc.; he is the virtual subject of all sorts of verbs; he periodically accomplishes, along with the other things, an act of love without essentially being a *lover*. He is not even a "someone." The truisms that one can formulate about substantiality hardly suffice to provide substance for his emptiness. An altruist by dint of egoism! A fortiori one can provide a more dramatic and more passionate meaning to the paradoxical correlation of the contrary with its contrary. Indeed, one would not be able to remain on the weakest side of the glow of altruism without becoming as coarse as a moral rhinoceros, as voracious as a crocodile. But one would also not be able to go beyond an infinitesimal philautia without altruism itself dissolving into the ecstasy of nonexistence and inconsistency, without itself being annihilated in the zero of the me: if an atom of egoism, a suspicion of sensuality, or a few seeds of self-love happen to tarnish our moral transparency or coarsen our pneumatic purity, then there is no abnegation either; altruism, in turn, evaporates for lack of an altruist.—At best, the apparently compact subject, the subject deprived of a conscience, the blind subject, overwhelmed by the inflation of his being-proper, chooses to love himself, or to love his own love, to feel again [*ressentir*] his own feelings [*sentiments*]. But love of oneself is a wholly fictional opening since it does not open on to the alterity of the other like a wide-open window that faces outside, but on to the self [*soi*] and on to what is the same [*le même*], literally on to oneself [*le soi-même*]. The egoist diverts an efferent influx whose natural vocation would be to be directed toward the society of men, and squanders it by loving himself; such are the monstrous undertakings of *amor sui:* the very circularity of this love is the sign of a failure, of an abuse, of an introverted and even retroverted movement, of a movement that does not succeed; such a love pretends. Or, in other examples: the man who is bloated by philautia is in reality only full of himself; all of which means that he is perfectly empty; the aptly named vain person who is sick with aerophagia, and even with autophagia; he eats air, devours clouds, and above all, he devours his own substance; he sinks into his own satisfied good conscience, with his good digestion and his self-importance.

Let us recapitulate here the comings and goings of the elusive correlation that is established between being and love and that leads to the inconsistent reversal of the two poles.

1st: Here you have, first, a body without a head and without a soul, the being completely devoid of love, the ogre of egoity, the monstrous diplodocus. And yet . . . much is still needed for the ego to be the constant negation, the pure and simple negation of love. We refused the simplism of a Manichaean polarity; and our refusal was formulated in the following manner: being is not universally the obstacle, it is in more complex and even contradictory terms an organ-obstacle. To love, it offers as a first step a base and a support, and all this at the risk of diluting its fervor, of cooling down amorous high temperature. As long as it remains attached to a body, the loving-being maintains an anchorage point or a mooring in the world of physical forces and in social reality. There is more! The ego indirectly affirms love, not only with its corporeal point of attachment but with the fact that the *point of attachment* is also a *fulcrum* [*point d'appui*] and acts upon love like a foil: this is what we were calling the dynamics of the trampoline: the inert weight with which the loving-being is ballasted gives love its spring, its trigger, and its dynamic impetus, an impetus that projects it upward. A force checked by gravity that thus overcomes the obstacle by liberating its energy: here is the secret of the impetus. Without a doubt, the ego itself would not develop such a dynamism if a chronic bad conscience were not already dozing within it, if it were not virtually full of haunting remorse, of nagging scruples, and of supernatural worries . . . if a latent moral conscience did not anticipate this very being that nevertheless exists before it. But conversely, this virtual conscience would not have become painfully real without this tiny bit of space one calls the body, in which it finds its point of attachment and its fulcrum. It is the body that makes it hear the voice of the exhilarating and dissonant contradiction. The passionate resistance and the desperate protest of the ego kindle, fuel, and exacerbate for me the alterity of the other.

2nd: At the extreme that is opposed to being-without-love is the fairyland of a love-without-being! Absolutely separated from the first person, love would be a troubled love, a love in the void, an immaculate and mystical love, and it would not even float between heaven and earth but above the heaven of angels; it is superficial and hazy like a phantom, impalpable like a thought; it dissolves or, better, vanishes into the air; it has relinquished its ego on the sand of the shores, and it is no longer anything but a miserable, cast-aside frock. This is an ecstatic love: it has wholly become, by extroversion, another than itself, it has fully flowed out into the other, without the frame of reference of the same; it is searching for the welcome incarnation and narrowness that will revive it. It is annihilated in that respect by indetermination. The wholly loving lover, the lover without being-proper, vanishes into smoke. The purest lover dies of his purity, and his purity itself makes him incapable of loving.

3rd: The loving being in himself implies the confrontation of pure love and ogreliness; sometimes this conflict degenerates into an acute crisis, sometimes it holds moral life in a state of instability and chronic ambiguity. The loving-being accepts being impure: he does not lay claim to impurity for the pleasure of being impure; but he *accepts* it. Being is not always the negation of love, but love is by no means the negation of being. The being that is an ego without love resembles a monster; he is not even a "someone," he is no one; an egoity without alterity, an ego without a second person; this is not even a first person; this is not a person at all; he is merely a log! And indeed, in this case there is *no one to do the loving,* or a person *to love,* either; for a lover who loves no one, a lover without a beloved is a burlesque contradiction. However, the love that one feels for the beloved founds and constitutes the first person itself (the subject) simultaneously as a lover and as a being-proper. Thus, it is an understatement to say that love is not nonbeing; it is more and much more than being, and that a fortiori; it is literally *super-being* [*sur-être*]! The ego itself and the intentional transitivity are born on the same day and they form, starting with their double birth, an indissociable correlation: the reference to the beloved is not a luxury, a supplementary pleasantry that would be additionally accorded to the lover, it belongs to love itself and only forms with this love a single gift, a single benediction. The being, we were saying, is not someone. And as for the ego, it is barely someone; but it will be someone when it itself loves someone; beginning with the moment in which the subject loves someone . . . what am I saying? when it believes sincerely, and in complete good faith, it loves this someone, even if the partner is imaginary, even if the beloved is superficial if not nonexistent, like the ghost of the *Amour sorcier*,[17] the subject receives an interiority. Well, it is its loving intentionality that is its interiority. The direct complement par excellence of the verb 'to love,' that is, the Thou [*Toi*], the person number two, who is the person outside who is immediately the closest to myself; this second person, so near and so far, is my accusative of love. It is my intentional correlate; it is the object of my aim, and of the acute aim par excellence (*kat' exochen*): first, because the lover loves his second person with an exclusive passion that does not admit of any division, then because he aims for the very center of the ipseity in its most concrete, most immediate, and most essential particularity. Beyond being and physical thickness, but on this side of Platonic love and mystical difluence, is space for love strictly speaking, which is an acute and precise relation of one to the other. The Thou immediately and without beating around the bush designates the intimate truth about the beloved; but it also and at the same time designates, although tacitly and indirectly, the truth about the lover; it reveals the lover to himself. Love renews, enriches, and intensifies the life of the lover: mesmerized and in a manner of speaking magnetized by the pole of its accusative of love, the grammatical subject exits the realm of shadows and feels itself to live with an impetuous and fervent life in which the entire organism has a part; the lover is no longer a forlorn nominative: it is this presence of someone outside himself that maintains a mild intoxication inside himself. The beloved whom one addresses as Thou [*tutoie*] and who is the truth of the beloved, and paradoxically and mysteriously the truth of the lover, the truth of loving-love and the truth of loved-love, the two simultaneously, this double and simple truth is called quite simply the truth of love; the true truth of love and its raison d'être; the proof of its sincerity, the touchstone of its reality; the guarantee of its authenticity. A love that loves "in general" and that is not capable of saying the name of the one whom it loves, such an anonymous love is a tall tale. Or better yet: a lover who has no one to love is comparable to a man of action who is an agent "in general," an agent "in himself," who has nothing to do, and who idly mopes around: the phantom-agent dies of boredom and of *idleness* among his phantom-affairs, like the phantom-lover among his imaginary mistresses . . . unless the do-nothing is itself an *Actus purissimus:* for the purest of acts has no need of "occupations" to fill up its leisure time activities!

10. Being Preexists Love. Love Forestalls Being. Circular Causality.

The contradiction of being and loving is complicated by an inextricable ambiguity. The confusion is at its height when one poses the alternative in terms of priority. 1st: By all accounts, being logically and grammatically preexists love (and duty); the existence (the preexistence) of the loving-*being* is, by its very definition, substantially presupposed as the minimal condition of this love. Substantialism, as we know, sings this haunting refrain, which is that of a disguised tautology; and hardly more than a vicious circle! And we were saying that being is the precondition of preconditions . . . *Being* preexists the love—for it was already there. 2nd: But love *forestalls* [*prévient*] being: the love was not already there, hence it intervenes [*intervient*], it happens [*advient*] or arises [*survient*], it hurries, it gets ahead of that which, however, was forever always there. Being *was* first, for it is the inert and silent, the negative and implicitly implied condition in existent things . . . First, because it is old, even immemorial. But love is also first in its own way, although in a completely opposite sense: Love, according to Diotima, is that which comes (*ites*); the future is announced with its arrival; always moving and always young, Love is a prophecy! Love is first because it is rapid and youthful; *neotatos,* says Agathon in the *Symposium*[18] . . . This is why, according to Pascal, we represent it as a child. But Agathon, being more conventional, immobilizes the god of love in his eternal and unmovable youth: Eros, the god of love, is not able to age; he is happy and his quite smooth face does not know the wrinkles of worry. Diotima is a philosopher and prophetess: she conceives of love as a becoming without an end, as a springtime that is always disrupted by adventures. Throughout a thousand ordeals, springlike inspiration does not cease to improvise a world; love is always nascent, always *on the verge of* . . . Love is a commencement, or rather a recommencement, that, infinitely, will continue to commence! Love is an event that happens. Love is first in that it posits and founds being; in that it is a founder, in that it is a poet. This is its life-changing energy, this is its quickness which is a priority. And in the same way: being preexists the having-to-be [*devoir-être*], but the having-to-be, by virtue of its preeminence, that is, of its eminent moral dignity, is the raison d'être of being; it justifies the value of it; well, the value of being is infinitely more precious than being itself, the value of being is immeasurable to this being that without it would not be worth an hour of trouble. We thought we could detect the same reciprocity, the same paradoxical circularity in the relations of love and death. In short, in order to love one must already be, of course, and that is a trivial truth, a truth of the crossroads—but to be it is necessary to love, and that is the esoteric truth of mysteries; an intoxicating truth, which one finds at the bottom of a glass of wine. Being preexists love, which forestalls it, but thoughtful [*prévenant*] love forestalls [*prévient*] the being that nevertheless preexists it . . . Being and love go out ahead of each other, they are stronger than each other! How is this possible? With what is it necessary to begin? What is the competition with no way out and no solution? One is tempted to admit that the response is in the question, and the solution is in what is itself insoluble! Bergson said, following Aristotle, when speaking of apprenticeship: *the action breaks the circle.*[19] This drastic solution is not only the Gordian violence of the conqueror who cuts the knot with his sword without taking the trouble to untie it: it explains why one learns to walk by walking, to will by willing, to love by loving, because love always begins through itself—that is, begins through the continuation . . . This fallacy of the circular argument is neither an ingenious paradox nor a sophism nor a vicious circle: or rather it is the so-called vicious circle that is a mysterious circle; the mystery is here the mystery of *aseity* and the *causa sui;* or, more simply, this mystery is the mystery of commencement and the creative act. And that is, thus, the mystery of freedom.

Since being and loving, to the disdain of all logic, precede each other mutually, if we may say so, one understands that the alternative is not rigorous, that they are able to rub off on each other; far from playing hide-and-seek, they often join forces in unstable and suspect complexes; sometimes they are in inverse proportion, and sometimes, and paradoxically, in direct proportion to one another; and just as the ambivalence goes to infinity, they push one another away and attract one another completely together; being and loving outdo each other in fleeing, and they warm each other up over and over with a type of passionate outbidding. Overabundant being prevents loving, but it knows that it must sometimes be; the one so often reviled, it knows how to be the natural blooming and the spontaneous radiance of love; like blossoming in springtime, it thus expresses in an immediate manner the positivity of an impetus turned wholly toward life and toward plenitude. Sometimes hypocrisy allows the false voice of egoism to be discordant in the harmony; sometimes it is love that itself is, in a way, a hymn to light.

11. A Total Gift: How to Tear Oneself Away from the Hinges of Being-Proper? Abnegation.

We have not, strictly speaking, posed the problem of pure love, which was Fénelon's problem after having been that of Clement of Alexandria and Gregory of Nyssa:[20] for this problem would not be able to be *posed;* one can only graze, with an imponderable tangency, the extreme limit and the acute edge of the aporia: a most pure lover, one who would love with a most pure love, that is, with an ecstatic and mystical love, isn't that a love without being, an unutterable love, a troubled love? Philosophical discourse has a hold only on the dialectic of an utterable love in combat with self-interest. As long as one holds forth about a pure love, about a devotion riddled with ulterior motives and stuffed with unadmitted reservations, about a disinterestedness tarnished by a thousand and one opacities and clandestine complications of concrete psychology, then that is splendid! These are everyone's loves, the loves whose protectress is the Aphrodite of the Crossroads. There will still be good days for the analysis of motivations, for measuring out doses, for posology, and for the evaluation of merits. The psychoanalyst awaits you! In fact, devotion is always episodic and intermittent: it alternates with long periods of eclipse during which the altruist is above all devoted to his own self-interest; devotion is the often occasional virtue of a subject who is not always generous, who is something wholly other than devoted, who is devoted and still a lot of other things, who is, among other things, envious, vindictive, etc., and who is also not devoted the entire time: the virtue of Sunday and of holidays, in short, the virtue of days consecrated to good actions and to pious works. And the gift itself is essentially partitive, defining itself as a gift with respect to all that is not given and that one prefers to keep or have reserved for oneself. A literally chronic sacrifice is almost inconceivable and unsustainable. For sacrifice is a heartrending crisis. And likewise, a "total" gift, a gift that gives everything without exception, without preserving anything, without cheating, without concealing a humble viaticum in its bag, without safeguarding any *except,* were it as a reference, were it for the effect of relief, in a word, the gift of a giver who incomprehensibly gives of himself and completely, such a gift is either something nonsensical, or the flash of lightning of a sublime and supernatural grace; and this grace could not be perpetuated without absurdity. Can one imagine that the impossible tour de force, the superhuman exploit of an ascetic who, not content with renouncing this or that, not content with setting aside his small pleasures as the doctor invites him to do, would aim at the horizon of the *total gift?* Totalization contradicts the very intention of giving, or else it is the relativism of the gift that refutes the totalitarianism of integral abnegation . . . Gone are the half-measures and the small gifts whose sole goal was to economize on the total sacrifice! Starting from here, "privations" no longer suffice! For the pseudo-ascetic adapts himself to privations with a disconcerting elasticity, he soon reconstitutes a small bit of comfort within his shrunken life, like valetudinarians who get by cozily with their regimen and would not give it up for a sumptuous banquet. It is the case that we omitted distinguishing the humdrum routine of austerity and the infinite demand of asceticism. Austerity does not demand of the austere man to dissociate himself wholly from his being-proper; but asceticism demands of the ascetic to extricate himself wholly from himself! An *ecstasy* is now necessary: "to dissociate oneself" no longer suffices . . . Such a gesture is still too empirical, too superficial, too readily complicit in bad faith. No, one is not quits for giving lip service to having dissociated oneself! It would be necessary that the me ignored itself and exiled itself from its own essence. Like Baron de Crac, the man in perdition, on the verge of getting bogged down, extricates himself from the swamp all alone by pulling himself up by his hair: the man who sinks into the moving sands and the rescuer who believes himself to be on firm ground are one single and same man; a single man still, the one who is already alienated from himself and the one who brings aid to the first one and succumbs to the same distress. In communal immanence, where will he find a transcendent fulcrum? How, by what transcendent and absurd techniques, will the distressed man who sinks into the moving sands of egoity succeed in staying afloat?

12. The Disappearing Appearance Between the Ego and the Vivid Flame of Love . . . The Threshold of Courage.

We were saying roughly this: the man of heart and duty is an altruist not *despite* his egoism but *qua* egoist: however much he is scandalously mired in his philautia, he is, paradoxically, all the more altruistic the more egoistic he is. Isn't this a paradoxical and literally *unexpected* challenge to the sage logic of identity? The moral man is obviously altruistic in spite of the egoistic resistance, an altruist of a diminished, contested, contradicted, and undermined altruism, thus miserably and shamefully enough altruistic, all in all: for the acts of revenge and counteroffensives of the ego are contained with difficulty . . . However, it is egoistic negativity itself that passionately, desperately, fanatically sharpens the protest of altruism. The "despite," a concessive preposition dictated quite naturally by good sense and a goodwill that wills correctly, gives up its place to cynical causality: no ego, no sacrifice! no ego, no merit! Here still, the dialectical complication born of contradiction imposes on us the zigzags and detours of the mediate path. One is tempted to say, using manners of speaking that are a bit simplistic and schematic: abnegation has need of a vigorous, vital, and sensual ego so as to rebound off it. Otherwise, where would it find the necessary elasticity and spring? And of what voluptuous pleasures would abnegation be the negation? So as to elevate itself toward the heavens of altruism, the ego needs to dump some ballast. Where will it find this ballast to dump? But be careful! The maneuver is risky and the margin is more than narrow: it is necessary to weigh and physically to feel the weight of the imponderables with an infinite delicacy on ultra-sensitive scales when one evaluates the good and bad faith of an option; if one has a hand that is too heavy, one risks going beyond or staying on this side. At the two extremes, the situation is perfectly unambiguous. If the obstacle is equal to zero, then there is no sacrifice; when altruism no longer costs anything, there is no altruism; when the practice of virtues costs just as little as the functions of a vegetative life or the circulation of blood in one's arteries, merit is no longer meritorious; or rather, with merit itself being the relation of a perfectioning to an effort, there is no more merit; as an example, angels are not deserving; as an example, saints are not "virtuous," humanly virtuous: having transcended *agony* and its pangs, they live in glory (provided that one can say that they "live"!). And conversely, just as a suffocating sensuality, which generates irresistible temptations, would make the weak, moribund spark of a moral scruple disappear, one is inclined to think that the proper measure of an adequate moral conscience must be found somewhere halfway between the too much and the too little. But can one seriously speak of a median "sensuality"? The determination of this proper equilibrium is still riskier and more delicate when one aims for the evanescent minute of courage and especially for the infinitesimal instant of the heroic decision. If the brave person has nothing to brave, if he has absolutely no fear, be it because he has no consciousness of danger or be it that he feels himself invulnerable, if he, the unruffled person, the intrepid person, does not even know what it means to tremble, then we have no reason to admire his courage. And even less, after the fact, if the horror has driven off the brave person, then the brave person was only a swaggerer, a braggart! Where will we thus find the intangible, the most subtle bravery of this brave man? One cannot, without ridicule, in the language of the golden mean label a man brave who is moderately cowardly, cowardice being repugnant in all cases and regardless of the amount of it. To the arithmetical determination of a mean or to the measurement of equidistance, we will perhaps prefer an intuition of the fine truncation and an infinitesimal mutation. It is in the present of the confrontation that it would be necessary to assign the instant of courage, it is at this point that in moral auscultation one would hear the heart of this courage beating. Before, it is too soon; after, it is too late! The occasion of courage, *kairos,* is undoubtedly somewhere between the two. But where is it necessary to situate this somewhere? We say 'situate' and not 'localize.' There is, indeed, a "threshold" of courage, but one perceives the introductory nature of it only in a hit-or-miss and dubious search; for a courageous instant occurs almost imperceptibly in an ocean of pusillanimity, as the good movement appears-disappears in an ocean of egoism, as the trembling spark of sincerity glimmers in the fogs of hypocrisy. Between the fearlessness of the not yet and the bragging of the no more that, once the fear is surmounted, infinitely sing the praises of imaginary exploits, there is a place for a passionate, serious, and indeed even tragic debate about courage and fear. The debate about fear and courage is summed up in a contradiction whose appearance alone is paradoxical: *to be courageous, it is necessary to have fear!* To be courageous, it is necessary to be attached to life, to a life that one feels to be fragile, threatened, and infinitely precious; to be courageous, it is necessary to be entirely attached to life yet to hold it cheaply! Fear creates an obstacle for courage, whereby it slows down, that is, *discourages* its impetus and simultaneously its raison d'être. This critical moment of extreme tension is not that of surmounted fear, but of fear to be surmounted; consciousness has not yet had the time to make a spectacle of the danger, or to go on and on about its own merits. The mystery of courage amounts to an infinitesimal shock of willing that is almost immediately carried away, eclipsed, and, so to speak, submerged by the infinite stream of exhibitionism, by unbounded bombast, and by verbal inflation. In the same instant, freedom is for the free man a *clear-obscure* glimpse and a dazzling certitude; in the lightning flash of this instant, the *disappearing-appearance* is, as it were, *equi-univocal*.

More generally and at any rate: if the accent is placed on the obstacle of the organ-obstacle, this is not in order to water down even more the blandness of a median sensuality, it is to increase the concern of a tormented, anxious, and worried sensuality, it is to make the bad conscience more vigilant. A conscience on alert is harassed by maniacal purism, kept in suspense by pointillistic scruples and merciless aphorisms, and persecuted by demands that allow nothing to happen. Gone, thus, is our sleep; the conscience is no longer just vigilant, but insomniac: the agony will last until the end of the world . . . "It is not necessary to sleep during that time."[21] A chronic bad conscience disturbs the sleep of people who are just: for "virtue" is essentially precarious. Obsessive, acerbic, and merciless, for La Rochefoucauld, is the denunciation of the omnipresent egotropism: the author of the *Maxims* tirelessly brings us back to the refrain of an ego that is the object of its exhausting perspicacity and that one finds again at every detour, at every junction or bifurcation of systematic misanthropy. Everyone feels himself to be guilty, impure, and thwarted. La Rochefoucauld, tracking down from maxim to maxim the pretexts, excuses, and sophisms of hypocrisy, inaugurates the era of suspicion well before Kant. The interpretation of statistics of duplicity—there you have the great strategic occupation of Baltasar Gracián. Even the sweetnesses of rhetoric can become a weapon of war. Even obsequious flattery is a form of belligerence, and the most perfidious kind . . . This weapon is called the ruse.

13. Unction. The Minimal Feeling of Abnegation (the Afference of Efference). The Pleasure of Giving Pleasure.

Nevertheless, *unction,* when it is preached by Saint Francis de Sales, and even by Fénelon, who, by the way, is so austere in matters of purity, so uncompromising on the subject of charity, unction is not necessarily deceitful sweet talk; or, in other examples: its velvety smoothness does not always conceal scratches. It evokes at first the thought of softness and tenderness. When it is not corrupted, it would instead be an appeal to confidence and leniency: a confidence restrained in the seduction of appearances, a leniency for the one who allows himself to be tempted by it. Better yet: there would undoubtedly be a bit of bad faith, some corruption, and a lot of unrealism to be displayed in these matters, of a rigor without nuances or of an overly merciless lucidity.

To discourage a goodwill with the prospect of an impossible task is a worthless precaution when it is not a mark of bad faith. For good faith pushed to the extreme (does this even merit the name good faith?) is generally indiscernible from bad faith or, at the very least, from a bad will. It is the radicalism, the Machiavellianism, of overly good faith that serves to waken the suspicion of a simple and upright soul; and these are, on the contrary, wild approximations of hope and chimeras of an illusion that justify faith in the effort.

In using Fénelonian concepts, here is how we would express ourselves: it is indeed necessary that the disinterested man, however disinterested he may be, feel at the very least a *sensitive interest* for the object of his disinterestedness; and it even happens that the altruism that is the altruism most detached from every egoistical pleasure experiences, for lack of another pleasure, the pleasure of being devoted. This, in an elementary logic, brings us back again to a substantialist truism. This vicious circle is clearly virtuous enough! Who devotes himself? *It is indeed necessary that* the verb "to devote oneself" have a subject! Always, "it is indeed necessary . . . " The inexterminable nature of the ego and egoism interacts with an inverse indestructability, that of altruism. For the optimism of pessimism is as stubborn as the pessimism of optimism, and one is referred endlessly from one to the other. Leibniz, speaking of meaning and the intelligible order, said that they are reconstituted infinitely and regenerate infinitely, that they cannot be nihilized. Beyond the most arbitrary whims and the absurd assaults of asceticism, beyond a masochism that is counter to nature and, by the way, contradictory, the attraction of pleasure and the positivity of the attractiveness resist all the persecutions and have the right to our leniency! Despite the reservations that we ourselves make in speaking of complacency, the simple and natural attraction of the thing that attracts cannot be genuinely rejected: our grimaces will not matter: and the contortions of a tortured ascetic can themselves become a suspect sign of contentment, even a reason for vanity. It is not always easy to distinguish between the joy of devoting oneself and the stupid satisfaction of a duty said to be finished, or to determine at which moment one passes from the former to the latter! As long as it is about the former (on condition of being certain of it), one can indeed ask, What harm is there in feeling such a joy? This is not a crime. The pleasure of giving pleasure is the greatest of all pleasures. In courtesy, allow me this pleasure.

This pleasure is not only excusable, it is innocent; and it is indeed not enough to say that this pleasure sticks the closest to the generous act; it is the immediate emanation of it. And one can even say more: this pleasure is simply one with the generous act: the gift and the pleasure of giving are the two sides, the one efferent and the other afferent, of one same benediction and one same joy: the pleasure is exhaled in a manner of speaking directly from the donation—or, conversely, it is the gift that is the generous expansion of the pleasure; pleasure and gift, they are, the one and the other, simultaneously effect and cause, and the two movements are synchronous that go from one to the other and from the other to the one. Each time the militant will acts, begins, does this or that, each time it anticipates or meets its second person to assist it, to help it, to save it, this spontaneous will suffers as an aftereffect, like a return wave, the centripetal reaction inherent in its helpful action; the charitable impetus and the receptive moment, the giving and the *feeling,* the primary impulse and the secondary "affect" are not consecutive but are part of the same process; it even happens, as in the innocent spontaneity of pity, that the emotion is not only concurrent with the helpful gesture but predates this gesture. How can one claim in that case, owing to the physiological theory, that piety amounts wholly to the theatrical ritual of holy water, and pity wholly to the perception of peripheric modifications, and that the merciful person feels pity for his own tears? Pascal never wanted to say that. Pity and gentleness of tears are only "egoistic" if one artificially isolates the passive side of compassion from helpful charity, or if one separates the emotion from the generous activity. This separation results in the simultaneous atrophy of generosity and feeling; it has as its solution the desiccation, the shriveling, and in the end the degeneration of the moral being: affective interiority is thus a pallid phantom without efficacy or consistency, while alms amount to mechanics and drivel or, better stated, to the pantomime of a learned monkey.

The same haunting question does not cease to pursue us: starting from what degree of philautia can the ego be accused of egoism? Starting from what ontic density does the necessary preservation of the subject become suspect, then guilty, and must it be condemned? More precisely: where does permissible self-love stop? At what point does guilty philautia begin? Where and how can one assign a limit? Up to what point can the ecstasy, up to what point can the rarefaction and the exhaustion of the substantial subject be pushed without the being sinking into the void of nothing and without dangerously compromising its survival? For the risk of nihilization is not negligeable in this game with nonbeing, in which the chance of escaping alive is at the mercy of a prodigious and perilous acrobatics. How much? Where and when? Admittedly, the passage from the good will to the bad will takes place at thus and such a moment: at a given moment . . . But what is this given moment? At a given moment . . . But when? But how? Not too much in any case . . . The circumstantial and especially quantitative determinations are as uncertain and arbitrary as the hour of death. Whatever the envisioned category may be, one can respond with precision, set the dosages, and assign the limit of what is too much and too little. These aporias, used by the Megarics as sophisms, sometimes evade the discontinuities in the specious and misleading continuity of the "sorites paradox," sometimes they fail to recognize the continuity of becoming and the mutation. Here again, it is necessary to say: it is especially with average dosages that our faculties of evaluation grope around in the equivocal; the extremes, on the contrary, are perfectly univocal. And yes, even in the mixed and tricky zone of our finitude, it seems that the proper rule is to avoid the petty hagglings of posology and agree to the most natural, obvious facts. The one who asks sophisticated questions cannot be surprised if he himself plays into the hands of the sophists and if he falls ill with the illness of scruples.

For man, a finite and impure being, the most pure of acts is a chimerical limit just like the ideal being of a most pure love: these are two names for a single pure, perfect ecstasy of all concrete reality, of all lived psychological experience, of any associative context. But the law of the alternative disrupts the reign of grace: the centrifugal impulse undergoes a clash of the forces that comes flooding back onto it and neutralizes it, or at the least compensates for it; every creative activity thus receives, as an aftershock, the effects of its correlative passivity. For there is no "pure act." The aftershock is the afferent wave that immediately follows the efferent act and is even part of this act . . . The aftershock is a repercussion and in a manner of speaking a resonance induced by the primary activity; when the affectivity is nascent, the man of action acquires a taste for, or more simply adheres to, his own initiative; the good movement's self-indulgence is the most fugitive, but also the most diabolical of the moral fatalities. Now, it sometimes happens that the body speaks loudly and even cries at the top of its lungs: in this case the sensitive aftershock manifests itself in the form of an explosion, of a violent protest of its organs. Passionate and almost imperceptible, this participation is sometimes a thinking and indiscreet adherence, it is sometimes an adherence of the ego to its own physiology, sometimes an impalpable but always discernible shaking of the conscience.

The interpenetration of the efferent influx and the afferent influx is still more intimate in love, even without admixture, than in the pure act. It is the case that love already implies affectivity and that it is itself the lived and sensible side of charity. Love simultaneously means *someone to love* and *someone for loving.* The first "someone," the object of the transitive intention, is simultaneously the accusative of love, that is, the aim of the lover, and what ignites and maintains the "vivacious flame of love." Wholly extroverted, turned toward the other, and in this particular case toward the second person, the love, with a limited love, tends toward the forgetting of itself, toward a sort of ecstatic perdition and an interior anesthesia. But the lover himself is neither an invisible breath nor breathing without a body or weight nor an impalpable thought: the lover is something existent and a substantial subject, and one cannot prevent the lover from loving love and, one thing leading to another, from feeling himself as he loves, from feeling the loving, from feeling himself in general and doing so in a progressive degeneration whose last term is self-love, and from, in the end, loving himself and taking pleasure in it. By the effect of being aware of itself and of the complacency that develops a taste for this conscience, love takes up space and acquires all the dimensions of existence. And not only does love become more existent, but by an aftershock the lover himself becomes warm and gains in fervor. Undoubtedly, Fénelon is an absolutist and above all not a realist when he condemns without compromise *sensitive taste* in general . . . This sensitive aftershock that one cannot nihilize belongs to the afferent side of moral experience, just as the disinterested gift is the efferent moment of it; and it is in the indissoluble union of these two moments that what is human in the human is expressed. Can one distinguish between the austere and costly renunciation of pleasure itself and tender solicitude for the second person? Without this loving solicitude, ascetic love would be only indifference and abstraction. The other is thus, in a manner of speaking, another myself, but not in the atomistic and substantialist egotropism of Aristotle, who is a bit too petit bourgeois: the love, because it is dead to itself, is miraculously, passionately, and ecstatically reborn in the being of the beloved. And that is why the act of *feeling* [*le sentir*], which is the minimal afference inseparable from disinterested efference, this feeling *again* [ce *ressentir*] is neither an effect of reflexivity nor a duplication in a mirror, but it is at the same time the second time and the first time; the act of feeling again [*ressentir*] is jointly a loving echo and a pure spontaneity. The alternative of the other and of myself is thus gone beyond, exceeded—transcended! So it is that love supposes the fulfillment of two series of apparently contradictory conditions. On one hand, and in the order of efference, the abnegation that inexplicably permits us to live for the other and in his place, and to think only of this other, as does intuition . . . Isn't the ecstasy, in its own way, a lived intuition? And on the other hand, in the order of afference, happiness, the ineffable gentleness of feeling oneself live intensely and in fullness: paradoxically the ecstasy becomes one with the vital fulfillment.

From this point on, it is no longer a sin to taste of the fruit of devotion, when by accident the devotion has a taste, or to feel the joy of sacrifice, if by chance the sacrifice implies such a joy. There is no harm in that. Suspicious judges reproach us for these innocent pleasures, and scrupulous souls in hearing these reproaches feel remorse for them. But as for us, we do not justify the "impassive" gnosticism of Clement of Alexandria; we do not hear the suspicious judges, and we refrain from anxiously dissecting maniacal scruples: for once, we rely on the voice of good conscience.

However, the vocation of love is aimed in the opposite direction from having, from conservation (from "keeping"), and even, up to a certain point (a point that one cannot assign), in the opposite direction from being, tout court; being is indeed an accomplishment, but it is no less a gravity, since it is ready made, in the passive past participle—and even, we were saying: precisely because it is an obstacle, it will be an accomplishment; being is an accomplishment that is an impediment; or, conversely, it is a weightiness that is a fullness. The being of love, in order to accomplish its vocation, must preserve its being-proper, and even, if needed, enlarge it, without us being able to determine in each case to what size it must enlarge it, or if this enlargement is pleonexia or if it is a necessary condition of loving fullness. There is thus no shame in holding fast to one's being. And if by accident one insisted and if one asked, At the end of it all, how much is necessary to keep and how much is necessary to give in order to be an accomplished man? we would again respond: in any event, it is not about creating two halves out of what one keeps and what one gives, as such a partition would soon be established in the static economy of the daily routine, and would degenerate into a shopkeeper-like management; in moral life, it cannot be about calculating the happy medium . . . Even less is it about a "negotiation": for that at which negotiators aim by alternating between blackmail, bluff, and intimidation with hypocritical concessions is the institution of a static order, a new relation of forces, and a new equilibrium; such a negotiation is only a cunning continuation of belligerence, a muted belligerence. Rather than a negotiation, we would prefer to speak of an infinite adjustment: the solution is far off, like the horizon—that is: it retreats as one comes closer to it. Every equilibrium is unstable, precarious, and perpetually put into question again; not anything established, or final.

The moral demand, just like a vulgar negotiation of vulgar negotiators, in fact, admits to compromises; it admits to them with a heavy heart and kicking and screaming; it admits to them by closing its eyes and turning away its head; but in fact and tacitly it admits to them, even though theoretically it abhors them, and even though it vomits them up; after all, it is an action in general that has need of approximations in order to achieve something, and that, without the approximations, would achieve nothing; so it adapts itself to the circumstances . . . Aristotle never closed his eyes to the natural opportunism of practical experience! A few misunderstandings here, a little bit of approximation there, a few drops of ambivalence, a lot of love and goodwill—and as best as can be (but probably more bad than good), and somehow or other, what is unviable makes itself viable and what is impossible proves to be possible! But the moral demand implies a clever negotiation that weighs and physically feels the weight of imponderables on its scales, calculates infinitesimal quantities, and makes exceptions for the most secret of motives. Perhaps it was necessary to contrast the supersubtle *approximation* that goes to infinity and the rough *approximately* that is common in merchants' transactions. Surely the purist demand is uncompromising, and it repudiates the art of crafting together [*composer*]²² alloys: but pure love can sometimes coincide, in the instant of an intuition, with its own contradictory. That is not the least surprising paradox of moral extremism . . . This is the supreme irony: love and being do not combine between themselves clever arrangements and ingenious mixtures that would be their modus vivendi, but they recognize one another suddenly in the flash of the *coincidentia oppositorum,* and they fall into each other's arms.

14. The Horizon of the Almost. From the Almost-Nothing to Nonbeing. The Unstable Resultant of Ambition and Abnegation.

The horizon of the *almost*—that is, of this infinitesimal approximation in which we were recognizing the third escape— permits us to understand how the being, by the effect of love, tends toward nonbeing as toward its limit, without ever disappearing into nothing [*rien*], without ever being nihilized. Let us first indicate the essential stipulation, the one that is the condition of all the rest: *barely* [*à-peine*] is negative, designating that which "barely" emerges from nonbeing; but *almost* [*presque*] is timidly affirmative. *Barely,* a disguised miscarriage, alludes to a failure; but, just the opposite, *almost* relates to a failure that foretells any future success; *almost* expresses in a single word that one misses the mark, but that one misses it by little . . . Except for that—a fortuitous failure, a simple misfortune—*almost* is wholly positivity: it is an adverb of modesty, but also an adverb of hope for the use of the man of courage and action, who, even if he were a hero, that is to say, confronting death and accepting with the sacrifice the possibility of dying, says yes to life and to the future, and preserves, if possible, his own existence in order to devote it to the existence of others, since that is the imperative of imperatives; he takes on the risk of becoming nothing [*s'aneantir*], but he needs to pull through and survive: for being is better than nothingness [*néant*]. Nothing is simpler, or clearer, than this gamble. The *almost,* in contrast with every nihilism, thus presupposes an act of faith and a will to live. What am I saying? the limited abnegation, in contrast to every crushing negation, every suicidal annihilation, presupposes values and reasons for living that are more sublime than life itself; abnegation is thus a fortiori vital; it renounces being in order to reach, in the light of love, to a super-being [*sur-être*]. Is the loving tangency to nothingness a failure or a triumph? Such an alternative at this level seems to be transcended. The supreme sacrifice is at first a failure to the extent that the loving-being, reduced to an almost-nothing [*presque-rien*], has become inconsistent and quasi nonexistent; but this failure, transfigured by the moral optics of duty, is also the most miraculous of chances, and the most triumphal, since in the last second of the last minute, what is barely existent is saved from nonbeing; it *is nec-*

essary that it be saved; by an acrobatic recovery the one who *almost* succumbed will survive . . . *On the verge of* succumbing, like Mazeppa, he comes back to life. Isn't this indeed a miracle? For *there was little* keeping the survivor, who was still breathing, from succumbing; *there was almost nothing* keeping the lover from being nothing; between the nothing and the almost-nothing, there is this infinitely little thing [*ce peu*], this infinitesimal break of the *almost,* this flickering glimmer that is also a boundless hope, vast, like the world.

The third escape is perilous, but the fourth is vertiginous; it is more mobile, more worried than the third, and about it we were calling to mind the zigzags and the buzz of a panic-stricken insect that is searching for an exit to its glass prison and bangs against the transparent walls: in this coming-and-going we recognize a characteristic beating and, in a manner of speaking, the vibration of a conscience in search of the almost-nothing; as for this conscience, the two extremes send it back and forth; alternately it grazes the beyond, that is, the supernatural world of love, without being able to gain a foothold there, then it regains its strength in the hither, and once again bounds toward the inaccessible subsequent patrimony on which no astronaut will ever land. The acrobat of the fourth acrobatics will not allow himself to be convinced by Descartes's relatively optimistic rationalism.[23] One recognizes the advice that the second maxim of the "morals by provision" gives to the lost traveler in the forest: this traveler, like the panic-stricken bumblebee, twirls, "sometimes to one side, sometimes to the other," and Descartes compares him to "weak and unsteady minds," who—an obvious sign of disarray—are shunted about by the oscillations of remorse and repenting; Descartes recommends that these disoriented travelers walk straight ahead in the same direction: for according to this method, they will at least arrive somewhere, the proper rule being to adopt a direction, even if by accident, and stick with it. Anything rather than wandering into the double darkness of the forest and the night! Rather the clear-obscure of what is practical and of probabilism than this double darkness! From the moment there is an irrational zone of what is practical, a hypothetical and pragmatic choice, dictated by the imperative of urgency, is undoubtedly preferable to despair . . . Now, when one speaks not of the obscure forest and of the lost path, that is, of space, but rather of unfathomable, unattainable, intangible realities, then it is permissible not to refuse any virtue related to becoming and to movement. Indeed, the rapid and frequent repetition of a coming-and-going does not take the place of omnipresence: nevertheless, the coming-and-going of the loving-being when he runs from being-without-love to love-without-being and from one way out to the other way out, this back-and-forth can, at the limit of approximation, appear to be indiscernible from ubiquity; just as the army of a genius strategist, compensating for the insufficiency of its forces with the lightning rapidity of its movements, seems to be present everywhere at the same time. The back-and-forth between being and loving calls to mind with its agility the intangible "games" of humor: if ironic reversal is a second-order seriousness, then the seriousness of humor is always infinitely somewhere else. Endless omnipresence and oscillation are not a miracle here: this "miracle" is quite simply the grace of mobility. And its name is mystery.

A single essentially equivocal maxim is thus valid for the impossible passage to infinity—a passage that always goes in the same direction—and for the shuttle movement, which is indefinitely possible. The moral imperative minimizes the necessary evil that the body and egoism set up in its path and into which it rightly makes a *least evil;* it rotates the necessary obstacle, which it turns into an organ-obstacle, and it does not thus imply that the negativity of the obstacle is integrally abolished and transfigured into a means. Abnegation necessarily takes into account this inert, irrational, and insoluble, inexplicable, and unjustifiable residue, which is the squaring of the circle in every theodicy. In the absolute, the moral imperative would require that one consider this residue nonexistent, which one makes as if null and void: this is what Leibniz called the antecedent will. But when one asks to what degree, in the relative, love can make an exception for being, the response is, theoretically: the least possible—and *in principle:* no more than is strictly necessary to survive; anything more is a luxury! In this minimum is implied, on one hand, the positive presence of being, for a minimum is not nothing, a minimum is at least something! Stable and finite, this something is merely tolerated and is the opposite of the pneumatic almost-nothing as austerity and sobriety are the opposite of asceticism, indigence is the opposite of mendicity, and modesty is the opposite of humility. But we have also said that the density of tolerated being cannot be quantified! And on the other hand, this "minimum" indirectly implies the limitation that infinite love imposes on it. If infinite love, in throwing us the bone of the *almost-nothing,* is a sublime abnegation, if being is the ambition of egoistic pleonexia, then the *something,* which is minimal, would instead be the resultant of this ambition and this abnegation, the unstable equilibrium that is continually undone and continually reestablished between the one and the other. Starting from that point, maximum and minimum are not so much exclusive antagonists of each other as they are correlatives and complementaries in an alternative. The more there is being, the less there is love. The less there is being, the more there is love. The one offsets the other. The tricky problem of moral life resembles a tour de force, but one carries off this tour de force almost without thinking about it when one loves: this is, if we may repeat it: *to fit the maximum of love into the minimum of being and volume* or, conversely, *to measure out the minimum of being or evil necessary that is compatible with the maximum of love.*

4
The Scheme of the Conscience.
How to Preserve Innocence

1. The Plethora and Sporadicism of Values. The Plural
Absolute: A Matter of Conscience.

The most diabolical of all the obstacles is the obstacle that
has as its origin value itself. Value is the space of transparency and communion. How can this transparency become
a source of confusion and misunderstanding? There is, as
we were saying, an opaque, inert, and irreducible residue,
a thickness that, without being confused with the "physical
minimum," is in its own way a type of least evil: this paradoxical least evil comes from, if one can say this, an over-
abundance of normativity, nay, even of infinite duty. The
obstacle in this case is not of course a mere material road-
block or a mere impediment, as is for example the temptation that theologians call concupiscence or lustfulness: that
is, a "necessary evil." And that being the case, this necessary evil is an integral part of a defensive strategy justified
by man's wickedness, by the paucity of his resources, and
by the miserable finitude of our lives; the moral law—and
why not?—will perhaps ask us one day to preserve the lascivious part of our being, to leave its luck to this being, and
to spare it any mutilation. Thus my personal responsibility
will become the objective and fortuitous auxiliary of devo-

tion; thus my duties toward myself (if there are any) will indirectly command me to strive toward the direction of duty *tout court*. The necessary obstacle is sometimes an apparent infidelity that, owing to the effects of the circumstances, finds itself in the service of a more profound and more serious fidelity, albeit more perplexing. And in second place in the temporal order: pneumatic fidelity is a long-range fidelity; it orders to us to live as long as possible; it forbids us prematurely to shorten our lives by sacrifice; the same imperative that would command me to love the other so as to die of it orders me, conversely, to live, and to live precisely out of love for this other . . . and, *which is the same!*—to live and, at any rate, to survive! At the last moment, and contrary to the absolutist demand, with literal rigorism, we *will preserve* an extension of life so as to *reserve* it for a militant mutual aid. It is indeed necessary, is it not, that I live *a little for me* if I want to live *a lot for you!* This concession does not in any way arouse a crisis of conscience: a solution is offered to helpful activism, and this solution, refusing every utilitarian mediation, every adjustment, and every saving that is a bit too ingenious, postpones the tragedy of the dilemma for us. The moral imperative is by no means refuted by this solution. For it is literally a "solution," and the optimist adopts it. Isn't the optimum a maximum for a minimum? A maximum for the least cost? Isn't the optimum the very relative superlative of an ingenious economy?

There is only that which is "tragic," in the proper sense of the word, in a *crisis of conscience*—except, of course, if the crisis of conscience is the effect of an optical confusion or an approximative analysis. And there is nothing insoluble but the isosthenia of two equally valid values that contradict or refute each other. The conflict of contradictory duties inexhaustibly furnishes excuses and pretexts to all the resignations, to all the capitulations. A true windfall for the idleness and the cowardice of the sophists! And what is the origin of such a competition? The origin of this absurd competition is the *plurality of values;* and the essence of this plurality, in turn, is very generally the mystery of the *plural absolute.* How can the absolute be plural? Absolutism supposes sufficiency and independence, solitude and autarky. And as for multiplicity, it generally has as a consequence relativity; the paradox of an absolute in the plural is thus neither less absurd nor less contradictory than the nonsense of a singular in the plural . . . A plurality of misfortune! Each value is for itself infinitely valid, valid up to the absolute; each one wants to be single and sovereign, and wants the entire space for itself, and absurdly claims to go to the core of its rights; no value in itself makes an exception for rival values, or for its own limitation; values sometimes repeat themselves and are duplicated, sometimes refute each other; if values emphasize the same virtue, highlight the same norm, even if under different yet analogical forms, one would be able to speak of a world of values, a relatively harmonious cosmos composed of complementary values. Well, there aren't any. One would say that values have carried on no matter how, independent of one another, without taking one another into account, like liana in a tropical forest. Indeed, there is something tropical in this profusion in which norms inextricably become entangled and overlap with one another. The disorder and incoherence linked to the sporadic nature of values, far from constituting a harmony, stir up a civil war. If one confines oneself to axiological objectivity, then these antagonisms and the conflicts of value that come from them lead to collisions and end up immobilizing and inhibiting the action. But if one considers the lived heartbreak and the moral despair that in a torn-apart soul result from the conflict of values, it will be necessary to speak, literally, of a crisis of conscience. In vain, one would search out in the hidden corners of the world of values a this-or-that, a cursed entity, a false note, maybe a gremlin, something that would be the palpable cause of the dissonance: it is impossible to put one's finger on this dissonance, to foil the cheating, to localize the evil, or to ascribe its origin. It is, in fact, the excess of value that is the evil! Evil, with its ambiguous and transient nature, is to a certain extent the superabundance of value, just as sickness in certain cases is the superabundance of vitality. For the Too Much is the enemy of the Good. It is thus value, because of its own luxuriance, that keeps itself from existing. Or, more precisely still: evil does not lie in this or that rule of action but, in general, in the fact that such and such an action elevates its own demands independent of the other demands; but a virtue, separated from all the others, is a vice. This is why perversity most often does not have any particular content: the perversion that makes this perversity perverse rests almost completely with the refusal to take into consideration all the other values. Excellences and perfections thus become senile, perverse, and wicked by the effect of atomization, are thus dull and dry like dust.—However, atomization in itself is not evil; plurality in itself has no intention; plurality in itself is indifferent; plurality in itself is neither good nor bad. Disintegration and conflicts of duties are the forms that the degeneration of values takes, but these contradictions themselves and this ridiculous plethora have, in turn, one cause, and one alone, the simplest of all of them: desiccated "virtues" collapse into dust because love has left them. This was the only important thing, and this is not even a "virtue": it was perhaps even necessary to find a name for it! Separated from this anonymous and impalpable thing, from this I-know-not-what, separated from their soul, and consequently from everything that would make up their power and their life, the virtues are no longer anything: dreadful grimaces and a pious mimicry—that is all that remains of them. Drained of this love that had been their sole fullness, they become merely the masks of wretched hypocrisy; a truth without love is nothing but harshness and indifference; a justice without charity is drivel and sarcasm; a truth without love is only deceit and bad faith, a justice without charity is the height of injustice. It is thus intentionality that is everything! It is the death of the loving intention that is the cause, and it is the wicked disintegration of small talents that have become malevolent and hostile that is the effect. For egoism and it alone maintains the disjointedness, the confusion, the muddle, and the war of all against all.—The conflicts of duties, whetted by the petering out of love, seem to justify the existence of a casuistry: a casuistry that endeavors to reunite and glue back together dislocated values, to replaster cracks; it imagines, for this replastering, new forms of cement. In each singular case, for each problem and each aporia, taken alone, casuistry has laboriously applied itself to the insipid and patient task: buffoonery and the disparate and artificial aspect of these cosmetic changes have merited their sad reputation. If the man who is crucified by scruples remained loyal to the inspiration of love, he would not be obligated to search for, in conceptual solutions or in I-know-not-what ingenious combinations, the synthesis of crumbled values; he would not need the casuist in order to reconcile them. Abnegation itself, in the measure in which it is love, says yes: not only does it affirm the existence of others, but it indirectly, and a fortiori, implies the preservation of the ego; in the crystalline transparency of love and in the limpid simplicity of innocence, the contradictions of duties vanish, as if by a miracle; the cornucopia of virtues, henceforth, amounts to a single virtue.

One would say that there is an analogy between the tattered firmament of values and the city of persons: axiological disjointedness seems to be embodied in the monadological plurality. Certainly plural absolutism opens up certain gaps between people, certain discontinuities, and certain passages that mobilize the transitive influx of love. But more often still this absolutism fuels the fight for life. In the same way in which claims that equally provide evidence for all values under the same undivided suzerainty will create frictions and collisions, so the absolutism of each person and each freedom considered separately, with each one being an end in itself or *imperium in imperio,* simultaneously engenders mutual attraction and ferocious competition, that is, passionate tension. Or simultaneously, to use the language of Pascal and that of Leibniz: the monadic world of persons and contradictory egoisms is a totality whose center is everywhere. The other is my brother in humanity and *thereby* he is paradoxically my impediment to living, the foyer of all communion, and he is an object of jealousy and hatred. By virtue of the law of the alternative, the place of the one is occupied by the other, the portion of the one is deducted from that of the other; monads are solidary, but owing to their wholeness they are incompatible. And thus the plethora turns into penury.

Evil is an intention and nothing else. We were saying: it is not plurality in itself that is evil, as Greek metaphysics taught, but the Machiavellian and perfidious intention of exploiting this division and, in exploiting it, of weakening values and casting doubt and discredit on to their seriousness. Equivocal and ingratiating: such is the obstacle that we were calling axiology, which is due primarily to the plural absolute. Because this is an immanent evil, an internal fight contested between values, it is impossible to hypostatize it; because it is an evil hidden in intentions, one cannot make a claim about that to which it is due, in what it consists, or on which side its camp lies: it is intentional, and that is all. Is it necessary to accuse instinct? Or vice? Or Satan? A little bit of all this and none of all that. In any case, no enemy in particular is guilty: always fading, unceasingly being revived, malevolence hinders the reification of evil; it recommences infinitely, but it almost never exists once and for all. The very paradox of a plethora of value already indicates at what point corruption can be evasive and bad faith disconcerting. Let us here repeat it: Saint Francis de Sales spoke, in his own language, of a "spiritual avarice"! There is indeed a devout rapaciousness dedicated to that capitalization of merits which collects virtues. Odd, pitiful hoarders who collect not medals but virtues themselves! In any case, the category of quantity and the response to the question How many? does not enlighten us on the qualitative distinction of good and evil. If it is value that is in question, then how could it be over the top? Over the top of what? The word 'excess' is not applicable if it is an issue of courage and disinterestedness . . . We had pointed out as much when we were speaking of the loving *impetus* and of the "demonic hyperbole" . . . Isn't the word 'hyperbole' absurd, starting from the moment one applies it to excellence? The motto in this matter would instead be Never enough! never too much! It is a fact, however, that values contradict one another, that the one can be an impediment for the other and—a supreme derision!—that the moral set of problems is often weighed down by a sort of ethical "gravity."

2. Everyone Has Rights, Thus Me Too. A Claim.

Everyone has rights, thus me too. The "rights" that I claim or that one acknowledges for me are in some way the normative part of this gravity. *Thus, me too!* we were saying. *Et ego.* For my rights are deduced from the rights of man in general. Their gravity weighs particularly heavily in the deductive reasoning that is of use for me in claiming them and in the indisputable and irrefragable mechanics of this "thus." A deduction? What did I say! almost a syllogism . . . A right that is valid for the universality of thinking subjects in consideration of their equal dignity is, hence, valid for me, who is one of these subjects; a right that is valid for all the others, and consequently for this one or that one, is a fortiori applicable to me, to me who myself is one of these others and, like the others, one of these subjects in favor of which one claims justice and right. There you have an application that is not specially provided for in my honor. There is nothing to say against that logic, for it is, all in all, the elementary logic of identity: what holds for the whole holds for the part: what holds for the collection of beings gifted with reason, first person included, holds ipso facto for (even more so? even less so? according to the point of view) for this first person himself: for I am part of, I as well, the human race; for I am encompassed by, I as well, what is universally human; I am one of us all! After all, I am, like anyone else, a citizen of the republic of free moral subjects . . . Neither more nor less than another—than every other! Neither better nor worse . . . On condition, however, that these microcosms in the plural coexist in the plenitude of their rights! For monads, if they do not make concessions to one another, if they affirm one another up to the absolute, that is, up to the absurd, then they violently contradict one another. On the other hand, the human community, which is entirely by my side and of which I am a representative, gives its powerful, its irresistible moral guarantee to instinctive philautia: the universality of the rights of man in general confers to our instinct for conservation and preservation in being a normativity that is nowhere to be found, a legitimacy that is our welcome good fortune. And vice versa, the lived aspect of instinct, by rubbing shoulders with moral ideality, makes it more concrete; it livens up consciousness of moral fraternity, and apparently seems to head in the same direction as it; with a providential osmosis, I carnally relive in myself the right of all men, while, vice versa, my vital needs—the passion of freedom, the right to live, the need to love—acquire in this amalgamation the dimension of universality. Into the passionate reflex deductive logic injects, thus, several drops of ideality, of objectivity, and of impartiality; thanks to this injection, the affirmation of my right is no longer simply the effect of egoism or voracity: it is a *demand;* that is: it has a juridical character; what I ask for is not an arbitrary claim or a wild requirement; what I ask for I have good reason to demand; I demand it nobly, with all the dignity of the frustrated good conscience.—The affirmation of my own right is particularly energetic when it protests against that which contests it. There is no "reason" for me to be frustrated by my right; for the spoliation is violent at first, that is, irrational; there is no reason for me to remain all alone like a poor, abandoned, disinherited, forgotten orphan, excluded from privilege, which is itself a paradox, since it is the "privilege" of all men. One single exception to this *almost* universal privilege, universal by right but suspended in my case and for my misfortune, a single exception at my expense would in one fell swoop refute the general law; either the privilege is universal, and it is thus not a privilege, since all men, from first to last, possess it, or it inexplicably leaves me outside, but in this case the principle that claims to protect what is human in all men in general and the dignity of each man in particular, this principle is a folktale: the two words, *except me* will have been sufficient; one single exception would send the great principles, the rights of man, the immortal truths, and theodicy itself into full-blown retreat; worse yet; the great principle was only an absurdity and a contradiction? Quite simply, just nonsense! At a minimum, the shocking inequality is a complication that expressly requires an explanation, something like an anomaly that waits to be normalized, a dissymmetry that requires being offset, a violence whose consequences have to be equalized. But the denial of justice is not only an illogicality that runs counter to reason: it provokes passionate responses and vindicative reflexes, anger, indignation, and resentment. The unjustifiable injustice is absurd, but the revolting iniquity causes a scandal. The iniquity was in reality an unmentionable, a scandalous persecution, and I protest against it: the insurrectional refusal joins the reasoning of reason, the reasoning confirms and legalizes the refusal. I do not accept being damned, I do not accept being personally excommunicated from the juridical and moral community, the one that extends to all men up to the last one, to all humans by definition, without exception or with any exclusion: I protest against this impossible supposition that is against me, against this irrational discrimination that is to my detriment.

In the providential interaction of a philautia legitimized by philanthropy and a philanthropy reinforced and vitalized by philautia, there is something suspect: a worrying exchange of good processes! This suspect something is assuredly not a miraculous coincidence, or an exceptional occasion, even less, as one could vulgarly claim, a "windfall." In fact, this "good fortune" rests on a harmony that is permanent . . . and approximative of personal interest and general interest. Indeed, the incorrigible optimist is always tempted to help out good fortune; he tells himself that in working for himself, he also works for others; he deploys for this purpose improvidences of ingenuity, of bad faith . . . What flair! What a stealthy complacency! There is nothing here other than mercenariness, the commutation of service, tit-for-tat . . . But love, in all this, where has it gone? What has become of it? love, that is, the loving vocation? love, that is, an inspired heat? As with my power, which is the latitude to act and a zone of possibilities beyond the real, "my rights" are an affirmative zone around the ego that enlarges my being-proper. The collection of my rights-proper constitutes a sort of "juridical minimum" that is, in its own way, the normative form of the least evil. One will be surprised to hear that my rights, those to which *I have the right,* and with full right, are an "evil" . . . But that is the lesser—at least given the collection of circumstances! How can this positivity which for me is an assurance and a power, how can this Plus that is a guarantor of my security, be an evil, be it the least, be it the smallest possible? To be surprised by something that is so unsurprising is to misunderstand the fact of the alternative and of finitude, and this is thus to misunderstand the paradox of happy misery. My rights simultaneously amount to *a little* [*un peu*] and *little of anything* [*peu de chose*]: a little, that is to say, more than nothing, that is to say, a humble assurance against brutishness, plunder, and violence; a little, that is, almost-nothing, or barely something, or in any case the least possible, all that is necessary so as not to be annihilated . . . Rights, owing to their normative character, are worth more than the arbitrariness of violence without belief or faith, but love itself is worth more than anything! As with having, and as with being itself, inasmuch as being is a fixed deposit, my rights are an opaque region in which light penetrates only with difficulty, an inert world in which the impetus of love raises itself up with some effort and falls back down immediately. But in the measure in which my right-proper, even the most personal, is never absolutely deprived of all ideality, one should be able to say: this particular zone is that of the clear-obscure. Me, the beneficiary of the rights of man, I am thereby the titulary of a moral credit that however moral it may be, is a credit all the same, a credit whose management for me is a source of delights, of worries, of content. Justice for me, just as for the entire human race! Justice . . . for the entire human race: that is the part for open morality. But first, justice for myself! Justice for the small, closed world, for this pretty garden, for this microcosm that is closed in on itself and which has the I as its center. Does this immanent harmony whose intrinsic elements are so dense and so well balanced and polished merit being called justice when it does not even make an exception for the other person [*l'autre*]? In the substantialist language of egocentric logic, my rights are wholly a positivity, and it is they that anticipate and condition my duties.

Can one admit that *my* right, closing the loop, secondarily returns to me via *your* duty? that my rights are simply a fortuitous consequence of the duties of others [*autrui*]? somehow a ricochet effect? Far from it! This would be worse than derisory good luck: this would be a true poverty! But there is more: the demand, when it is a matter of my right, is not only forestalling, it is also, as we were stating, essentially protesting and consequently jealous and touchy, even arrogant: the demand immediately gives rise to a revolutionary gesture that would make up for the injustice. My right is not the object of a Platonic declaration: even less is this a favor or alms for which I beg and in exchange for which I would owe to those who grant them to me gratitude and heartfelt thanks. After all, this right is due to me. And I only claim my right. That's the least of it! The man who demands speaks loudly and strongly. For his right itself has the strength of the coalition (of the complicity?) that connects the norm to instinct: the cartel that justice enters into with pleonexia, if it is the source of misunderstandings, represents, however, a double force; the man assured by his right suppresses scruples and ulterior motives, if there are any; anger smolders within him, ready to explode.—The man assured by his right believes himself to be equally assured of his intimate good conscience, and this apparent good conscience is the conscience of not "postulating" anything; the demand of the man who speaks loudly endeavors to be clear of any gratuity, of anything arbitrary; nothing vague, ambiguous, or allusive; no timidity, no sunset clause. Everything is strict and rigorous. This good conscience excludes up to the suspicion of a nascent bad conscience; nothing that is phobia or masochism, mania for persecution or martyr's passion touches its assurance lightly. Will it be necessary for justice to make a pronouncement against me so as to appear just to me? for justice to be just only when it is at my expense? I do not make an exception to common law, even if common law for once favors me! even if justice serves my interest! It is not, after all, a scandal that the law grants me my right, and neither is it a reason to consider this law suspect. Independent of every egoistic or reasonable justification, in certain cases it is necessary to admit an advantage with simplicity.

3. Everyone Has Rights, Except Me. I Have Only Duties. To You Belong All the Rights, to Me All the Responsibilities.

But precisely: the deafening and resounding good conscience [*bon conscience*] of my legitimate right [*bon droit*] speaks at the top of its lungs only so as to cover up deep within itself another voice buried in my heart of hearts: this other voice is the humble, secret voice of the bad conscience. This good conscience that is so assured and, in fact, so profoundly ambivalent wanted first to convince itself. In the tone of its voice a hesitation was detectable—in its insolence itself a profound incertitude, in vociferation itself a hidden timidity and one that is like an imperceptible tremor . . . Let us reestablish the thread of paradoxes that has been momentarily broken. And first, what is paradoxical with the first generation is directly related to what is doxical and to the truisms stemming from the principle of identity: everyone has rights, thus me too; my right then appeared as a link in the continuity of a reassuring deduction. And now, conversely, we would rather say: everyone has rights except me; here the preposition *except,* digging a hole in lieu of a *therefore,* occurs with the brutality of a break, an injurious and scandalous break that, in this pitiful world in which everyone has a right to defend, gives a halting blow to the generalization of the moral right over itself and a blind denial of its universality. *On condition of* not myself being a Machiavellian and subtly hypocritical candidate for heroism, I voluntarily profess the offensive exception, the unmentionable *numerus clausus,* that forever excludes me from any claim. I will only be a disinherited person and a pariah. Even though he has not expressly wished for his own dispossession, the man without rights renounces everything connected with becoming bourgeois and accepts the purity of absolute destitution. For his part, this is neither affectation nor coquettishness nor masochism: for all that, both the mania for persecution and the delectation of the martyr still represent for the hypocrite ways of securing his right. The just person, a victim of extreme injustice, such as Job and his scandalously unmerited trials, ultimately is mistaken for the disinterested, desperate lover, who loves without consideration.

The cynic does not know any other rights than his own rights for himself; and these are not, thus, *rights* in the normative sense since it is an issue of bare fact. My own rights for me are quite simply the absolute of violence and pleonexia without measure or limits. That is the beautiful axiom of egoism. And justice rectifies, brings nuances and alterations: the rights of man are my rights of man for me, limited, adjusted, and, if need be, suspended by the rights of others, by the rights of the greatest number of men possible; this is at least what is left of them. And here now is the austere truth: the rights of man are the rights of others, without concessions or compensations, without accommodation of any sort. Far from right and duty being able to be con-

sidered as the positive and the negative, the right side out
and the backward of one same moral reality, the dissymmetry between the one and the other is radical. The paradox of
paradoxes, for whoever does not want to fall back into the
pious hypocrisy of good conscience, is summed up in this:
a priori and theoretically, I have rights, but strictly speaking and ultimately, I do not have any right. And first: I have
rights. My rights—those at least to which *I have the right*—exist or, rather, consist in juridical objectivity and social reciprocity: they overlap each other, stick to one another, form
a system of intelligibles, a sort of staged theater piece that
somehow constitutes our ethical assets; better yet, they
are reified, enumerable, and we do not cease reciting, with
many variations, the list of them; we name them as the ancient astronomers named the stars in the sphere of Fixed
Stars. They do not change color according to the light and do
not depend upon the point of view. Compared to the speculative optics of the monad of monads, every monad, as the
bearer of intangible rights, is ideally worth another. And
the bearers of rights, in turn, are theoretically equal, if not
interchangeable.

4. The Reification and Objectivity of Rights, the Inequality and Irreversibility of Duty.

In this firmament of rights and norms, duty brings to the
fore a principle of destabilization and worry: our axiological patrimony is put on hold. The transformative action
that is our vocation accentuates the contingent and amend-
able character of that which is given; the given seems to be
wholly other . . . Duty brings disparity with it, or even in-

equality [*l'imparité*]. For duty is essentially *uneven* [*impair*]! Scruple, humility, the passion for completing and amending are born in its wake; in humanizing juridical equality, in overturning egoistic unevenness, which is all for my benefit, duty institutes unevenness at my expense . . . Put differently, the man of duty is fundamentally *disinterested.* Beyond every mercenary aspect, the man of duty professes (if one can say "profess"!) a magnificent negligence with respect to the regularity, with respect to the equilibrium, with respect to the symmetry of the *tit-for-tat.* The relation called duty has the same meaning as generosity, mercy, or love, and this is a relation in *one direction;* but the dominant feature of this relation is rather the voluntarist rigor of devotion than anxious and tender solicitude. In any case, be it imperative exigency or loving spontaneity, duty thwarts the transformation of the good movement into merit or into a thing; it keeps us in suspense; it mobilizes and unceasingly remobilizes the good movement that is always tempted to admire itself in the mirror of contentment and to turn in circles; the extreme tension of duty prevents the hoarding of merits and the capitalization of virtues; duty progressively breaks our baby's rattles and little toys. An exhausting and passionate tension, duty maintains an open conscience. Open on to what? on to which future? The magnetic pole that attracts from a distance and orients the intention is called the second person; this future is simultaneously close and distant . . . So close, so distant! It is the neighboring future [*le future prochain*],[1] because it points a finger at the first thing that is a non-me outside me and in its immediate tangency with me, because it is *barely* a non-me, because it is *almost* me without being me; in time it thus designates an *urgent* duty or at least relates to an *imminent* task. And in addition to this, duty aims at another always other, infinitely other than me and even other than every other; other with an infinite exponent. The fascinated and, so to speak, magnetized moral will is no longer where it was: across the void, the will in its willing has made the perilous jump to meet instantaneously the thing willed and miraculously to identify with it; the magnetized will, as we were saying concerning ecstasy, is off its hinges. Isn't this the sort of ecstasy that would have to be called intentionality? The will on this point is as miraculous as love: the space left empty by the forgetting-of-self, if one dares say it, causes a draft: provided that the relation of the one to the other, or more simply the relation tout court, will have a meaning. And not only is the subject no longer where it was, it is no longer what it was, it is no longer itself. This second enchantment, all in all, is but one with the first. Omnipresence and metamorphosis, ultimately, are confounded. Whether a loving subject or a willing subject, the subject is simultaneously here and there, and it is simultaneously the same and the other, itself and wholly other. In the empty space, there is no thing, or even something else, there is an end that is passionately willed, and there is the accusative of love, which is entirely impetus and entirely fervor. The vocation of duty calls me to live for the other while remaining inexplicably myself. It will be shown that this impetus is innocence. Indeed, obstacles are not lacking that would make it go off course. Here are the three principal ones that are among the most dangerous: the first naturally is villainous instinct and ogreliness [*ogrerie*], the *autos* and its bestial *philautia;* for the human being to be transformed into a human person and a subject of duty, he must first drain out his substantial egoity. May he become a type of nothingness under the gaze of the other! The second obstacle is professional altruism, which creates out of philanthropy a specialty for the use of a clientele: the altruist begins again to be lethargic and to chug along. And the third obstacle is the movement of a scrupulous retroversion of the man, who in denying the vocation of duty and forgetting his distant-neighbor [*prochain-lointain*], would fall back on the self not reflexively but pathologically so as to deepen his own manias.

The egocentric optics that is based on the persons of the various conjugations entails at every instant the most paradoxical reversals. Likewise, it is necessary to stipulate and specify unceasingly the irrational stipulation of the *point of view:* this stipulation is an apparently circumstantial, even anecdotal and derisory and as a result negligible, detail; however, it reverses all the judgments of value, and it is thus morally decisive. The circumstance is more essential than the essence. Small causes, great effects. Gracián and Pascal, as one knows, are quite attached to this metaphysics of derision. In the interpersonal objectivity of the monad of monads, all the rights of the human person are eternal, absolute, and equally and infinitely valid. But the mystery of the *plural absolute,* which is that of persons, upsets this serene heaven. The moral being is also a psychosomatic being; he is at the mercy of his carnal finitude and of derisory stipulations: by imposing a partial optics on all humans, the unilateral privilege of the first person, egocentrism is somehow the lived image of a caricatural universe in which only monsters live. Can one say that the centrism of this center is organized in us in the manner of an a priori? This would be to forget that the a priori is rational, that the priority of the me [*le moi*], conversely, is rather biological and instinctive. Can one say at least that *the me* is the center around which is ordered my own microcosm—my egoistic microcosm? *The me* (with an article) is a general entity, a concept that already presupposes the reduction of deformities born of egocentrism and that in some measure neutralizes or compensates for, explains or excuses these deformities: in saying 'the me' from the height of my objectivity, 'the me' and not 'me' [*non pas moi*], not 'me' [qua 'the one'] who speaks to you and who writes this, in this very place and in this very moment, I [*je*] already take my distance with respect to this unmentionable, egoistic preference: I got rid of it; me and myself no longer form a one-piece block; I relinquished my state of substantial indivision with myself. It is the act of awareness that established this fission. Later the split consciousness can return on purpose to the stage of indivision, can profess in doctoral fashion, that is, cynically, the original egocentrism and make its religion out of it: sometimes it abounds in insolence and builds on instinct; sometimes it consents in complete lucidity to the egoistic inclination; its egocentrism becomes egotropism, and it gives in to all temptations: retraction into the self, moral gravity, and phobia of the other and of opening up. But if it adheres to its own naturality, it is because it has already theoretically dissociated itself from it. The history of consciousness will do the rest . . . For one does not limit the infinite consequences of an act of awareness!

5. The First Person Passes Last, the Second Becomes First. I Am the Defender of Your Rights, I Am Not the Policeman of Your Duties.

The conversion from one extreme to the other, from one extreme to the diametrically opposed extreme, marks for the conscience the advent of a moral life: the first person, first for myself according to grammar and conjugations, passes last: always for me; the second person, that of the partner (the Thou) pneumatically becomes the first, the entirely first for me, dislodges me from my egoity, and takes my place . . . all while remaining a numerically different person: it will be, because of the passionate interest that I take in its existence and happiness, my new first person! *Esontai hoi eschatoi protoi kai hoi protoi eschatoi:* the last will be first and the first will be last;[2] this revolutionary interchanging of the ordinal number is the sign of a still more radical reversal, of an ascetic and literally supernatural reversal that serves as a prelude for the reversal of reflexes and the advent of a naturality that is counter to nature. Supernature simultaneously transcends nature and the nature that is counter to nature . . . which is never anything but nature in reverse! Or rather, supernaturality will never be, in action, counter-natural, will never become habituated to walking with its head hung low: a relentless fight, at least, becomes possible between disinterested love and reflexes harassed by scruples. The preservation of the being-proper and the augmentation of its assets-proper will henceforth come in the very last place, after the tender solicitude that our neighbor inspires in us. The most elementary forms of courtesy and sociability are like a timid but still quite conventional approach of abnegation: the glutton restrains his gluttony and serves himself last; he habituates himself to choosing the smallest portion, not for teaching a glorious lesson to the gallery, but, if it is possible, out of pure kindness; the captain of a sinking ship leaves the vessel last, not theatrically and to immortalize his example, like the admiral in the film *Kind Hearts and Coronets,*[3] but so as to save the most men possible.

With a conversion that is sudden and often without a to-morrow, my duty toward others thus dislodges the egocentrism that was occupying the first place—all of the place. This *primacy* of duty, of my own duty for me, is not, as is the *priority* of instinct and of my right, a simple biological and chronological priority: but neither is this an *ontological* primacy, like that of the impersonal rights of man qua man. If the priority of instinct is rather *preexistent,* then the primacy of duty is *forestalling* [*prévenante*]: the problems that it poses for us we face in connection with a crisis of conscience, that is, a conflict of values. Ultimately and in principle I have only duties with respect to my neighbor, without morally having the least right over him, and notably without having a right to the least recompense: such is the disinterested truth, the austere and ungrateful truth of duty! And as for you, my neighbor, you merely have rights over me without having duties with respect to me, at least duties for which I could morally require respect: your duties toward me do not concern me! To you all the rights, to me all the duties and all the responsibilities! And as if that were not sufficient: my duty, more than any other thing, is applied to the preservation of your rights, it encompasses and commands this preservation as one of its most imperative requirements. What is sacred for me and the object of my daily worry and my constant solicitude is not so much the rights of the human being in general, among which are mine, but above all the rights of the other and, more specifically, yours—for I work for your rights, and not for mine: the first of my duties is respect for others [*autrui*], for their dignity, for their rights, for their honor; for this honor that is not mine, I fight and if need be sacrifice myself; I have to be capable of dying for that honor. Not because your honor or dishonor would be a part of mine, or would be shared by me, as in tribal morality, but solely because this honor is yours and for that reason alone . . . which is not *a reason!* I am not the policeman of your duties, but I am the defender of your rights.

Rights are a *more* that is a *less;* and conversely, duties are a *less* that is a *more.* Rights are a Plus, of course, when one considers them in their relation to norms in themselves, to the eternal and metaphysical values of which these glittering medals, these crosses, and these multicolored ribbons are the reflection and the symbol, or rather, the memory . . . ; somehow the summary! But the signs of a past courage are no longer courage itself: for courage is in the present instant: and merit needs to be continually renewed and renovated, rejuvenated, and updated; one is not able to live all one's life on claims to fame from forty years ago: what happened before, in matters of heroism, does not count! The rights that are inscribed, that are spread in capital letters on the chest of the brave person, a man covered with rights, armored with titles, and adorned with prizes, these rights have become a mere power, that is, a static, inert, and desiccated possession like all possessions: the meritorious man, overwhelmed by these relics of a defunct past, ends up suffocating under their weight. Just as a virtue isolated from other virtues is a vice, so the truth of my right, exiled from duty, is nothing more than an abstraction, that is, a lie.

A less that is a more: such is duty. But first, a less: for its arid and thankless tasks require the sacrifice of my own interest and are taken from my leisure time and my freedom. Your rights, it is you to whom they come back or belong, but it is I on whom their defense *is incumbent:* and in this form they are the most sacred of *my* duties: it is not my role to enforce my own rights, or to demand what is due to me, or even to speak of it—for the consciousness of my own right, considered reflexively and in the first person, is never moral; it remains the prisoner of interest and sordidness. The man of duty himself does not work to justify more or less hypocritically his own right and his own ambition, he is rather there to sanctify the happiness of others. The positive and the negative, by joining forces, impart the contours and the relief of ambivalence to duty. Sublimity and misery, Pascal would say . . . Our finitude invariably comes up against the same alternative, against the same insurmountable barrier. One cannot have all the advantages at the same time! Anguish will thus be, as always, the fatal ransom of our dignity . . . The charge that incumbers us is our weighty responsibility, and it holds a lot of grief in store for us. Noblesse oblige . . . Dignity obliges! But it is not, of course, *on account* of nobility that the man of duty pursues this exhausting, eternally unfinished undertaking . . . It is not so as to play the role of a noble that he remains loyal, without any hope of reward, to the endless opus.

The relativity of the persons of the conjugations is summed up in the end for all men in the opposition of two universes, and one could even say of two landscapes: the first, which is a point of view, my point of view, and which is the egocentric cosmos, distorted and ceaselessly changing, viewed through the tiny dormer windows of my body; the other, which is the non-me on the whole, the objective universe, the universe of others [*autrui*], and of all the others [*autres*]. The impalpable fact of being another, that is, of being my own similar-different person, monadically distinct from myself, is, if one can say it, the cause of a love that is without cause. The impalpable cause can have as an effect only an inexplicable love. To love the other simply because he is another, without any reason and independent of his merits, this is the distinctive feature of a pure and disinterested love, an unmotivated love. Because it is I, because it is she: this circular *because* that does not respond to a why and refers to itself, here you have the absurd formula of gratuitous love. When the response is ultimately the simple repetition of the question, this signifies: there is no other reason to love than the fact of pure alterity . . . which is obviously not a reason, at least not a sufficient reason; the fact that the other is the other—my other—whatever this other may be, this fact is a tautology and could not suffice. But what use is it to spin one's wheels? It would thus be necessary to claim that it is precisely the absence of any reason that is the reason. But to desire at all costs that the absence of reason itself be a reason is to interpret the incomparable gratuity of love in a pedantic way. Outside even the verbal character of this sleight of hand, one can observe that the taste of humans for absurd or ridiculous loves is still an affectation, and of the most alienating kind . . . Disinterested love, unmotivated love is not the passing fancy of a stubborn lover. No, pure love is not a whim. But it is also the opposite of an absurd obstinacy: the truth is that being itself a founder of a causality, it anticipates every etiology; it is categorically imperative precisely because it is unconditional; like restorative perfumes, it is paradoxically, absurdly an inspiration. On the other hand, our love for the alterity of the other is a pure love because it is meant for the very essence of the beloved being. That which it loves is not this or that eminent quality of such and such a beloved person (an exceptional gift in this person here, a remarkable talent of that person there), for love in that case would be second with respect to what is lovable, and would die out with the quality that gave birth to it: this poor, mercenary, motivated and conditional love lags behind a because; it breaks up and dissipates among the reasons for loving, and its high temperature is lowered; the fervent flame of love, always forestalling, which burns in loving ecstasy and in the forgetting of self, will never come to know it.

The reasons for loving, when they claim to motivate love, are transformed into bankable commodities, into negotiable, and as a result revocable, securities. Let us go farther: the precious, the inestimable movement of intention, as soon as it becomes aware of itself, becomes an inert schema and counterfeit money; all moral scaffolding rests on the fragile point of innocence: the edifice, deprived of the inspirational instant, collapsed in one fell swoop, and all that remains of it is rubble. Better still, and using other images: to debunk the bluff of the vain person one word was enough, a monosyllable, a possessive adjective . . . *My* good movement, *my* disinterestedness. Thus the merits the ego is claiming deteriorate, thus the eminent virtues the subject is claiming for itself atrophy: these virtues ring hollow not because such meritorious qualities would in themselves be condemnable but on account of the presumptuous fact of claiming them and taking advantage of them, and even quite simply of speaking of them. A caricature of consciousness, the complacent "reflexivity" of the me [*moi*] is a deleterious poison. There are qualities that are immediately or ipso facto contradicted, refuted, and annulled by the reflexivity of the possessive adjective (my modesty, my humor, my innocence!), others that are made farcical and doubtful by the mere addition of the I [*Je*] (my dignity!): the grandeur of soul is, if not obliterated, at least made smaller by conceit and pettiness. Even when the satisfaction of the one who brandishes his beau-

tiful soul like a saber is not without an agenda, it is nevertheless suspect and questionable, to say the least.—Here is,
then, a truth that is objectively true . . . and that I, none-
theless, do not have the right to say: as soon as I say it (and
precisely me and not you or such and such another person),
it becomes immoral, ridiculous, and even completely false!
Such are the two opposite and apparently arbitrary forms of
one same aseity: truth pneumatically becomes a lie (while
remaining literally true), solely because I profess it and because I am of bad faith; a falsehood pneumatically becomes
a truth (while remaining false) because I love with a sincere
love and because a sincere love has neither accounts due nor
justifications to provide. In all cases, forestalling love is *causa
sui!* Depending on whether I speak the flattering truth about
my soul myself or someone else says it for me (if it is, and
make note of this, the same truth), flattering truth changes
meaning completely, it changes lighting and range; and if I
scream it from the rooftops it becomes, to be frank, shocking and absurd. And all this, and make note of it again, solely
because this is I and for that sole reason! One will say again
that this sole reason is still not a reason, that it is instead a
counter-reason. The most veridical veracity, even made up
for by the reductant that one calls "a personal equation," is
still imperceptibly falsified: it is the a priori of egoity that is
in question here. Is the excuse of the first person a simple
grammatical precision? Far from it! This irritating precision
is not a vain, anecdotal, and circumstantial detail. If the dis-
tortion that it reveals to us amounts to an arbitrary and gratuitous whim, it would be nothing: an insignificant peccadillo,
a mere emphatic and picturesque exaggeration. Well, it is
about a constitutional fatality, and this fatality is more perfidious than the discord of appearance and essence: for it con-

cerns not the relation of truth to error but the moral qualifi-
cation of the person. My virtues, provided that I boast about
them, become vices, that is, tics and ridiculous obsessions,
or turn into comical gestures. My merits—the very ones that
at the time and objectively were dazzling merits—have been
drivel for quite some time. My talents are nothing more than
a bluff, boastfulness, and an instrument of ambitiousness.
What is, ultimately, properly irrational and even a bit diabolical is the inexplicable contradiction inherent in the *ethical
minimum:* the ethical minimum, when demanded, becomes
juridical, and the juridical minimum, when demanded, becomes in turn a deposit without life, an asset, and a certifi-
cate of ownership; the ethical minimum is, at the end of the
day, locked in a strongbox, and that on account of the sole
effect of the demand, by virtue of the most legal of claims,
and thus with full right. Normativity is demanded here, it is
not usurped, it does not result from a misappropriation. It is
this normativity of one of the two contradictions that made
us say: perhaps the contradiction is diabolical? The contradiction is perhaps a malediction? The *I* [*Je*] that poisons our
just rights is perhaps cursed? Who knows whether the malediction of the contradiction is not a trick of the evil genius! In
any case, one would thus explain the sometimes somewhat
terroristic nature of a repression that, in language, prohib-
its and censures the first person and that contrasts the phobia of the *I* [*Je*] with the malady of conceit. It is forbidden
to whisper the cursed monosyllable. It is forbidden even to
think about it. All these vetoes for a monosyllable! Indeed,
we were saying 'phobia' where it would be perhaps necessary to say 'propriety.' A phobia is a pathological anomaly,
but propriety is the rarest, the most delicate, and the most
exquisite flower of moral existence. Here the monosyllable is

only a breath, a light breathing, a barely audible confession. Rights—do understand: my rights, not yours—verify and justify this discretion: they want to remain incognito, they ask us for anonymity. It is forbidden for us to accept our own rights! It is forbidden for us to profess them . . . Good-bye, my rights! And yet my rights are just and true. *And yet* (*eppure*) . . . These two words express the stubborn truth of the paradoxology that scandalously protests against the vulgar and continually reborn obviousnesses of common sense. In the end, the status of my own rights and dignity is not founded either upon that which is obvious or upon that which is not obvious: it is rather shrouded in ambivalence and ambiguity; it is essentially disconcerting. Mitigated by the soft pedal of propriety, the claim claims sotto voce, becomes timid, evasive, and sometimes almost private; in the dark, what is obvious becomes blurry, and what is insolent becomes certitude, void of its dogmatic assurance, appears doubtful and foggy. The universal rights of man are ultimately intangible and, in a manner of speaking, impalpable rights, ones that it is scandalous to deny to others, and that I cannot, however, claim for myself. Isn't this an unjustifiable injustice? an insoluble contradiction? The me [*moi*] is hateful. Hide this me [*moi*] which I would not be able to see. Without a doubt, isn't the *I* [*Je*] made for seeing itself? But in the end . . . so many scruples concerning a monosyllable? so many scruples and all the agonies of the bad conscience? The insignificance of the petty truth and the meditation that it brings us—now here is a very Pascalian subject of meditation. Derision of derisions! What a derision! Again, everything depends upon this petty detail, everything depends upon this detail: the number changes everything, decides everything. By the way, the irony of this caricatural disproportion between the me [*moi*] and truth—an irony that is similar enough, owing to its un-bounded consequences, to Cleopatra's nose, isn't that rather a mystery? Indisputably, such a contrast has its comical sides and it is to this mysterious comedian that it is necessary for us to give the name *paradox*.

6. Opening of One's Eyes. The Loss of Innocence Is the Ransom That the Thinking Reed Must Pay for the Price of Its Dignity.

In the interior of the ethical minimum, the consciousness-of-self can appear, in certain cases, as the heaviest part of our baggage, when the stock of our memories, of our traditions, and of our prejudices builds up in it. For the consciousness of self is, like freedom itself, a double-edged sword: it is the reflexive liberation that puts an end to vegetative indivision; but in the measure in which it sometimes is introversion and retroversion, it is also perversion and diverts us from our vocation, which is to act and to love: in this very way it can become quite perfidiously and very subtly fallacious. The disparity of the effects of consciousness [*conscience*] is implied in the narrative in Genesis: the appearance of conscience [*conscience*] is the principle of the opening of one's eyes, that is, of clairvoyance, but this clairvoyance itself is the discernment of Good and Evil, *dignoscentia,* knowing the Good by Evil, and Evil by the Good, a relative knowledge linked to the effect of relief, and it has as a consequence shame, the phobia of nakedness, the search for shade: "The man and his companion hid from the face of God among the trees in the garden."[4] The shameful knowledge, which looks for the clear-obscure in paradise, is thus not compatible with a blessed eternity. This alternative of felicity and a knowledge split-in-two would somehow be the original tare. Let us say more: simultaneously lucid and generative of opacities, consciousness is that which makes innocence so fragile, so unstable; innocence asks only to veer off: one single grain of dust suffices to render purity impure, to make the immaculate whiteness into a grayness—an infinitesimal shaking of consciousness, an imperceptible fold in my simplicity—and the superlative of innocence is already far away. Good-bye, innocence. Consciousness and shame have killed candor in me. The serpent does not need eloquence to instill in my heart of hearts the drop of venom of a false promise: the key to its art of persuasion lies in a light whisper . . . Man is weak, credulous, accessible to temptations! But here it is, with its insoluble alternative, the tragedy of the contradiction—a tragedy that is still more acute than that of merit and legitimate pride—: innocence is the vital condition of a love without ulterior motives, of a courageous and spontaneous action; and the conscience is my irreplaceable superiority over the thinking reed![5] For one can call tragedy a crisis of conscience in which it is the conscience itself that is in question. This crisis of conscience is a hopeless dilemma. The *priority* of innocence and the *a priori* of the thinking consciousness [*conscience*] are as "forestalling" as each other; they vie to preempt one another over and over. Consciousness is wholly reflection; but the conscience is also a nascent affectation that is always ready to split itself in two, to gaze at itself and admire itself in the mirror, to listen to itself, quite busy, all in all, with looking good; instead of looking straight ahead of itself at the goal that is its intentional aim, it squints toward its own image and watches itself out of the corner of its eye play the comedy of its own life. That too is the conscience! The conscience, it too, is a means that stands in the way. The warped conscience becomes vicious starting from the moment in which the obstacle wins out over the organ. Consciousness exists only in the act of *becoming aware [prendre conscience]*. So how can the thinking being prevent itself from becoming aware? For that, it would be necessary to become a little child! It would be necessary not to become aware of this consciousness [*conscience*], to shun all the way up to the thought of this thought . . . Thus, do not think about it, and above all . . . shhh! do not speak about it. It is forbidden to think about the thought of the thought! Provided that the superconsciousness [*surconscience*] of the conscience [*conscience*] lightly grazes you, as imponderable as this may be, complacency and affectation have already put on their masks and inscribed their grimace on your face; the comical gestures have chased away innocence. *Do not pretend,* Alain counsels us in one of his most subtle "statements."[6] For pretension, ambition, and demands weigh heavily and indiscreetly on the conscience; they crush its fine point without one being able to say at what moment the insistence becomes suspect.

The superconsciousness has a refined ear: so it does not remain ingenuous for long. It hears it said and whispered that everyone has rights; and this philanthropic truth does not fall on deaf ears. Moreover, it is endowed with memory, which makes it capable of skimming over the instantaneous reality of the present. Why would this universal nobility apply to all human beings except to itself, except to myself, a reflective subject? There is nothing privileged about that type of nobility, and there is no reason, let us recall, to exclude myself from it; every excommunication in such matters is arbitrary, discriminatory, and scandalous. Likewise, the thinking conscience, threatened by a scandalous denial of justice, by an incomprehensible numerus clausus, does not take long to apply to itself, to claim for itself, with a direct extrapolation or a simple deduction, these rights of man that are valid without any exception for all men. The respect for this elementary asset is indeed the least that one owes us.

7. Your Duties Are Not the Foundation of My Rights.

But I can become aware of the reverse: if it is true that I have rights like you, then it is no less true that, after all, you have duties like me. From this recognition of your rights to the thought of my correlative rights is only one step. And this step is quickly traversed. For the ego does not lose its mind ... To construe the duties of others as translating in intaglio that which in relief would justify my own rights, to annex to one's own assets and to one's own credit the duties and obligations of others, here you have without a doubt a less direct inference than the first one, but more ingenious and just as convincing. A somewhat casual and gratuitous speculation, in fact! We were saying: I have only duties. But just as everyone is, thank God, in the same situation, the set of these duties of other people assures me of a certain latitude in acting, clears around me a notable freedom of movement, and like a fringe of authority; in other words, the consciousness of the subject, aerated by the duties of others toward it, has available to it several rights to undertake and a small margin for finishing the work undertaken. In one way or another, whether I wanted it or not, the universality of the rights of others toward me will make my life more livable, the action more viable, the coexistence more breathable, and the world more habitable; I will be somewhat discharged of my charges; I will experience a tiny bit of relief. So that in fact the question of the impossible duty will not arise in its literal rigor: there will not be an aporia; a modus vivendi, thanks to this misunderstanding, is found in advance! However, your duties were not made expressly for enriching and reinforcing my rights; the rights of others did not originally have as a goal to ensure my ease and my welfare. This is simply a fortuitous occasion that is offered to me, which I exploit to my advantage, an unforeseen opportunity of which I eagerly make use. This opportunity is the correlation, or better yet the specular symmetry, of your duty and my right, a symmetry that makes possible the sleight of hand of the interchanging: your duty will be my right. This opportunity is unexpected and even unlocatable since, in addition, the protection of my rights has become an obligation for the partner . . . as if the unique protection were not sufficient! as if it were part of its moral code! In fact, and ipso facto, my right stems from your duty, and that without any express intervention on my part, without my claiming anything, without my even thinking about it . . . This unexpected favor that I have neither solicited nor in any way sought, and this supplementary right that I did not expressly claim, are somehow a happy surprise, and I receive them innocently as my personal opportunity or rather as a grace; after the fact I find myself in possession of several unexpected facilities. I welcome these duties of others toward me, fraternal aid or duties of assistance, with a relaxed soul and an incredulous heart, almost timidly, and while resisting all arrogance. Blessed is the surprise that rang one morning at the door of my dwelling, like a friend on whom I was no longer counting.

Everything for me is duty. And consequently, your rights

are perceived and lived by me as being the first of my duties, the most urgent, and the most imperative: they would have to be my worry, my intention, my daily anguish, and the object of my solicitude. The rights of the other are themselves for me so many duties that I must accept and jealously preserve, as one watches over an infinitely precious treasure. But that does not mean, however, that the reverse is true and that your own duties are automatically my rights, corresponding obligatorily to my own rights . . . This would be too beautiful, too convenient! This would be a fairy tale, a veritable enchantment, a providential harmony; but above all, this symmetry would be too exemplary, the reciprocity too fake . . . with, in addition, a suspect whiff of bad faith: if your rights sketch in relief my duties, then the proposal is far from being reversible. I thus cannot morally apply to myself any of these two interested reasonings, any of the two supporting sophisms devised for my benefit: or deduce my own rights from the rights of man in general, or even less, profit from the welcome moral latitude that the moral rectitude of others allows me, and merrily avail myself of the facilities that are for me the result of it. Or at least, isn't it for me to judge that, and no more in the second case than in the first case: these are only contrived tricks for avoiding my duties.—In reality, the rights that result for me from your duties are like relapses and leftovers of these same duties; forgotten crumbs . . . specks of dust! Anyway, I allow these unexpected rights to come to me via your duties; they come back by a stroke of good luck after having swerved suddenly, and I pick up a few paltry crumbs at the moment in which I least expected it.—So your duties will perhaps be my rights, and I will benefit from them . . . *on condition* of not indiscreetly watching this swerve effect, *on condition* of not counting too much on it, as on something owed, *on condition* of not insisting too consciously, too reflexively, too expressly. On condition of, on condition of . . . This condition, always the same, is to avoid the excess of consciousness that gets in the way of innocence, that plays fast and loose with its secret. Such a speculation about the duties of others can transpose a great absence of tact, a great moral vulgarity. I do not ignore that my partner, too, has duties, duties that once the moment has come will ease my effort and help me to live. But for now, it is better to forget that. Until further notice, it is preferable that I do not count too much on your duties to lighten my task. First of all, the jobs of the one and the other do not form a single job in which it is the result that would count, one single task in view of which the solidary drudgeries would be able to help each other and join their efforts, a unique oeuvre that would be completed morsel by morsel thanks to the effort of all . . . In this case, your work effectively releases me from mine, and the substitute would be able to replace the one for whom it substitutes: for that which is done is no longer to be done . . . in the measure in which it is about *doing* something! That which is done by the one would be deduced from the task of the other, would be deducted from the duty of the other; that which is done would be *at least done!* Well, it is not! We must renounce all these ingenious conveniences . . . Good-bye beautiful economy of effort and the harmonious complementarity of tasks. The intention, the responsibility, the moral decision of sacrifice are essentially solitary initiatives that no one can make in my place and from which no one can release me. Each here must work and toil for his own reckoning instead of relying on his neighbor. A man can devote himself in the place of another in such-and-such a determinate circumstance: but in the ultimate instant each dies alone; and in the same way each has to toil and suffer for himself, as if he were alone in the world; no one can do anything for him. More exactly still: I fight for your rights and for your existence, and I would even be ready, if this were not absurd and even contradictory, to accept your duties myself and in your place. There is in all cases a crude trick we can avoid: I do not have to supervise the exercise of your duties, or dictate to you the list of them; I do not check the benefit that I could derive from them or the advantages that I expect: these suspicious precautions do not concern the disinterested man, the man of duty and rectitude. In this opinion, there is no direct communication, no osmosis between your duties and my rights. I do not have to throw myself like a starving man, with an unseemly eagerness, on the duties of Peter and Paul: Peter and Paul are themselves busy with what encumbers them, and that in complete innocence, just as we ourselves work, suffer, and toil for them without expecting anything from them, neither a salary nor remuneration nor recognition. This is why it is necessary to tell oneself and tell oneself again tirelessly: I am the unconditional defender of your rights, I am not the policeman of your duties. *To each his duties,* henceforth, could not be the pathetic formula of egoism, but quite the contrary: the currency of universal disinterestedness and of this universal innocence in which men meet and, outside every mercenary relationship, exchange among themselves the kiss of peace.

The one who preserved and justified his moral values and safeguarded his honorability and his ethical *minimum* runs medium risks. But what do we call the totally destitute man who reaches this extreme edge of a limit-devotion whose name is abnegation? We will call him a daredevil: for his mortal adventure and his super-acute dilemma would summon him to opt between love-without-being and being-without-love. Well, how do you make the choice? One responds: it is necessary to choose a minimum of being so as to survive, because there is no love if there is no lover, and because the ego, the substantial subject, is the condition sine qua non of the loving relation: a few bubbles of love, if you please, to mitigate the dejection of the being, and to relieve adipose deterioration. But as we have shown starting with La Rochefoucauld and Fénelon, the superlative of loving purity and disinterestedness is so fragile and so unstable that the least thickening suffices to degrade it: an imperceptible complacency, an imponderable insistence, a barely detectable sluggishness, a suspect distraction, and the immaculate whiteness, as we were saying, becomes grayness. Where does pure love end up when one goes in the direction of being? At the very point at which self-love, that is, impure love, begins, immediately. As with ultrasensitive microscopes in which the image becomes blurred with the slightest pressure of one's hand, a love that is *still* pure, that is, "*nonexistent,*" which is beyond being, becomes blurred with the least tangency of a thousandth [*millième*] of a millimeter and a millionth of a second, of an impalpable and fugitive movement of our mood; an infinitesimal dose of self-interest or the light touch of a distant ulterior motive would suffice to blemish and muddy this purity. And in the reverse direction, up to what point is it necessary to go in the rarefaction of being-proper when one dreams of a new purity for a love that has become muddy? Starting from what moment does the rarefied, almost nihilized being run the risk of dying from exhaustion? For if love-without-being is infinitely unstable, then being-without-love is essentially vulnerable. Between these two extremes, in which miracles of acrobatics are necessary for holding steady, all the varieties of impure love and all the degrees of intermixture are represented. How can one squeeze between Charybdis and Scylla?—In an extremist and hyperbolic logic, in the absurd logic of moral exigency, that which is not the purest, and consequently 100 percent pure, is impure: and likewise, that which is not certain is doubtful, beginning with the instant in which the thing that is certain enlightens us not about an absolutely transparent certitude but about a certitude that is half certain and half uncertain. There is no middle ground. The Stoics said, A peccadillo is already a great sin. A little bit, when it concerns a misdeed, is already too much, infinitely too much! And the quantity has nothing to do with the case. Theoretically, the moral paradox would not even allow me the consolation of thinking that I am a human being among others and like the others. For I am not even one of these others and as capable as they of picturing the human race in my own person: it could indeed be, given the diabolical sophisms of self-love, that this modest concession was itself an excuse for reinstating in one fell swoop all the prerogatives of my precious person, for retrieving all my privileges, for deducing all my rights again, including those to which I never had any right! At most, the paradoxology would acknowledge that my rights can be a fortuitous consequence and not demanded on account of the duties of others . . .

8. The Precious Movement of the Intention.

With that said, such excesses will no doubt seem absurd. I am a little thing? Then I am something! I am, at least, a little; I am not a less-than-nothing. Less than nothing? such a humility would be pure madness! The little that I am, I am it. This very modest, lived tautology, which one could call "tautousy,"[7] is essentially positive; it protects me, at least, from the infinite annihilation of humility: between the nothing of this humility and a swelling boastfulness, it safeguards this precious movement of the heart which is a fine beam of light, an internal forgetting of self and an infinite openness to others, vast just as the sky is. But neither is it objectively true that in all cases your life is more valuable than mine: it is true only that I will do my best not to be aware of it. If morality were a simple, abstract speculation, a work of lofty fantasy, and if the moral paradoxology were aimed at I know not what utopian and theoretical limit, then in a pinch one could imagine a pure love that was a zero of being and a loving nothingness. Indeed, the moral paradox has relations with action or with praxis, and in principle it must be lived in actuality: it is made for that! Without this entirely positive plenitude, it would be only a folktale, a Platonic wish, or a mere rhetorical figure. Is moral extremism something serious? It is not serious, and it is even a bit phony if it promises us a definitive elevation of the entire being, a perfectly stable chronicle, and permanent advancement and transfiguration: but it is serious if, as with abnegation, it quits every professional sublimity and if, in the instant, it accepts the spontaneity and the freshness of innocence. This fine and transparent innocence is like the extreme point of the soul. So fine, so transparent! It takes nothing for it to be nothing anymore! Or better, it takes *almost* nothing: but this *almost* decides everything.

"A paradoxical life" or "a lived life," the paradox of morality is undoubtedly a contradiction, a challenge to the conditions of social life and even to the laws of physiology and biology—and better still, a challenge to common sense and reason; this is what the sages and saints always thought, the Stoics and the Cynics, Plato, and even Aristotle, and, on the other hand, the spiritualists of the Philokalia and the author of the *Imitation*. Acrobatics in a spectacular and perilous form, movement in the most familiar forms of daily life, and temporality itself renew at every instant the miracle of a delayed fall that is a continued reestablishment: the solution is given at the same time as the challenge to the laws of equilibrium and gravity is initiated. And man in his infinite gratitude gives thanks each morning to his adventurous fate for having escaped one more time from the perils of death. The miracle of movement of which Bergson tells us is in its way this perpetual thank-you that man formulates in his own heart for the new extension that was granted to him. The paradoxical life is livable at the same time it is unlivable, viable and at the same time inviable, simultaneously possible and impossible, or, which amounts to the same thing, infinitely possible for a desperate and passionate goodwill that itself is capable of willing infinitely. One indeed says: to want is to be able . . . Not that wanting is, literally, being able to do what one wanted, by virtue of an act of omnipotence, like that of pixies and sorcerers: it is rather infinitely "to make possible" an impossibility that is forever impossible. Willing asymptotically tends toward a limit that it will not be able to touch by physical contact, or that it can merely graze with an imponderable and instantaneous tangency.

Disconcerting and inconsistent, disappointing as well as evasive, moral existence infinitely contradicts itself: not only is it paradoxical, but it does not even fear sometimes appearing "paralogical" . . . that is, irrational. To love, it is necessary to be. But the more one is, the more one flows and overflows, generously and richly, in the density of being-proper; the more love suffocates; and by dint of suffocating, it dies. But if one *is* not, then where is the lover who will be the subject of the verb *to love?* This lover has not yet been born; perhaps he will never belong to the world of the living . . . Again, where is the love? Hither or beyond, the same questions beset us concerning moral life, its intangibility, its values that are so controversial, its exigencies that are so often flouted. All that is perhaps nothing but myths and crazy ideas. Or indeed, is it a dream from which I have not yet awakened? More than once we have wondered where our moral life has fled to, what it consists in, and even if it consists in something at all! Well, it is precisely in these instants, in which it is at the point of escaping and in which we despair about catching it, that it is the most authentic: it is thus necessary to capture in flight the opportunity in its vivid flagrancy! Provided that consciousness does not disfigure its face with grimaces too quickly, or break off its impetus [*élan*] too soon . . . The moral *impetus* [*impetus*] resembles the fairy Anima, who stops singing when Animus watches her and who regains an innocent, most pure voice when Animus stops staring at her; in that, moral life is no more modest than the soul, or more evasive than freedom, or more perplexing than temporality, according to the testimony of Saint Augustine: if one asks me *what is* (*quid sit*), or if I attempt to explain its nature, I become confused and I stammer; but when one no longer harasses me with questions, and I consider time with simplicity, with a naive and relaxed soul, the ambiguity and the worry make room for what is obvious. For that, it was necessary to see things from high enough and far away enough, not in the fogginess of the approximately, but in the sane approximation of good sense. 1st: The vocation of man is to love and to live for others. 2nd: But in the elementary order that we were calling the *ontic minimum,* love would not be able to be entirely, or purely, or always loving: love presupposes a loving being which is, according to the point of view taken, either the substantial and irrational subject, the impure foundation and the passive condition of love, a vehicle, somehow, in contrast to the active principle, or, conversely, the indissoluble and so to speak opaque and massive residue of this same love. Residual or substantial, this irreducible element, in any case, blocks our path of limit-abnegation, thanks to which the compact being would be entirely sublimated and converted into love. If there were not other complications, one would not dare to give the name of evil to this impediment that is the fatal gravity of love, its congenital tare, and its inevitable coefficient of inertia: the being of the lover, insofar as it is flesh and matter or is the nonloving part of the loving being. Doesn't the resistance of this massive element, this blind ego bear the signature of our finitude? But it is necessary to take into account a complexity that almost immediately asserts its claims: the massive element is not a lead weight, it is called flesh: it itself implies a complexity that twice complicates the loving-being; this complication is not an extrinsic contradiction but an immanent negation. Extrinsic, it would be dispensable and curable; immanent, the negation is a necessary evil or, as we were still saying, an impossible-necessary, and all the more irritating because it is, indeed, necessary: the contradictory that is egoistic deeply penetrates into the intimate texture of the moral intention, not only because it conditions it, but because it borrows its face from it, because it mimics it, so as to be mistaken; hypo-

critical charity borrows the true mask of charity and ultimately it becomes indiscernible from it. We were speaking
of a hybrid called the organ-obstacle. More organ or more
obstacle? In a pinch, one would be able dialectically to interpret the univocal sense of this equivocal, the esoteric sense
of this appearance, if the obstacle were always a spring, a
trampoline, or a foil, an ingenious machine that permits us,
thanks to the relaxation or to the step back, to leap higher
and with a more energetic impetus . . . It is the tool that gets
in the way, and it is a waste of resources or quite simply lost
time; it is the instrument itself that is the impediment. And
more generally, in order to be able, it is necessary to be im-
peded and limited; this alternative is the paradoxical tare of
finitude. When the luxury and the ridiculous enormity of resources used themselves become cumbersome or threaten
us with suffocation, one can reduce them to a minimum
and thus equivocate with the contradiction; this relation of
a minimum of resources to a maximum hope is the aim of
a wise economy. Indeed, the entanglement sometimes is inextricable. When the moral being is not constrained by the
weight and the consequences of its offerings but is a priori hampered by the intimate corruption of the intentional
movement, attained in its essence and in the totality of its
existence, then there no longer is a solution, and the tragedy
is coupled with a very bitter irony: for it is thus the very being of the contributor that belies the loving gift: that which
by its very definition makes the disinterested gift possible
makes the egoistic deterioration of it possible. *Neither with,
nor without.* Well, such is the desperate formula of the insoluble dilemma and the situation that has no exit; such is the
double impossibility that forever blocks every response.

The being of the individual, whether it is physical or biological, is, in comparison with love, just like rights in comparison with duty. One can consider rights as an ethical display of the being. Rights bring to an existing situation (isn't this a veritable windfall?) the normative justification and the consecration it was lacking; they confer on the naturality of the ego a type of aureole—the aureole of idealizing sublimation, or at the very least honorability; stabilized, jealously claimed, sometimes even encoded, often reduced to the state of a virtual deposit, the ethical minimum is more akin to having than to being: it thus becomes something like the moral viaticum that accompanies us and protects us in the trials of existence. We have shown that in the relations of being and love there is a malicious derision that is due to the constitutional finitude of man or, more precisely, to the ambivalent and contradictory relations of being and love: it is the being of the lover that makes love possible, but a lover who is too happy, too healthy, and too well nourished is the negation of love; and, conversely, if he only has as a vehicle a rarified being, then love vanishes into the void. Vital fulfillment favors it, up to the moment in which satiety suppresses in him this sacred dissatisfaction, this need for something else, and finally this worry that was the aerial side of his nature: weighed down by a ridiculously plethoric being, bourgeois love loses its wings and crashes to the ground. And so love comes and goes between what is too much and what is too little; it necessarily renews its strength each time it bathes again in the wellsprings of life, periodically finds a new youth and new blood, and somehow or other, as best as it can, haltingly succeeds at surviving.

But as concerns the debate about rights and duties, the predicament, if it is less bloody, is more subtle, the malice is more insidious, the alternative is more ambiguous; for it is the moral man himself who discovers the normative truth of rights—of my own rights and of the rights of others, which sanctify these rights and assert them. The moral paradoxology forces me to profess, against everything obvious and my conviction itself, that I do not have rights and that everyone has rights except me. This contradiction at my expense is certainly not a bloody sacrifice as is, ultimately, the impossibility of love and being, as is ultimately the impossible necessity of being annihilated for loving with a pure love, but it is nevertheless, in its own way, an agonizing renunciation . . . and all the more heartbreaking in that this denial *in adjecto* has normative values at stake and can pass for a cynical attack against truth and against the principle of identity; it is indeed good to say that the sacrifice is here literally sacrilegious! This scandalous inequality, this appalling injustice to my prejudice that reason refuses to admit, does moral pessimism, for all that, make it plausible? One is tempted to consider this scandal as an appearance that would conceal I know not what perplexing finality and perhaps even a tacit promise. Would we thus support the denial of justice in the name of a promise? This is how rationalist speculation, always wise and considerate, seeks to reassure us: you lose nothing by waiting, it tells us, whoever laughs last will have a good laugh! The hope of a better future will help us bear the present frustration. Nothing is wiser or more reasonable! But then what difference exists between day-to-day mercenariness, indeed even on a weekly basis, and the sordidness of this all too easy calculation? Because the renunciation of my right-proper is a long-range speculation and a far-off deadline, it is no less utilitarian or less interested for all that. This tortuous calculus is a hypocrisy and nothing more. I must *in principle* bear the insupportable iniquity of which I am the victim, without claiming any compensation, without demanding the least compensation, without even having the right to complain. Doesn't my neighbor have all the rights over me?

Each moral being should inwardly confront the double trial to which the disparity of duties and rights submits his egoism. And first, everyone has duties, including me, especially me, since duty, expressing the infinite incompleteness of the moral being is above all a call and a vocation. Indeed, I do not have to watch over the duties of others: my duties encompass all the duties, and I am responsible for them. And on the other hand, as we had said, everyone has rights except me, who incomprehensibly, inexplicably does not have them: I am then in principle, devoid of everything and cannot thus count on anything, not even on the freedoms and the powers that the duties of others, fortuitously but also fatally (together) will allow me; here is in some way my opportunity in this unjust misery. Am I condemned to live in mendicancy? I will receive, if not what is due to me—since nothing is due to me—at least the crumbs of the banquet and what is left behind, that is, the surplus that comes back to me, somewhat contraband, from the merits of others. Indeed, these crumbs are not nothing, since they allow me to survive in a grueling and very bitter fight to which I am condemned. They are the aleatory food that a compassionate hand throws to the birds in the sky and that, mysteriously, almost never lacks recklessness. But the grip of paradoxes that moral philosophy throws to us as food is not always a system of truths. Here we touch the ultimate truth, the one that is rooted in the most impenetrable of mysteries. I do not have the right to anything and, notwithstanding, I will finally receive what is due to me without being due. I

will receive it on condition of not calling for it, of not even
having thought about it; I will receive it in total humility and
in total innocence. I will receive it . . . but hush! do not repeat it . . . Let no one know anything about it. Alas! we have
just said it! We have already divulged the secret, and it could
not be otherwise. How can one keep a secret by divulging
it? divulging it by keeping it? Indeed, one can do this, if it is
true that the alternative of the contradictories, both being
impermeable, is from time to time overcome. The oracle of
Delphi, according to Heraclitus, neither talks nor hides, but
it suggests by signs, without having to spell things out or co-
vertly. Or, more simply, it does not speak, but it *leads us to listen,* and it whispers hidden truths into the ear of our soul.

Notes

Footnotes in the French edition often supplied only a short form of a title with perhaps a publisher, page number, or, for older works, section number. Where possible I have supplied a full citation for either a French- or an English-language edition. I have also added a few notes for clarification. [Trans.]

1. MORAL EVIDENCE IS SIMULTANEOUSLY ENCOMPASSING AND ENCOMPASSED

1. Jankélévitch here has the Greek term for "evaluation"; I have transliterated his parenthetical Greek terms and phrases throughout. [Trans.]

2. This is the title Victor Hugo gives to the drama of Cain in *La légende des siècles* [The Legend of the Ages].

3. [Clément Rosset, *La logique du pire* (The Worst-Case Scenario)] (Paris: Presses universitaires de France, 1971).

4. [See Aristotle,] *Nicomachean Ethics* 10.2.1172b15–16 [trans. Terence Irwin (Indianapolis: Hackett, 1999). English edition supplied by translator.].

5. [Henri Bergson,] *The Two Sources of Morality and Religion* [trans. R. Ashley Aurda and Cloudesley Brereton (Notre Dame: University of Notre Dame Press, 1935/2002), 31, 143, 164, 184. English edition supplied by translator.].

6. Cf. Xenophon, *Mémorabilia* 4.4.11: *e ou doxei soi axiotekmartoteron tou logou to ergon einai* [trans. Amy Bonnette (Ithaca: Cornell University Press, 2001). English edition supplied by translator.].

2. THE CONSPICUOUSNESS OF MORALITY IS SIMULTANEOUSLY EQUIVOCAL AND UNIVOCAL

1. [Nikolai Berdyaev, *La destination de l'homme: Essai d'éthique paradoxale*] ([Paris:] Éditions "Je Sers," 1935).

2. [Baltasar Gracián,] *El Héroe,* 7: "Excelencia de primero" [First-Class Excellence].

3. Or prosopolempsia; notably Romans 2:11; James 2:1,9; Acts 10:34; Ephesians 6:9; and Colossians 3:25.

4. Jean-Louis Chrétien invites us to distinguish between a truly generous donation that sacrifices its most precious possession and a somewhat indifferent generosity that, like the diffusion of light, is an imperturbable radiance and superabundance, but that does not know the tragedy of sacrifice ("Le Bien donne ce qu'il n'a pas," *Archives de philosophie* 43 [1980]: 263–77).

5. [Plato,] *Republic* 7.518c; cf. 4.436b [trans. C. D. C Reeve (Indianapolis: Hackett, 2004). English edition supplied by translator.]. Aristotle, *Nicomachean Ethics* 9 (What Is Serious).

6. Cf. notably Syméon, "Le nouveau théologien," in *Petite Philocalie de la prière du cœur,* ed. Jean Gouillard ([Marseille]: Cahiers du Sud, [1953]), 173–74, and 118, 136.

7. [Plato,] *Republic* 6.509b.

8. [Plotinus,] *Enneads* 1.7.1: *epekeina ton onton . . . ousias . . . energeias . . . nou . . . nueseos* [trans. Stephen McKenna et al. (London: Faber and Faber, 1956)]. Cf. 1.6.9 and 6.8.14. [A pdf of this translation can be found at: https://classics.mit.edu/Plotinus/enneads.html].

9. [Plotinus,] *Enneads* 1.8.2.

10. "L'amour est enfant de bohême" (Love is a Gypsy child) is a line from the "Habanera" in Bizet's *Carmen.* [Trans.]

11. [Syméon,] *Petite Philocalie,* 174.

12. 1 Corinthians 3:19. [Trans.]

13. [Plato, *Phaedrus*] 265a [trans. Alexander Nehemas and Paul Woodruff (Indianapolis: Hackett, 1995). English edition supplied by translator.].

14. [Plato, *Phaedrus*] 244a.

15. Revelation 3:16.

16. Song of Songs 8:6.

17. Matthew 26:38; Mark 14:34; [Blaise] Pascal, "Mystery of Jesus" (*Pensées,* part 7, §552): Night of Gethsemane [*Pascal's Pensées* (trans. W. F. Trotter), introduction by T. S. Eliot (New York: E. P. Dutton, 1958). English edition supplied by translator. Jankélévitch gives the citation as §553.]

18. *Somewhere into the Unfinished* [*Quelque part dans l'inachevé*] is the title of a book published by Jankélévitch in 1978. [Trans.]

19. [Plato,] *Symposium* 203d [trans. Alexander Nehemas and Paul Woodruff (Indianapolis: Hackett, 1989). English edition supplied by translator. In "The Speech of Diotima" in Plato's *Symposium,* Diotima of Mantinea, one of the noted speakers at the banquet in which the topic of discussion is love or Eros, claims that Eros is the son of Poros (Poverty) and Penia (Way, Resource). See *Symposium* 203b–d. Trans.].

3. THE LEAST EVIL AND THE TRAGIC SIDE OF THE CONTRADICTION

1. [Plato,] *Symposium* 211c; [Plato,] *Republic* 6.511b.

2. [Plotinus,] *Enneads* 1.6.1.

3. Baltasar Gracián, *The Courtiers Manual Oracle, or, The Art of Prudence* (London: M. Flesher, 1685). The pdf for this book can be found at https://quod.lib.umich.edu/e/eebo/A41733.0001.001?view=. [Trans.]

4. [Gracián,] *The Courtier's Manuel Oracle,* Maxims 73, 130, 140.

5. Leonardo Cremonini created a poster titled "Against Forbidden Meanings/Directions [*Sens*]: The Streets of What Is Possible." In French, the sign for a one-way street reads, *Sens unique.* However, the word *sens* means both "direction" and "meaning." [Trans.]

6. [Plato,] *Republic* 7.518c; Matthew 22:37; Luke 10:27; Mark 12:30–33.

7. Matthew 22:37.

8. [Plato,] *Symposium,* 203d.

9. Revelation 3:15–16. [Trans.]

10. [Georg Simmel,] "Der Begriff und die Tragödie der Kultur," in *Philosophische Kultur* (1911), 245–77. It appeared in the same year in the Russian [journal] *Logos* (Moscow: Musagète, 1911), 2:1–25.

11. [Henri Bergson,] *Creative Evolution,* chap. 1, p. 93; chap. 4 [trans.

Arthur Mitchell (1911; Mineola, N.Y.: Dover, 1998). English edition supplied by translator.].

12. [Bergson,] *Creative Evolution,* 88.

13. Jean Wahl, *Études kierkegaardiennes* [(Paris: Librairie philosophique J. Vrin, 1974)], 614.

14. Franz Liszt, *The Legend of Saint Elizabeth,* first part, number 2.

15. [Plato,] *Republic* 6.509c. Cf. 509b.

16. Victor Hugo, *The Legend of the Ages.*

17. Manuel de Falla's ballet-pantomime *L'amour sorcier.* [Trans.]

18. [Plato, *Symposium*] 195a,c (Agathon); 203d (Diotima).

19. [Bergson,] *Creative Evolution,* 192.

20. Fénelon, *Le Gnostique de saint Clément d'Alexandrie* (le P. Doudon, 1930); *Explication des Maximes des saints sur la vie intérieure* (A. Chérel, 1911); *Les principals propositions des Maximes des saints justifies* (*Oeuvres completes,* 1848, vol. 3); *De amore pura* (vol. 3); *Condamnation du livre des Maximes* (vol. 3); *Instructions et avis sur la morale et sur la perfection chrétienne,* 19 (vol. 6). *Sur les oppositions véritables entre la doctrine de M. de Meaux et celle de M. de Cambrai* (vol. 2).

21. [Blaise] Pascal, "Mystery of Jesus" (*Pensées* part 7, §552) [*Pascal's Pensées* (trans. W. F. Trotter), introduction by T. S. Eliot (New York: E. P. Dutton, 1958). Jankélévitch gives the citation as §553.]; Miguel de Unamuno, *The Agony of Christianity and Essays on Faith* [vol. 5 of *The Selected Works of Miguel de Unamuno,* trans. Antony Kerrigan (Princeton: Princeton University Press, 1974), 11 or 73–85. English editions supplied by translator. The citation from Jankélévitch would seem to refer to a passage in an early part of the book, translated by Jean Cassou, his brother-in-law and friend, in which Unamuno refers to Pascal and "agonic doubt." "The Faith of Pascal," occurs in chapter 9 (pp. 73–87); but there is a specific reference to P. L. Couchoud's *Mystery of Jesus* on p. 20. (Trans.)].

22. The French verb *composer* can also mean "to compromise" [Trans.]

23. René Descartes, *Discourse on Method,* part 3 [in volume 1 of *The Philosophical Writings of Descartes,* trans. J. Cottingham, R. Stroothoff, and D. Murdoch (Cambridge; Cambridge University Press, 1985), 122. English edition supplied by translator.].

4. THE SCHEME OF THE CONSCIENCE.
HOW TO PRESERVE INNOCENCE

1. Jankélévitch here plays on the French phrase, "*le future proche,*" which means the "near future," and the word "*prochain,*" which means "neighbor" or "next one." [Trans.]

2. Matthew 20:16, 19:30; Luke 13:20.

3. In the French version of this 1949 British film the title was changed to *Noblesse Oblige.* [Trans.]

4. Genesis 3:8.

5. Pascal wrote that "man is but a reed, the most feeble thing in nature, but he is a thinking reed"; see *Pascal's Pensées,* part 6, §347, [trans. W. F. Trotter], introduction by T. S. Eliot (New York: E. P. Dutton, 1958), 97. [Trans.]

6. [Alain,] *Préliminaires à l'esthétique,* statement 72 [(Paris: Éditions Gallimard, 1939)].

7. "Tautousy" is a Jankélévitch neologism stemming from the notion of tautology. [Trans.]

Translator's Acknowledgments

I need to acknowledge several people whose help made this translation possible: Abbie Storch and her colleagues at Yale University Press have been supportive from the beginning, and I am indebted to Susan Laity, a manuscript editor at Yale, who made many extremely helpful suggestions for improving the translation. A long while back, at a time when Jankélévitch was completely unknown in the English-speaking world Alan Udoff encouraged me to translate his work, and subsequently Joëlle Hansel connected me with Jankélévitch scholars in other parts of the world. Bradley University, my home institution, provided me with a sabbatical leave in spring 2022, during which most of this translation was completed. My wonderful colleagues in the Department of Philosophy and Religious Studies at Bradley had to take on extra teaching and service duties during my sabbatical leave. Finally, I need to thank family members: Jennifer in particular, but also Eamon, Neve, Mom, EJ, Dawn, Tim, SuLin, Sheila, Maura, Dan, Maeve, and Fergus.

VLADIMIR JANKÉLÉVITCH (1903–1985) was a French philosopher and musicologist. Born in France to Russian-Jewish parents, Jankélévitch was educated at the École normale supérieure and served as an infantry officer and later in the French Resistance. After World War II, he returned to the Sorbonne, where he held the Chair of Moral Philosophy from 1951 to 1978, and where he taught and wrote until his death. He is the author of twenty-eight books, ranging from musicological illuminations of Ravel, Debussy, and Fauré to philosophical considerations of death, the possibility of forgiveness after the Holocaust, the ethical consequences of living under a regime built on lies, and the ineffability of art. A friend and contemporary of Emmanuel Levinas, who credits Jankélévitch with originating his ethics of otherness, Jankélévitch infuses his body of work with a deep engagement with metaphysics, mysticism, and morals. Several works by Jankélévitch have been translated into English, including *Ravel* (1959), *Music and the Ineffable* (2003), *The Bad Conscience* (2014), *Forgiveness* (2005), and *Henri Bergson* (2015).

ANDREW KELLEY is professor of philosophy at Bradley University. He teaches and writes on ethics and logic, Kant, modern philosophy, Levinas, and Bergson. His translations of French and German philosophy include Vladimir Jankélévitch's *Forgiveness* and *The Bad Conscience,* as well as Josef Popper-Lynkeus's *The Individual and the Value of Human Life* (1995).